A FAMILY WORSHIP RESOURCE:
Devotionals for parents and youth, plus stories for children

Faithful
FAMILIES
Stimulating Trust in God

HOWARD BEAN

Christian Light Publications

Harrisonburg, VA 22802

FAITHFUL FAMILIES
Christian Light Publications
Harrisonburg, Virginia 22802
© 2017 Christian Light Publications, Inc.
All rights reserved.
Printed in the United States of America

ISBN 978-0-87813-795-4

Cover Design: Clement Ebersole
Interior Design: David W. Miller
Interior Illustrations: Diane Horst

Cover Graphics: Clement Ebersole, Getty Images

2703181

DEDICATION

I dedicate this book to Brenda, our second oldest daughter. I recall her cheerful, enthusiastic ways in childhood. I recall her coming to us at bedtime as an adolescent and telling us she wanted to become a Christian. I recall the vibrant testimony she left in her work as a nurse in a local nursing home. I recall her marriage to Stephan Gingerich in 2001 and her readiness to serve with him wherever the Lord would call them. I hear about and periodically observe her busy missionary life in the jungles of Guatemala, which she has called home for many years.

Brenda wrote about the extortion attempt directed at Stephan and her, and about the fire in the trees. You can read about this in one of the stories for children.

I appreciate the faith, courage, and patience that Brenda demonstrates in Guatemala. She is also very hospitable, having cared for six boys who needed a home, plus her son Jeffrey and daughter Jasmine. She also typically serves hundreds of meals a year to traveling missionaries and a variety of visitors in her role as a pastor's wife.

ACKNOWLEDGEMENTS

- I appreciate the contribution of my faithful wife Barbara in typing and formatting this book. She is a continual inspiration to me.

- Special thanks go to Dorcas Hoover, Juliann Good, and Jasmine (Shantz) Martin who wrote stories for which few other people could have had accurate information.

- I am grateful for the skills of the people at Christian Light Publications.

- I am thankful for the example of heroes of faith recorded in the Bible, and also for those who have lived faithful lives in times since.

Books by Howard Bean

Devotionals for teens and adults
  Daily Truth for Godly Youth
  Daily Strength for Growing Youth

Devotionals and stories for families
  Fruitful Families: Cultivating Spiritual Fruit
  Worshipful Families: Marveling at God's Awesome Creation
  Faithful Families: Stimulating Trust in God

Devotionals for courting couples
  Keepsakes: Courtship Meditations and Memories

Handbook for Christian leaders
  A Good Minister: How to Preach, Pastor, and Serve Effectively

TABLE OF CONTENTS

Dedication   *iii*
Acknowledgements   *v*
Books by Howard Bean   *vi*
How Parents Can Use This Book   *xiii*

NOAH

Noah Found Grace   *3*
Noah Walked With God   *5*
Noah Had Faith and Fear   *7*
Noah Obeyed   *9*
Noah Preached and Persevered   *11*
Noah's Faith Was Rewarded   *13*
Noah Was Perfect, Yet Imperfect   *15*

Have Faith in God   *17*
John Chambers

ABRAHAM

Test of Leaving Family   *31*
Test of Truthfulness   *33*

Test of Unselfishness   *35*
Test of Patience   *37*
Test of Faith   *39*
Test of Befriending Strangers   *41*
Test of Obedience   *43*

Asking in Faith   **45**
Jean Chambers Cober

ISAAC

Is Anything Too Hard for God?   *59*
Isaac's Trust and Submission   *61*
A Unique Courtship   *63*
He Loved Her   *65*
Parental Favoritism   *67*
Live at Peace   *69*
Isaac, a Man of Faith   *71*

From Canada to China   *73*
Jonathan Goforth

JACOB

Jacob Values the Birthright   *87*
Jacob Lacks Faith and Integrity   *89*
The Staircase to Heaven   *91*
Facing Fears and the Future   *93*
Wrestling with God   *95*
Keys to Reconciliation   *97*
Faith and the Future   *99*

Faith Found in the Early Church   **101**
Polycarp, Justin, Symphorian, Maximilian, Justus

JOSEPH

Joseph and Jesus: Relating to Siblings   *117*
Joseph and Jesus: Relating to Parents   *119*
Joseph and Jesus: Purity   *121*
Joseph and Jesus: Falsely Accused   *123*
Joseph and Jesus: Faithful   *125*
Joseph and Jesus: Exalted   *127*
Joseph and Jesus: Forgiveness   *129*

Faith Facing Danger and Death   *131*
Stephan Gingerich

MOSES

Moses the Baby   *145*
Moses the Prince   *147*
Moses the Shepherd   *149*
Moses the Leader   *151*
Moses the Teacher   *153*
Moses the Intercessor   *155*
Moses the Deceased   *157*

Two Kinds of Faith   *159*
John Troyer and Gary Miller

RAHAB

Rahab's Faith   *171*
The Scarlet Cord   *173*
God's Mercy   *175*
Rahab, a Type of the Sinner   *177*
Faith That Works   *179*
Hall of Shame   *181*
Lessons from Rahab   *183*

Trust and a Steamboat   *185*
George Grenfell

GIDEON

A Brave Coward   *197*
Gideon Finds Peace   *199*
Faith in Action   *201*
Faith and the Fleece   *203*
Gideon Conquers His Fears   *205*
Faith Conquers   *207*
The Good and the Bad   *209*

Greater Than Guerrilla Guns   *211*
José Benito

JEPHTHAH

Getting Past the Past   *221*
Make Peace by Persuasion   *223*
Appreciate God's Providence   *225*
Have Faith   *227*
Don't Be Rash   *229*
A Living Sacrifice   *231*
ID'd by One's Speech   *233*

Fearless Woman of Faith   *235*
Mary Slessor

SAMSON

Samson's Strength   *247*
A Strong Weak Man   *249*
Compromise Can Kill   *251*
What Samson Lost   *253*

Don't Despise Godly Parents   *255*
Lessons from Samson   *257*
More Lessons from Samson   *259*

A Jump of Faith   *261*
Tim Whatley

SAMUEL

Asked of God   *279*
Building Proper Self-Esteem   *281*
Eli's Wisdom toward Samuel   *283*
Samuel's Intercession   *285*
Samuel's Faithfulness   *287*
Samuel's Courage   *289*
The Importance of the Heart   *291*

Missionary With Faith and Fervor   *293*
Hudson Taylor

DAVID

The Lord Looks on the Heart   *307*
Lessons from David's Family   *309*
David Confronts Goliath   *311*
David Behaves Wisely   *313*
David Faces Discouragement   *315*
Admirable Qualities of David   *317*
David's Kindness to Mephibosheth   *319*

Trust in Times of Terror   *321*
Sabina Wurmbrand, Robert Haddad, Mentu

A GREAT WOMAN

Great Perception   *335*
Great Hospitality   *337*
Great Kindness   *339*
The Rewards of Hospitality   *341*
When Children Are Sick   *343*
The Shunammite's Faith   *345*
Be Fair   *347*

Man of Narrow Escapes   *349*
John Paton

TITLES, VERSES, AND READINGS   *363*

HOW PARENTS
CAN USE THIS BOOK

Faithful Families is a resource for the family altar. I hope it helps to meet a need my wife and I felt when we were rearing our four children—the need for something on a child's level that would interest and instruct them.

This book follows the pattern of *Fruitful Families: Cultivating Spiritual Fruit* and *Worshipful Families: Marveling at God's Awesome Creation*, both published by Christian Light Publications.

The book consists of two parts for each day. The first part is for Mom and Dad and the older children in the family. It consists of a suggested Scripture reading, a theme verse, and a devotional meditation on the topic introduced by the Scripture reading.

The second part consists of a story for children on the theme of faith. You as parents (or a child) may read the story. Here are various possibilities about how you could use the story.

- You may read a portion of the story as part of your family worship each day. A symbol indicates a suitable stopping place.

- You may wait to read the story portion until evening (assuming your family worship is in the morning).

- You may read several portions or the whole story on days when you have a more relaxed schedule (such as Saturday for some families).

The goal of these stories is to create interest and enthusiasm for family worship in the hearts of children, while making application of Bible principles. This is hard for parents to do if the devotional thoughts are solely on an adult level. Parents, as well as children, have urged me to write this third devotional book for families.

The devotionals follow Bible characters mentioned in Hebrews 11, "The Faith Chapter." (The Shunammite woman is not named in Hebrews 11, but it alludes to her in the phrase "women received their dead raised to life again.")

Parents should note that several of the stories in this book include references to cruelty to other people, violence, and the existence of cannibals. Just as you may wish to omit or rephrase some parts of certain Bible stories for young children, you may want to alter a few parts of some stories, in particular, the stories about John Troyer, José Benito, George Grenfell, Mary Slessor, and John Paton. You may wish to glance over these stories prior to reading them to your children. Although I have de-emphasized the atrocities of heathen and wicked men, I needed to include some aspects of them.

All of the stories are true except that in a few cases some conversation and details have been added to help the story to flow. All of them demonstrate remarkable faith. I know personally nearly all of the characters in the stories who have lived in the last forty years.

I have provided ten questions based on the story of each week's theme that you may use if you wish. The *Questions for Review* are easier, largely factual questions that younger children may be able to answer. *Questions for Discussion* are intended for older children and provide opportunities for applying the theme to your family life.

You will notice there are thirteen themes divided into seven days each, thus encompassing ninety-one days—approximately one-quarter of a year.

May this book stimulate worship and faith in the Lord in the hearts of you and your children. He is absolutely trustworthy and faithful to us.

~Howard Bean

NOAH

Noah Found Grace

But by the grace of God I am what I am: and his grace which was bestowed upon me was not in vain; but I laboured more abundantly than they all: yet not I, but the grace of God which was with me. 1 Corinthians 15:10

READ GENESIS 6:1-8

As the sun rose on January 2, 2000, in Tehran, the capital city of Iran, a noose was placed around the neck of a seventeen-year-old who had quarreled with and killed a fellow citizen. With tears running down his pale face, the teenager awaited the signal for his death on the gallows in front of a large crowd. Just then the victim's father stepped forward and granted the teenager forgiveness, canceling the death sentence as he could do under Islamic law. Instead of receiving justice, the teenager was given grace. The teenager repeatedly thanked the father whose son he had killed, as he was taken away in the vehicle that had been waiting to take his body to the morgue.

The daily reading tells us that "Noah found grace in the eyes of the Lord." God extended His favor and help to Noah. A.W. Tozer defined *grace* as "the good pleasure of God that inclines Him to bestow benefits upon the undeserving." Unlike his neighbors whose wickedness was great and whose thoughts continually evil, Noah's life found favor with God.

3

How can you find grace? First Peter 5:5 tells us that "God resisteth the proud, and giveth grace to the humble." In addition to humility, prayer is necessary. "Let us therefore come boldly unto the throne of grace, that we may obtain mercy, and find grace to help in time of need" (Hebrews 4:16). Ultimately, we find God's grace in Jesus. "Grace and truth came by Jesus Christ" (John 1:17).

There are two aspects to God's grace: His favor and His enablement. Surrounded by sin, Noah's life shows us that God's providence will never place you where His grace cannot keep you.

John Newton, who wrote "Amazing Grace," said, "I am not what I *ought* to be. I am not what I *wish* to be. I abhor what is evil and I would cleave to what is good. I am not what I *hope* to be. Soon I shall put off immortality, all sin and imperfections. Yet though I am not what I ought to be, nor what I wish to be, nor what I hope to be, I can truly say that I am not what I *once was*—a slave to sin. By the grace of God I am what I am."

If we love and obey God less under grace than under law, it is a disgrace.

NOAH WALKED WITH GOD

By faith Enoch was translated that he should not see death; and was not found, because God had translated him: for before his translation he had this testimony, that he pleased God. Hebrews 11:5

READ GENESIS 6:9-22

Regular walking is one of the best things you can do for your health. Regular walking strengthens the heart. In the 1950s it was observed that postmen who walked the rounds had less risk of a heart attack than postal workers who worked at desks (although the risk of dog bites was greater). Walking also lowers blood pressure by improving the efficiency of the heart. Furthermore, walking reduces the likelihood of diabetes. Walking aids the body not only by reducing weight, but also by helping the body handle sugar, according to research in Sweden. In addition, walking is an excellent way to fight osteoporosis. Even the frequency of headache attacks may be reduced by exercise such as walking.

Noah walked with God, as the daily reading says. And his great-grandpa, Enoch, walked with God too. What are the characteristics of walking with God?

- A willing walk. No one is forced to walk with God. He is not a father who drags His children along. Rather, He walks with those who love Him.

- A humble walk. To walk in humility is the only way we can walk with the Lord. The three-fold divine requirement of Micah 6:8 includes "to walk humbly with thy God."

- A directed walk. God is unchanging. If we are walking with Him, it is because we have chosen His way. We need to agree with God. As Amos 3:3 says, "Can two walk together, except they be agreed?"

- A trusting walk. The essence of our walk with God is faith. That's how Enoch pleased God, "for before his translation he had this testimony, that he pleased God. But without faith it is impossible to please [God]" (Hebrews 11:5, 6).

- A continued walk. The Hebrew word suggests he "walked and continued to walk." And then he began walking with God in glory, "for God took him." One little girl imagined it this way: "One day they went for an extra long walk and they walked on and on, until God said, 'You're a long way from home. You had better come in and stay.' And he went."

Do you want to walk with God?

The poet wrote:

> Just a closer walk with Thee,
> Grant it, Jesus, this my plea,
> Daily walking close with Thee,
> Let it be, dear Lord, let it be.

NOAH HAD
FAITH AND FEAR

*By faith Noah, being warned of God of things not seen as
yet, moved with fear, prepared an ark to the saving of his
house; by the which he condemned the world, and became heir
of the righteousness which is by faith. Hebrews 11:7*

READ GENESIS 7:1-10

Kara, a little orphan in India, begged a missionary from another
village to take her home so she could go to the mission school.
The missionary said sadly, "We have no room. We have no
money to build more rooms." Seeing Kara's sadness, the missionary's
heart was touched. "You pray to God to send us money so we can take
you. I will pray too."

When the missionary returned to her home, she found a letter from
America. The letter contained the money that was needed to build
lodging for Kara. Early the next morning, the missionary sent a messenger for Kara. It was a long day's journey to Kara's village. But in just a
few hours, the messenger returned with Kara to the mission compound.
Little Kara said, "You prayed to God to send the money and I prayed to
God to send the money. I knew He would hear us, so I thought I might

as well start." She had walked half the way to the mission compound when the messenger met her.

The orphan girl had acted by faith. Noah built a big boat by faith. Noah had no indication that a supernatural phenomenon was approaching, except for God's Word. And that was enough. By faith Noah, being warned of God of things not yet seen, built an ark. Noah had a lengthy test of faith: no visible confirmation, no public opinion support, and no precedent for a worldwide flood. He had been building a character and he had been building a family and then he began building a gigantic floating zoo.

Like Noah, we are called to live by faith in the fear of God. Like Noah, we should take seriously divine warnings. Examples:

- "Be sure your sin will find you out" (Numbers 32:23).

- "Therefore be ye also ready: for in such an hour as ye think not the Son of man cometh" (Matthew 24:44).

- "The wicked shall be turned into hell, and all the nations that forget God" (Psalm 9:17).

Faith is the simple confidence that God exists and that He will do what He has promised. Noah had faith, stepping out into the unknown, obeying God's commands.

NOAH OBEYED

* *

Though Noah, Daniel, and Job, were in it, as I live, saith the Lord
GOD, they shall deliver neither son nor daughter; they shall but
deliver their own souls by their righteousness. Ezekiel 14:20

READ GENESIS 7:11-23

In Zaire where the vegetation is thick and the animals are wild, a small boy played under a tree in a garden near the missionary house. Suddenly his father called to him, "Justin, obey me instantly. Get down on your stomach." The boy responded at once, and his father continued, "Now crawl toward me fast." The boy again obeyed. After he had come about halfway, the father said, "Now stand up and run to me." The boy reached his father and turned to look back. Stretched out on the branch under which he had been playing was a large snake.

Noah rendered complete obedience, and his life was spared. After God had given him specific instructions about the ark's construction, the animals, and the food for the animals and his family, "according to all that God commanded him, so did he" (Genesis 6:22). This was no small undertaking—it was long, laborious, and costly. Genesis 7:5 emphasizes that Noah obeyed God one hundred percent. And Genesis 7:9 and 16 indicate that Noah directed the animals as God had commanded him.

Early church leaders stressed obedience. For example, Hermas (150 A.D.) wrote, "They only who fear the Lord and keep His commandments have life with God; but as to those who keep not His commandments, there is no life in them."

Justin Martyr (160 A.D.) wrote, "Let those who are not found living as He taught, be understood to be no Christians, even though they profess with the lip the precepts of Christ; for not those who make profession, but those who do the works, shall be saved."

Jesus stressed the importance of obedience. He said, "Not every one that saith unto me, Lord, Lord, shall enter into the kingdom of heaven; but he that doeth the will of my Father which is in heaven" (Matthew 7:21). He also said, "If a man love me, he will keep my words: and my Father will love him, and we will come unto him, and make our abode with him" (John 14:23).

Like Noah, he is wise who learns to obey although others go astray.

ᒐ

NOAH PREACHED
AND PERSEVERED

*And spared not the old world, but saved Noah the eighth
person, a preacher of righteousness, bringing in the flood
upon the world of the ungodly. 2 Peter 2:5*

READ MATTHEW 24:35-44

"Well, Noah, I see you are still building that monstrosity."

"God is going to destroy the world with a flood. A big boat is the only way to escape His judgment for man's violence, wicked imaginations, and corruption."

"A flood? How ridiculous. There's never been a flood. Everything is going to continue like it's been for years and years. Besides, God (if there is a God) is too merciful to destroy people."

"You're wrong, my friend. Join my family and me in preparing to escape the flood. Trust God and obey Him. Turn from your wickedness."

"I don't believe that. You're a fool, Noah. Why don't you forget this nonsense? You've been preaching this for years, even for decades. You know what I believe? I believe we're going to have an especially good time at a party tonight. Come and join us. We are going to have a blast."

"Not interested," replied Noah. "I'm going to keep on building with my family."

I don't know what words Noah used or to whom he spoke, but I do know he was a "preacher of righteousness."

Noah preached and preached and preached and preached while he kept building. From the reference in Genesis 6:3, it seems that he may have preached and pounded nails for over a century.

Future judgment is a reality. Charles Spurgeon said, "He who does not believe that God will punish sin, will not believe that He will pardon it through the atoning blood. He who does not believe that God will cast unbelievers into Hell will not be sure that He will take believers into Heaven. If we doubt God's Word about one thing, we shall have small confidence in it upon another thing. Sincere faith in God must treat all God's Word alike; for the faith which accepts one word of God and rejects another is evidently not faith in God, but faith in our own judgment, faith in our own taste."

NOAH'S FAITH
WAS REWARDED

And God blessed Noah and his sons, and said unto them, Be fruitful, and multiply, and replenish the earth. Genesis 9:1

READ GENESIS 8:15-22

If you lived in the Amazon rainforest, would you be interested in buying snowplows to clean jungle trails in case it snows? If you lived in Antarctica, what would you think of the plan to plant a banana plantation?

Ridiculous? That's no doubt what Noah's neighbors thought about the construction of the ark. But God told Noah the ark would be needed because of the Flood. Noah believed God, and Noah and his crew of seven were saved.

I'm impressed with the story told by William Hacquist of the Evangelical Alliance Mission in China. He and some friends were trying to escape from danger in the days of the Boxer Rebellion. They had traveled six days and had come to a point where they needed to choose between land or river for farther travel. Because of drought, there was no water in the Han River in front of them. Further, their carriers and escort refused to travel other than on the land route.

They had a prayer meeting to ask God's guidance. They felt led to procure two large flat-bottom riverboats; they bought food and placed it with their baggage on board. But there was no water. William said, "The place where we stayed was surrounded by high hills. As we prayed and waited, in about midafternoon, heavy dark clouds came over the hilltops, and from them came pouring down the heaviest rain I have ever seen. It really looked like a cloudburst. In a very short time the riverbed was filled with water, so we could release the boats and nicely float down the river. We later learned why we were led not to travel by land. In a mountain pass, several hundred bandits were waiting to kill us. God sent us the safe way."

God rewarded Noah in various ways. God walked with him (Genesis 6:9). God spoke to him (Genesis 6:13). God invited him into the ark (Genesis 7:1). God shut him safely in the ark (Genesis 7:16). "God remembered Noah" (Genesis 8:1). "God blessed Noah" (Genesis 9:1).

If we have the character and faith of Noah, we too shall be blessed.

NOAH WAS PERFECT, YET IMPERFECT

Wherefore let him that thinketh he standeth take heed lest he fall. 1 Corinthians 10:12

READ GENESIS 9:18-29

Thomas à Kempis wrote: "No one is so good that he is immune from temptation. We will never be entirely free from it." To be totally free from temptation will be one of the blessings of Heaven where "there shall be no more curse" (Revelation 22:3).

David committed adultery, Peter denied Christ, Moses struck the rock instead of speaking to it, Solomon worshiped idols, and Noah became drunk.

How sad that Noah fell into sin. But the Bible is realistic; men are fallible, and our enemy is subtle and strong. Perhaps Noah didn't realize that he could become intoxicated by the wine and was too inebriated to realize his uncovered state.

The fact remains that a just man who walked with God lay drunken and naked. The man who Genesis 6:9 describes as perfect, meaning blameless, is depicted as imperfect. Noah lived another 350 years, but this is last incident in his life we read about in the Bible.

We have reason to believe that Noah repented and returned to a life of godliness. Ezekiel 14:14 and 20 imply that Noah was one of the three most godly men mentioned in the Old Testament. Second Peter 2:5 refers to him as a preacher of righteousness. And of course, Noah is listed among the heroes of faith in Hebrews 11.

Take a few lessons from this regrettable incident in Noah's life.

1. Don't be spiritually devastated if a godly hero succumbs to temptation.

2. Don't be overconfident.

3. One person's sins affect others. (Consider verse 22 of the daily reading.)

4. The time of achievement and rejoicing can be the hour of temptation.

5. As long as we live, we will need the promise and provision of 1 John 1:9, "If we confess our sins, he is faithful and just to forgive us our sins, and to cleanse us from all unrighteousness."

6. We may meet with temptation in farming or any other occupation.

7. Always wear the whole armor of God.

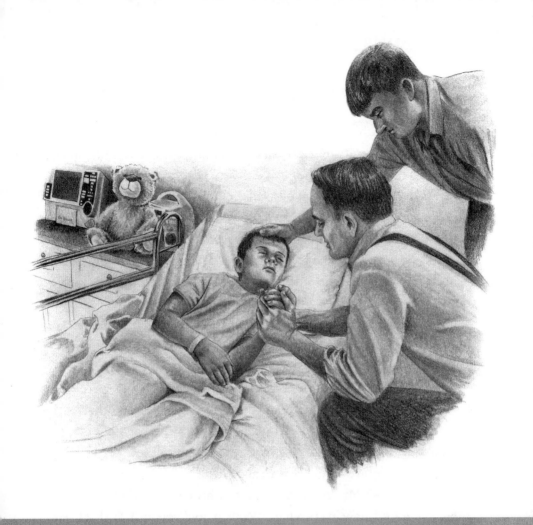

Have Faith in God
John Chambers

by Jasmine Shantz

"Good morning, children!" Eight-year-old Jean and her brothers and sisters looked up at the sound of Mr. Jonathan Lyons' friendly voice. They immediately left their game and raced to the fence, drawn by Mr. Lyons' kindness, as well as the knowledge that he often carried nuts or candies in his pocket and was generous about sharing them.

Jean lived with her family on Elizabeth Street, just a few houses down from a little city mission in Welland, Ontario. She and her family did not go to church, but they loved their Christian neighbors, Mr. and Mrs. Lyons, who lived at the mission.

"How are you all doing today?" he asked.

"Oh, we're pretty good," Jean answered for everyone.

"Feeling a little bit hungry," murmured her older brother Harry, rubbing his stomach. Jean elbowed him. She knew their mother would not approve of him hinting that some candy would be good. Not that she would turn candy down, if Mr. Lyons happened to have some.

Mr. Lyons chuckled. "Is that so? Hmm. I wonder if I have something here that could fix that."

He put his hand into his pocket and searched around, furrowing his brow with concentration. The children looked at each other with glowing eyes. He made a puzzled sound and pulled his hand out empty.

"Hmmm. That's strange," he muttered to himself.

"Maybe in your other pocket?" Harry suggested hopefully.

"My other—" Mr. Lyons reached into his other pocket, acting as though it were a new idea to him. "Well, would you look at that?" He pulled out several pieces of candy—one for each of them. Jean looked up him and smiled. He winked at her as he handed her a candy.

"Thank you," she said.

"You're very welcome, Jean," he replied. "Now, will I see you all in Sunday school this week?"

Jean wanted to go. She wondered what church would be like. Mr. and Mrs. Lyons were so kind and cheerful that she felt certain church must be a wonderful place, if it was full of people like them.

"Dad doesn't want us to," Harry said. Jean could tell that he was curious too.

Mr. Lyons sighed. "I see. Well, perhaps he will change his mind some day. Have a good day, children!"

They called out good-byes as they ran back to their game of jacks. Jean continued to think about church as they played.

"What do you think Sunday school would be like, Harry?" she asked.

He shrugged. "I don't know."

"Do you think that Dad will ever let us go?"

"I don't know. Dad likes to do a lot of things that Mr. Lyons doesn't do."

Jean knew that this was true. Her father liked to smoke and drink and invite friends over for card parties. Mr. Lyons never did any of those things. She wondered if people who did those things were allowed to go to church.

But as they played, Jean forgot about Sunday school. She didn't think about it again until supper time. "Dad, could we go to Sunday school with Mr. Lyons sometime?" she asked when the family was gathered around the table.

"Jean, you don't need to worry about going to church. You're already a very good girl!"

"I just wondered what—" Jean began, but was cut off by her father.

"I don't want to hear any more about going to church, Jean. That's all I'm going to say on the matter. Eat your supper. You're too young to be worrying about things like this." He reached over and pinched her cheek playfully, but she could tell that he meant what he said. She finished the rest of her supper quietly.

Later that night, after everyone had gone to bed, Jean woke up with a jolt. She lay stiff in her bed, wondering what had awakened her and why she felt as though something was very wrong.

She heard muffled voices and something else. It sounded like... crying? More than just crying. Someone was groaning in pain. She felt a sinking feeling inside.

She slipped out of bed and felt the cool wooden floor underneath her bare feet. She tiptoed over to the door, opened it a bit, and stuck her head out just in time to see her mother rush past.

"Mom?" she whispered. "What's happening?"

Her mom turned around, clearly surprised to see that Jean was awake. "You should be asleep, dear," she said, brushing the hair back from Jean's face.

"What's happening? Who's crying?" Jean asked again.

"It's Harry. He's not feeling well. We're going to take him to the hospital. Ellen will stay and take care of you here. Don't worry."

Don't worry? How could Jean not worry? Harry was going to the hospital! "Is he going to be okay?" she whispered.

"It's all going to be fine. We'll take him to the hospital, and the doctor there will know how to help him. We'll let you know how he's doing as soon as we can. Go back to bed now. It's far too late for you to be awake! Come. I'll tuck you back in." As Jean turned to go back to her bed with her mom, she saw her father helping Harry down the hallway.

He looked so different from the way he normally did. Her brother Harry was tall and strong. Full of energy and always hungry. She remembered how he had hinted about candy to Mr. Lyons earlier that day. This hunched-over, groaning boy seemed like a different person. It made her feel scared inside. She ran down the hall to him and squeezed his hand.

"I'll be okay," he said, but his face was pale and his lip quivered. She didn't know what to say, so she squeezed his hand again and ran back to her room. Hopping into bed, she burrowed under the covers and squeezed her eyes shut.

She felt the gentle weight of her mom sitting down on the edge of her bed. She tucked the blankets around Jean and whispered, "Ellen will take good care of you, Jean. We'll talk to you tomorrow. Good-bye."

With those words, she was gone, and Jean felt very alone in the darkness. She kept her eyes closed so tightly that her face started to ache.

She remembered the time she had worn her new watch to go skating and had fallen and broken it. Harry had taken it to the jewelers and gotten it fixed for her, and her mother had never known about the incident. Harry always took care of her.

She didn't like to think about him feeling so sick that he couldn't even stand up straight. She wondered what was wrong with him. Somehow, in the midst of all her wondering, she drifted off to sleep again.

When she woke up the next morning, it took her a moment to remember why her heart felt so heavy. Then she remembered and tears filled her eyes.

Breakfast tasted like sawdust to Jean. No one seemed to enjoy it very much. The Chambers siblings were a sad, quiet bunch that morning. They worked together to clean up breakfast and then drifted their separate ways. Jean went back to her room and tried to read. Ellen knocked on her door after a while.

"Dad's home," Ellen said. "He wants to talk to us downstairs." She smiled, but Jean could see the worry in her eyes.

They walked downstairs together and joined the rest of the family in the kitchen. Their dad was sitting at the kitchen table, looking very tired and sad. Jean ran to him and gave him a hug.

"Good morning, Jean," he said, smiling as much as he could, pulling her up onto his knee.

"How's Harry doing?" she asked eagerly, hoping that it would be good news.

"Well," he began, but then stopped and sighed heavily. Jean felt the same sinking feeling that she had felt the night before.

"Harry is very sick. His appendix burst, and that means that he has lots of poison in his body." He paused.

"But he's going to be okay, right, Dad?" Jean's older brother Arthur asked. They all waited anxiously to hear their father's response.

"We—" He stopped and took a deep breath. "We're just going to have to wait and see."

"You mean…" Arthur's voice trailed off.

"He might die?" Jean turned to see her father's face as she asked it.

"We don't know what will happen. The doctors say that he is very sick. We have to wait. Hopefully he will get better." Jean could tell by the trembling in her dad's voice that he really didn't know what was going to happen, and that he was scared. She didn't like to think about her dad being scared. He had always been strong. Seeing him so close to tears made her feel like crying.

Her dad cleared his throat and said, "I think that I'll go for a walk. I need some fresh air after being in that hospital all night."

Jean slid off his knee, missing the solidness of her father's arm around her. She watched as her father left the house. Once again, she was unsure of what to do. It felt so strange to be at home without her mother and without Harry.

What if she never saw Harry again? Harry had to get better. Jean wandered outside and sat down under the tree by the fence. After she had been sitting and picking at the grass for a while, she heard a familiar, cheerful voice. "Good morning, Jean."

"Good morning, Mr. Lyons," Jean replied.

"I have a special treat for you children today! Where's Harry? I'm surprised he's not out here waiting for me. He's not going to want to miss out on this treat."

Jean didn't know how to explain to Mr. Lyons that Harry was sick. That Harry was at the hospital. That Harry might be dying.

Mr. Lyons' took a good look at Jean and said, "What's the matter, Jean? Is something wrong?"

Jean nodded. "It's Harry." She had to swallow hard around the lump in her throat to keep the tears from coming. "He's in the hospital."

Mr. Lyons brow furrowed. "What's wrong? Is he sick?"

"His appendix burst, and we don't know if he's going to get better or not," Jean explained.

"I'm very sorry to hear that. It makes me so sad. Are your parents at home? I'd like to speak to them."

"Mom is at the hospital and Dad went for a walk," Jean answered.

"Ah yes. I see him coming this way now. I believe I'll go have a word with him. I'll be praying for Harry, Jean. Keep your chin up. With God, nothing is impossible."

"Nothing?" Jean asked.

"Absolutely nothing. God can do anything. Remember that." Mr. Lyons sounded very sure of himself and very sure of God. He smiled at her and then walked to meet her father.

Their voices carried down the street and Jean could hear their conversation from where she was sitting.

"I heard the unfortunate news," Mr. Lyons said to her father. "I'm very sorry. What are the doctors saying?"

"He's in very bad condition," her father said. "They don't know if he'll pull through or not. I came home to be with the children for a while, but I'm going back to the hospital soon."

"We'll certainly keep Harry and the rest of you in our prayers and help out however we can."

"You're going to pray for Harry?" Jean heard her father ask.

"Of course we will."

"If God hears you and heals my son, I will serve Him forever."

Jean was surprised to hear those words come from her father's mouth. Did he mean it? Would they be able to go to church? She remembered what Mr. Lyons had told her. *With God, nothing is impossible.* If that was true, God could heal Harry, and her father would let them go to church.

"Could I go to the hospital with you and pray for Harry right now?" Mr. Lyons asked.

"I suppose so," her father replied. "There's no harm in trying it, I guess."

All of a sudden, Jean felt hopeful. She knew that Mr. Lyons believed completely in God. She had even heard him tell about times in the Bible when God had done amazing things. Surely a God like that could heal Harry.

Her father headed to the hospital with Mr. Lyons a few minutes later, and Jean could hardly stand the waiting. All morning, she wondered how Harry was doing. She felt almost positive that he was getting better by the minute.

That afternoon, she couldn't wait any longer. She ran down the street to the mission and knocked on the front door.

"Why, hello, Jean!" Kind Mrs. Lyons greeted her at the door. "Are you here to ask Mr. Lyons about Harry?"

"Yes," said Jean. "Is he here?"

"I'm here," Mr. Lyons said, coming into the kitchen.

"Did you see Harry?" Jean asked anxiously.

"I did. I prayed for him."

"Is he better now?" She felt so hopeful.

"He was asleep the whole time. He's in God's hands, Jean. Remember what I told you about God?"

"Nothing is impossible for Him."

"Exactly. Don't forget it."

Jean headed back home, feeling less hopeful than she had before. She had hoped God would heal Harry right away.

All day she wondered what was happening at the hospital.

Finally, her mother and father came home for the night. Jean ran out to meet them. "Did you bring Harry with you?" she asked.

"Harry needs to stay at the hospital for now, Jean," her mother answered, reaching out and pulling Jean close.

Although Jean was disappointed that Harry hadn't come home, she could tell by her father's smile that he wasn't as worried as he had been that morning.

"Is he getting better?" she asked. "Is Harry going to be okay?"

"The doctors are very pleased with how he's doing. He should be able to come home in a few days."

Jean felt so relieved. She wanted to run and sing and laugh. "Mr. Lyons asked God to heal Harry, and God did!" she said. "Can we go to church now?" she asked her father.

"We'll have to see," her father said.

Several days passed, and the whole family was excited when Harry was finally able to come home. It was so good to hear his teasing and his laugh again.

Time went on and it seemed to Jean that her father had forgotten what he had said to Mr. Lyons that day. He never mentioned it and never went to church. Nothing changed until the day when Jean's parents were planning to have their friends over for a card party.

That very day, Mr. Lyons called Jean's mom and asked if they could have a prayer meeting at their house.

Jean heard her parents discussing it.

"I couldn't say no to him," her mom said.

"We're having our own company over," her father argued. "Are we just supposed to cancel it?" Jean could hear the anger in her father's voice.

"I already have," her mother answered. "Mr. Lyons prayed for Harry when he was sick. Who knows what would have happened if he hadn't? It won't hurt us to have one prayer meeting at our house."

Her father sighed heavily. "Fine. Just this once."

That evening, Jean and her family listened as people read from the Bible and talked about how good it was to belong to God.

When the prayer meeting was over, Jean's father stood up and picked up one of the pipes that he enjoyed smoking so much and said, "After this night, I will never smoke again." And after that night, he never did.

But even though he stopped smoking, he still did not want to go to church or learn more about God.

One day, Jean's father came home from work with a strange expression on his face.

"Is something wrong?" Jean's mother asked him.

"Something very strange happened while I was walking home from work today," he answered.

"What happened, Dad?" Harry asked curiously.

"As I walked, I looked up and noticed a beautiful rainbow in the sky. I was thinking about how nice it looked when I heard a voice talk to me."

"You heard a voice?" Jean asked. "What did it say?"

"It said, 'I kept My promise to man, but man does not keep his promise to Me.'"

"Who was it, Dad?" Arthur asked.

"I think," their father paused, "I think that it was God."

"Are you sure that you didn't imagine this?" Jean's mother looked skeptical.

Her father laughed. "I *know* I didn't imagine it. It was real. God spoke to me. I said that if He healed Harry, I would serve Him forever. I think He wants me to keep my promise. It's time for us to start going to church!"

Soon after that, there were special meetings at the church, and Jean's whole family went to hear the evangelist preach. During one of these meetings, Jean's father prayed and confessed his sins, asking God to forgive him. Jean could tell right away that her father was a different person. He threw away all of his liquor. He spoke kindly all the time and treated her mother very tenderly. As Jean's mother watched him, she saw that he really had changed and that becoming a Christian had made him a much happier, kinder person. Soon she also became a Christian.

Jean saw how much her parents loved God. She saw how they carried the Bible around the house with them, and how they took every opportunity to read and memorize it. She loved learning about God. She loved knowing that He was taking care of them. She would never forget the way He had healed Harry. She would never forget the way He had spoken to her father.

Jean truly believed what Mr. Lyons had said. Nothing was impossible with God.

Questions for Review

1. What health problem did Harry have?

2. Why didn't Jean and her brothers and sisters go to church when they were invited?

3. What did Mr. Lyons keep saying to Jean about God?

4. What strange thing happened to Mr. Chambers as he was walking home from work one day?

5. How did Mr. Chambers' life change after he became a Christian?

Questions for Discussion

1. What were some instances of faith in this story, and which one do you like best?

2. How was Mr. Lyons a good missionary in Welland?

3. Are there any children in your area that your family could invite to Sunday school or church?

4. Why did Mr. Chambers permit a prayer meeting in the Chambers' home?

5. Has anyone you know had appendicitis? a burst appendix?

It was my privilege to know John Chambers. He bore a very close resemblance to the man giving thanks for his simple meal in the famous photograph called "Grace" taken by Eric Enstrom. John Chambers died in January 1986.

~Howard

ABRAHAM

TEST OF LEAVING FAMILY

By faith Abraham, when he was called to go out into a place which he should after receive for an inheritance, obeyed; and he went out, not knowing whither he went. Hebrews 11:8

READ GENESIS 12:1-9

Amy Carmichael, born in northern Ireland, heard Hudson Taylor speak about missions when she was twenty years old. She sensed God calling her to missionary work. Although she suffered various physical ailments, she served faithfully in India, rescuing girls from immoral slavery in Hindu temples. Without a return home, she served in India for 55 years until her death.

Abram received a call from God, and he never returned to his homeland. The Lord asked Abram to make a complete break, forsaking his relatives, his home, and his community. Abram passed the test of leaving family in order to follow God's call.

Life for Amy in India was no bed of roses. While in India, Amy received a letter from a young lady who was considering life as a missionary. Her question to Amy was, "What is missionary life like?"

Amy replied, "Missionary life is simply a chance to die." Amy's life demonstrated a great personal sacrifice. It is unlikely that Abram's journey to Canaan was easy either.

Amy provided physical and spiritual shelter for over 1,000 children whose futures had looked very grim.

Through Abraham's obedience, over a thousand people groups have been given hope via Abraham's descendant, Jesus Christ. God told Abraham, "In thee shall all families of the earth be blessed."

Ideally, you will have the support of your family and be able to maintain contact with them as you endeavour to do the will of God. But if members of your family oppose your obedience to the Lord, the Lord must come first. Jesus said, "He that loveth father or mother more than me is not worthy of me: and he that loveth son or daughter more than me is not worthy of me" (Matthew 10:37).

Test of Truthfulness

*These are the things that ye shall do; Speak ye every
man the truth to his neighbor; execute the judgment of
truth and peace in your gates. Zechariah 8:16*

Read Genesis 12:14-20

What are some signs that a person may be lying to you? Dr. Alan Hirsch of Chicago, a psychiatrist, says that the Pinocchio syndrome can be one thing to look for. (Pinocchio, you may recall, was a fictional character whose nose grew longer each time he told a lie). Dr. Hirsch claims that blood rushes to the nose of a person who lies, and the sudden increase of blood supply makes the nose itchy. This may cause a person to scratch the nose or touch it more frequently than normal. He also claims liars may clear their throat more often or begin to stutter. Before telling a big lie, a person may lean forward, constantly change position, or rest his elbows on the table. Other body language signals of possible prevarication include tightening the lips, licking the lips, swallowing more, and taking deep breaths. (I suppose a lot of these signs simply indicate nervousness, so don't jump to conclusions that a person is lying just because he exhibits one or more of these signs.)

While I was conversing on a social level with a Canadian border official, he mentioned that he looks to see if the person he is inspecting makes direct eye contact or not. Liars tend to avoid looking you in the eye and roll their eyes as they speak as if they are thinking what they will make up in answer to the question asked them (which is, in fact, what they are doing).

I don't know if Abram gave any tell-tale signs of not telling the whole truth as he told Pharaoh that Sarai was his sister. But certainly Abram failed the test of truthfulness, as told in the daily reading.

The Israelites were commanded, "Ye shall not steal, neither deal falsely, neither lie one to another" (Leviticus 19:11). In fact, "lying lips are an abomination to the LORD" (Proverbs 12:22). The New Testament plainly teaches us, "Lie not one to another" (Colossians 3:9). We are warned, "All liars, shall have their part in the lake which burneth with fire and brimstone: which is the second death" (Revelation 21:8).

The "ability" to lie is a "lie-ability." It may appear to be an asset but ultimately it will prove to be a liability.

TEST OF UNSELFISHNESS

Even as I please all men in all things, not seeking mine own profit, but the profit of many, that they may be saved. 1 Corinthians 10:33

READ GENESIS 13:1-18

My mother taught her children this poem.

> A Tea Party
> I had a little tea party
> This afternoon at three.
> 'Twas very small—
> Three guests in all—
> Just I, Myself, and Me.
>
> Myself ate all the sandwiches,
> While I drank up the tea;
> 'Twas also I who ate the pie
> And passed the cake to Me.

Abram's attitude was altogether different. He unselfishly let Lot choose the best land for his herds, although Abram was the elder. As the latter part of the daily reading indicates, God promised to bless Abram abundantly.

Abram had a different orientation than the boy who was riding a hobbyhorse together with his sister. The boy said, "If one of us would just get off this hobbyhorse, there would be more room for me."

Jonathan was another unselfish Bible character. First Samuel 18:4 tells us, "Jonathan stripped himself of the robe that was upon him, and gave it to David, and his garments, even to his sword, and to his bow, and to his girdle." The Lord Jesus was the greatest example of unselfishness. "For ye know the grace of our Lord Jesus Christ, that, though he was rich, yet for your sakes he became poor, that ye through his poverty might be rich" (2 Corinthians 8:9).

An anonymous writer with considerable perception composed the following "Recipe for a Miserable Life."

- Think about yourself.
- Talk about yourself.
- Use *I* as often as possible.
- Mirror yourself continually in the opinion of others.
- Listen greedily to what people say about you.
- Expect to be appreciated.
- Be suspicious.
- Be jealous and envious.
- Be sensitive to slights.
- Never forgive a criticism.
- Insist on consideration and respect.
- Trust nobody but yourself.
- Demand agreement with your own views on everything.
- Sulk if people are not grateful to you for favors shown them.
- Never forget a service you may have rendered.
- Be on the lookout for a good time for yourself.
- Shirk your duties if you can.
- Do as little as possible for others.
- Love yourself supremely.
- Be selfish.

TEST OF PATIENCE

Take, my brethren, the prophets, who have spoken in the name of the Lord, for an example of suffering affliction, and of patience. James 5:10

READ GENESIS 15:1-6; 16:1-6

Phillip Brooks was a New England pastor who wrote "O Little Town of Bethlehem." He had a reputation of being very calm and unruffled, but sometimes he struggled with impatience. A friend told of being with Brooks one evening as Brooks paced the floor. "What's the matter?" he asked.

Brooks replied, "The trouble is I'm in a hurry, but God isn't."

Abram knew God had promised an heir to him and Sarai, with a multitude of descendants. Was Eliezer to be Abram's heir? Sarai had another idea that she soon regretted—let Abram have a child with Sarai's handmaid, Hagar. Abram needed much patience.

F. B. Meyer wrote in *Abraham*, "God has His set times. It is not for us to know them. Indeed, we cannot know them. We must wait for them. If God had told Abraham in Haran that he must wait all those years until he pressed the promised child to his bosom, his heart would have failed him. So in gracious love, the length of the weary years was hidden, and only as they were nearly spent and there were only a few more months to wait, God told him that according to the time of life Sarah shall have a son.

"If God told you on the front end how long you would wait to find the fulfillment of your desire or pleasure or dream, you'd lose heart. You'd grow weary in well doing. So would I. But He doesn't. He just says, 'Wait. I keep My Word. I'm in no hurry. In the process of time I'm developing you to be ready for the promise.' "

God sometimes lets us stay in a state of perplexity for a while so that we may learn patience. E. C. McKenzie made this evaluation, "The true measure of a man is the height of his ideals, the breadth of his sympathy, the depth of his convictions, and the length of his patience."

TEST OF FAITH

*Through faith also Sara herself received strength to conceive
seed, and was delivered of a child when she was past age, because
she judged him faithful who had promised. Hebrews 11:11*

READ GENESIS 17:1-8, 15-19

Have you wished for a change of name? Sometimes people shorten the name they are given: Michael becomes Mike; Rebecca becomes Becca; Thomas becomes Tom; Elizabeth becomes Liz. Both Abram and Sarai received changes to their names by the Lord. God changed Abram's name to Abraham when He made a covenant with him, that Abram would have a son in his old age who would be the ancestor of many nations. God changed Sarai's name to *Sarah*, meaning "princess." This indicated the role she was to play in being the mother of many nations, a mother of royalty (verse 15 of the daily reading).

To believe God's promise that Isaac would be born when Abraham was 99 and Sarah was 90 took considerable faith.

Jesus gave good instruction to His disciples, past and present. "Have faith in God" (Mark 11:22). The psalmist said, "Mine eyes are unto thee, O GOD the Lord: in thee is my trust; leave not my soul destitute" (Psalm 141:8).

D. L. Moody said:

Trust in yourself, and you are doomed to disappointment.
Trust in your friends, and they will die and leave you.
Trust in money, and you may have it taken from you.
Trust in reputation, and some slanderous tongue may blast it.
But trust in God, and you are never to be confounded in time or eternity.

Test of Befriending Strangers

....

Distributing to the necessity of saints; given to hospitality. Romans 12:13

Read Genesis 18:1-15

In the 40-line poem "The House by the Side of the Road," the author, Sam Walter Foss, states the following wish repeatedly: "Let me live in my house by the side of the road and be a friend to man." Mr. Foss wrote it after coming to a small unpainted house on one of his hikes through rustic England. Weary, hot, and thirsty, he saw a signpost, pointing to a well-worn path, which said, "Come in and have a cool drink."

Mr. Foss followed the path to a spring of ice-cold water. On a nearby bench was a basket of summer apples with another sign, "Help Yourself."

Mr. Foss decided to talk to the people who lived in the house and ask them about the signs and the fruit. He learned that they had no children and barely eked out a living on their poor farm. But they had lots of fresh cold spring water and apples in season, and so they felt rather rich and wanted to share with anyone who might pass by their place. The old gentleman said, "We're too poor to give money to charity, but we thought in this way we might help others a little on their way."

Abraham did very well at befriending the three men who appeared at his tent door.

- He was eager to be friendly. "He ran to meet them" (verse 2).

- He was polite. He "bowed himself toward the ground" (verse 2).

- He welcomed them. "Pass not away" (verse 3).

- He made provision for them to be comfortable. He washed their feet and he said, "Rest yourselves under the tree" (verse 4).

- He offered them food. "I will fetch a morsel of bread" (verse 5).

- He quickly arranged for the food to be prepared. "And Abraham ran unto the herd, and fetcht a calf tender and good" (verse 7).

- He gave the best he had and acted as their servant. "And he took butter, and milk, and the calf which he had dressed, and set it before them; and he stood by them under the tree, and they did eat" (verse 8).

It is, no doubt, Abraham that the Hebrew writer had in mind when he wrote, "Be not forgetful to entertain strangers: for thereby some have entertained angels unawares" (Hebrews 13:2).

TEST OF OBEDIENCE

By faith Abraham, when he was tried, offered up Isaac: and he that had received the promises offered up his only begotten son. Hebrews 11:17

READ GENESIS 22:1-6

Not only schoolteachers give tests; God does too. "God did tempt," that is, *test* Abraham in a very personal way (verse 1 of the daily reading). And what a test!

What faith Abraham needed: faith that God would show him the mountain (verse 2); faith that God knew what He was asking; and faith that God would resurrect Isaac (Hebrews 11:19).

Abraham and Isaac went to worship. *Worship* originally meant "to bow down." They were bowing down to God and His will. Not understanding but believing, they both showed perfect obedience to a perplexing command.

Isaac was submissive to his earthly father and his heavenly Father. Father and son "went both of them together" (verses 6 and 8). At first Isaac had questions. The fire and wood he saw, but where was the sacrifice? But as he let himself be bound and placed on the altar and saw the knife in his father's hand, the question of what the sacrifice would be was answered.

Note Abraham's prompt obedience. He "rose up early." It was a long journey, so he took two assistants along as well as Isaac. They traveled for three days before they arrived at Mount Moriah. Those three days must have been agony for them. Both father and son were fully set to do God's will from the moment they started out. Thus, in a sense, Isaac had been dead three days. The three days of apparent death correspond to the three days during which Christ was actually dead. The wood was on Isaac's back; Christ's back was bound against the wood on the cross. "Where is the lamb for the burnt offering?" The answer comes back across the centuries: "Behold the Lamb of God, which taketh away the sin of the world" (John 1:29).

Never was such a loving father or obedient son put to such a test as this. Abraham obeyed God because he believed God. "Was not Abraham our father justified by works, when he had offered Isaac his son upon the altar? Abraham believed God, and it was imputed unto him for righteousness: and he was called the Friend of God" (James 2:21, 23). He had received righteousness imputed by faith, but that faith was tested by works.

Asking in Faith
Jean Chambers Cober

by Jasmine (Shantz) Martin

Jean ran down the street and up the steps to her friend Marcy's house. She knocked on the door and bounced impatiently as she waited for someone to answer. She hoped Marcy would be able to come and play with her.

45

"Oh, good morning, Jean," Marcy's mom said when she opened the door. Jean noticed that she didn't greet her as cheerfully as she usually did.

"Good morning! Can Marcy come out and play with me?" Jean asked.

"I'm afraid not, Jean. Marcy is very sick. She's got whooping cough."

Jean felt the smile disappear from her face. "Oh, no! I'm so sorry. Will you tell her that I hope she feels better soon?"

"I will do that. Now you go along home and make sure you don't get sick too, all right?"

Jean nodded and waved good-bye. She trudged home and into their kitchen where her mom was baking. "Couldn't Marcy play today?" Mom asked.

"She's sick. She has the whooping cough."

"Oh, no! I've heard of several other children on this street who have it as well. It must be going around. I hope you children don't get it. We have special services at church coming up, and it would be a shame if you were to get sick." Jean knew that her mother was concerned with more than just missing out on the special services. People with whooping cough got very sick.

She hoped that she wouldn't get it. But Marcy had it, and Jean had played with her many times in the past few days.

The next evening, Jean started to cough.

Her mother put her hand on Jean's forehead and sighed. "You have a bit of a fever, I'm afraid. Better get to bed."

Jean crawled into bed, hardly able to believe that she was getting sick. Would it be whooping cough? Would she get better?

Jean's mother sent for Mr. and Mrs. Lyons. "How are you feeling, Jean?" Mr. Lyons asked as they came into her room.

Jean shrugged. "Not very well."

"We've come to pray for you."

Jean nodded. She remembered how God had taken care of Harry when his appendix had burst. Surely He would take care of her as well.

Mr. Lyons pulled out a small flask of oil and poured some of it onto Jean's head. He and Mrs. Lyons laid their hands on her shoulders and head. Jean felt the warmth of their hands seeping into her skin.

"Dear God," prayed Mr. Lyons, "we know that You are taking care of Jean. You know that she's sick. We know that You can heal her, if it's part of Your plan. Please take care of her and help her to feel better. In Jesus' name we pray, Amen."

As soon as they finished praying, Jean gave one very loud, large whooping cough.

And that was all.

She never got the whooping cough, even though most of the other children on her street did. In fact, no one from her family caught it.

Jean believed in God's power even more than she had before.

Several days later, Jean was outside playing with her doll buggy by herself.

"Ouch!" she said as she pinched her finger in the hood. Her thumb was cut and began to bleed onto her dress.

Jean looked down at her bleeding thumb. It hurt a lot.

God could heal it. She knew that He could.

Jean got down on her knees to pray right there on the sidewalk.

"Dear God," she said. "Please make my thumb feel better and stop bleeding. Amen."

Jean opened her eyes and peeked at her thumb. It was still bleeding.

She was closer to the mission than she was to her house, so she decided to stop there and ask for a bandage.

As she walked up the sidewalk to the mission door, she glanced at her thumb again.

She stopped walking and stared in amazement.

The thumb that had been bleeding heavily only moments before was no longer bleeding.

In fact, the cut had been healed. Jean could see where the cut had been, but the wound was closed now.

"Thank You, God!" Jean said out loud as she wiggled her thumb in astonishment.

The scar from that cut remained on her thumb for the rest of her life. It was a constant reminder to her that God was good, and that He was taking care of her.

"Where's my history book?" Harry yelled one morning as the children got ready for school.

"On the kitchen table," Jean calmly responded. Harry rushed to the kitchen and returned with his book.

"Thanks," he said. "I, uh—I don't suppose that you know where my math book is."

"Have you checked the coffee table?" Jean suggested.

Once again, Harry returned with the missing book.

"What would I do without you, Jean?" Harry asked, reaching out to tousle her hair. Jean laughed and ducked away, wanting to keep her hair neat.

Jean's family lived right across the street from their school, and they could be there on time even if they left just when they heard the first bell ring. It was very handy on mornings such as this one, where there seemed to be hardly enough time for everyone to get ready. Things were especially chaotic because Jean's father, John Chambers, had broken his hip while helping to paint the church and was confined to his bed. He kept saying that they could trust God to supply all their needs, but Jean knew they had hardly enough money to pay for the things they needed.

"Children! It's time to pray!" Jean's mother called. Each morning, before going to school, the family gathered to pray and read a passage from the Bible. The children ran from all corners of the house to their parents' bedroom.

The family knelt around the bed as their father prayed. "Lord, thank You for a good night and the beautiful day. Please be with the children as they go to school. And Lord, Ellen really needs new shoes. Would You please take care of that for us?" Jean's father then quoted part of Psalm 37:25 and 26 as part of his prayer. "Yet have I not seen the righteous forsaken or his seed begging bread. He is ever merciful, and lendeth; and his seed is blessed. Amen."

Just then, the first bell rang. There was a flurry of good-byes, and Jean and her siblings ran out of the house. Jean slid into her desk just in time and wondered how God would supply a new pair of shoes for Ellen. She needed a new pair badly.

But how would God send a pair of shoes?

Three days before Jean's father prayed about the shoes, Agnes Flagg, the deacon's wife, stooped in the hot sun, picking berries. She worked quickly and carefully to fill her last bucket.

"Phew!" she said to herself, standing up and stretching her tired back. "What a hot day!" Although she was tired, she had a smile on her face. She mentally tallied up the amount of money she had earned. Her daughter Elsie needed a new pair of shoes, and the five dollars that Agnes had finally earned would buy a pair for Elsie.

As she stood there, the smile slowly left her face and was replaced with a frown. She considered a thought that had just popped into her mind. *Send this money to John Chambers today.*

"But, God," Agnes said out loud, "I need this money. Elsie has needed new shoes for a while already! Do You really want me to give it away? I worked so hard for it! Not only do I need it for the shoes, but I also don't have a way of sending it. There's no way that I can get this money to John Chambers."

Just then, Agnes noticed her neighbor walking up the road towards her. "Good morning!" she called.

"Good morning! I have some extra time this morning, and I came by to see if there is anything I can help you with today," her neighbor offered.

Agnes knew right away that the Lord had provided a way for her to send the money to John Chambers. With purpose in her steps, she went into the house, put the five dollars into an envelope, and gave it to her neighbor to deliver to the post office.

She sighed gently as she watched the envelope of money leaving. With determination, she continued to pick strawberries with the contented look of one who has obeyed the Holy Spirit's nudging.

By the end of the day, Jean had forgotten about Dad's prayer requesting shoes for Ellen. But that evening, when the family gathered around the table for dinner, their parents looked very happy.

"Children, today we received something special in the mail," Jean's father said, unable to contain his smile. He held up an envelope and pulled out a five-dollar bill. "This!"

Five dollars would buy a new pair of shoes for Ellen! The children began to smile and laugh as they realized that God had answered their prayer.

"That's the fastest answer to prayer I've ever seen!" Harry shouted.

"Who's it from?" Jean asked curiously.

"It doesn't say," Dad answered. "There's no name anywhere."

"I suppose the only thing that we can do is thank God," Jean's mother said.

Dad quoted Job 14:15. "Thou shalt call, and I will answer thee."

"I can't believe that God sent money for a pair of shoes. God cares about my shoes," Ellen said joyfully.

Jean knew that what Job 14:15 said was true. God had heard their request and answered it, all in one day.

Jean's father recovered from his broken hip, and a few years later he was preparing his offering envelope. He sat thoughtfully at his desk before turning to Mom. "I think I should send some money to Isaac and Agnes Flagg."

"Why do you think that?" Jean's mother asked.

"Well, you know they are market farmers and their crops produced very poorly this year. I imagine that they hardly have enough money these days."

"Yes, I think you should do it," Jean's mother said. "Remember how relieved we were when we received those five dollars when you had a broken hip?"

"I do. It's our turn to give now."

Jean's father tucked some money into a separate envelope. "It's too much money to send in the mail. We'll drive it over to their house later today."

Jean climbed into the car to go along for the ride. When they arrived at the Flagg's house, Jean was surprised to see a large shiny car in the driveway that did not belong to the Flaggs. She craned her neck to see out the window. She wasn't sure exactly what was going on, but she could tell that it wasn't something good.

Some important-looking men, dressed in suits and stern faces were talking to Isaac Flagg.

Mom and Dad immediately saw what the trouble was. "I think we arrived just in time!" Dad said.

Jean's parents left the car and took the envelope of money to Isaac. Jean watched as Isaac looked inside the envelope. His face filled with relief when he saw what it contained. Even from inside the car, Jean heard him say, "Praise the Lord!"

Isaac straightened his shoulders and lifted his head. Then he used the money from Jean's parents to pay the debt that would have made him surrender his farm to the important-looking men. The men climbed into their shiny car and drove away.

"Praise the Lord!" Isaac shouted again. "He keeps providing for us."

Jean left the car and skipped up to the happy group just in time to hear Agnes speak. "God truly is amazing! Several years ago, I sent you some money in the mail because I felt as though God was asking me to. It was hard for me at the time because I felt like I needed that money for my own family. But I decided that if God wanted me to share my money, I would trust Him to supply my needs. And now, years later… God sent you to supply our need! Thank you so much for listening to Him!" Her eyes filled with tears.

The group was silent for a moment as they thought about how well God takes care of His people, if only they trust Him to do so.

"Amazing," Jean's father said softly.

Jean looked up at the faces of these grown-ups who loved God. She was so thankful that Agnes had allowed God to use her five dollars years ago, and that her father had promptly obeyed when he felt God wanted him to give money to the Flaggs.

A little bit of trust can go a long way.

As Jean grew, she continued to learn more about God and what it meant to follow Him. She saw her father and mother adjust their family's rules to teach their children to obey God. Her parents' belief impacted her greatly.

When Jean entered high school, she began to feel that God wanted her to wear a head covering to school. None of her friends—in fact, no one else in the school—wore a head covering, and Jean did not like the thought of standing out in that way. But she decided that she must obey 1 Corinthians 11 and began to wear a covering to school.

This, of course, attracted a lot of attention. Questions from her classmates were common. Her math teacher in particular did not seem to like Jean and inflicted on her a sort of persecution, drilling her relentlessly in front of the class.

God never failed to take care of Jean though. After a time, even that harsh math teacher became one of her friends. When Jean was about seventeen years old, she gave her heart completely to Jesus. She determined that she would never turn back, and she didn't. At

21 years of age, she married Alvin Cober. They had two boys and two girls.

Jean and her husband Alvin were doing some cleanup work in their orchard. As Jean worked, she hummed cheerfully, thanking God for such a lovely, calm day. She and Alvin each carried a load over to the burn barrel. They took turns dumping the sticks and trash into the barrel and then stopped to catch their breath.

"It feels good to be getting this job taken care of! We've made good progress," Alvin commented, wiping his forehead with a handkerchief.

"Do you think that we could burn this right away, or should we wait until we get a new burn barrel?" Jean asked, eyeing the old barrel a bit warily. "That old barrel worries me."

"I think we can use it one more time," Alvin replied. "It's a calm day, so it should be fine. If I start it burning now, it might be finished in time to burn the next load of trash. We'll keep an eye on it." Alvin started the fire, and the two headed back to work.

"I've got another load full!" Jean called as she finished filling another basket with trash.

"Why don't you take it over to the burn barrel and see how it's doing? We'll start a new pile over there until we can put it into the barrel," Alvin directed.

Jean lugged her big basket in the direction of the barrel. As she neared it, she could see that something was not right. Flames were licking out from the bottom of the barrel.

"Alvin!" she screamed. "Fire!"

Alvin ran over. "Please help us, God. Run and get the hose, Jean!" He yelled the last part, already running for a sack lying nearby. He began beating at the flames as Jean ran for the hose.

Never before had the hose seemed quite so heavy and awkward to carry. *Please, God! Please help us to put out the fire!*

Alvin kept beating even after Jean turned the hose on the flames. The flames didn't seem to be dying down. *The trees. If the fire reaches the trees, how will we ever stop it?*

"Get some mats from the house, Jean! We'll make them wet and beat with them." Jean did as Alvin had said, and they both worked with wet mats, doing their best to extinguish the flames.

But that fire seemed unstoppable. Nothing caused it to diminish in any way.

Alvin stopped and stood still. "Jean, it's time to stop."

"Stop?" The idea of stopping seemed crazy.

Alvin took the blackened, damp mat out of her hands. "We need to pray. There's nothing else that we can do."

Together, Alvin and Jean knelt on the ground. "God, You can see that we need Your help. We can't stop this fire. We know You can. Please help us," Alvin prayed. Jean silently begged God to stop the fire before it reached the trees.

Jean squeezed Alvin's hand as his prayer came to a close. Her head remained bowed in silent prayer.

"Jean," Alvin whispered. "Look!"

Jean lifted her head. "What?"

"The fire. It's dying!"

"Are you sure?"

"Yes!" Alvin stood up in his excitement. "It's definitely dying!"

Jean watched in awe as the very fire that had raged unstoppable died before her eyes.

Alvin laughed in relief. "Thank You! Thank You, God!" he called out.

"Look!" Jean said. "Look! There's a line exactly where the fire stopped."

"So there is!" Alvin laughed again. "God sure answered that prayer quickly!"

"He certainly did!"

"Well, Jean, I'm afraid these tests show that you have breast cancer," stated the doctor. "We'll have to book you for further treatment."

Jean was sixty-two years old. Her mind was whirling as she left the doctor's office that day. She remembered all the times in her life that God had done things that seemed impossible. She knew that He was able to cure her cancer.

That evening, Alvin asked how her appointment had gone.

"I have breast cancer," Jean answered.

"Oh, Jean…" Alvin said softly.

"It will be okay, Alvin. God has never left us before, and He certainly won't leave us now. I've been thinking—"

"Yes?"

"I would like to be anointed. I believe without a doubt that God can heal me."

"All right. Let's see what the ministers say."

When Jean expressed her faith in God's ability to heal her, the ministry agreed that they would anoint her. Upon her request, they anointed her with oil during an evening church service as the congregation prayed for her healing. Jean continued to trust that God had His hand of protection over her.

Jean went on to have surgery, but after that it was discovered—to the surprise of the cancer doctor—that no further treatment would be needed.

Some time later, when Jean was in the hospital for a different reason, the cancer doctor who had worked with her paid her a visit.

"Hello!" Jean said in surprise. "I wasn't expecting to see you!"

"When I heard that you were here, I just had to drop by."

"Why is that?" Jean asked.

"I wanted to make sure you knew just how much trouble you have caused me!"

"Trouble?" Jean was surprised. "How have I caused you trouble?"

"When I first diagnosed you with breast cancer, I was so certain you would require further treatment that I booked it in advance for you. After your surgery, when we found that no further treatment would be needed, I forgot to cancel the treatment I had scheduled. Some people were pretty upset with me!" The cancer doctor shook her head. "That was miraculous."

Jean smiled. "Yes, it was." She was thankful for the reminder that God was taking care of her.

Questions for Review

1. What sickness did God spare Jean from because of prayer?

2. What did Jean do when her thumb was cut?

3. How did God answer Mr. Chambers' prayer for shoes for Ellen?

4. Why did the Flaggs not have enough money to make their payments on their farm?

5. How did Jean and Alvin try to put out the fire in the orchard?

Questions for Discussion

1. What were some instances of faith in this story and which one do you like best?

2. Does your family know of anyone who has been anointed with oil?

3. When has your family especially needed to trust God?

4. What are some answers to prayer in your family?

5. Has your family ever helped others or been helped financially?

Jean was a member of the same church that I am. She had a ready testimony for Jesus and a strong faith. My wife and I often hosted her and Alvin in our home and listened to her tell her life experiences. She was strong in faith to the end. She died in 2012 at the age of eighty-four. ~Howard

ISAAC

IS ANYTHING
TOO HARD FOR GOD?

*Ah Lord GOD! behold, thou hast made the heaven and
the earth by thy great power and stretched out arm, and
there is nothing too hard for thee. Jeremiah 32:17*

READ GENESIS 18:9-15

For which Old Testament character does the Bible record his birth, youth, marriage, adulthood, and death? He apparently experienced love at first sight. He was an average sort of person, not a giant of faith like his dad, nor a go-getter like his son. He enjoyed eating venison.

Isaac's birth was remarkably predicted by angelic messengers, as told in the daily reading. Sarah was ninety when Isaac was born, and Abraham was a decade older. Genesis 21:2, 5 tells about it. "For Sarah conceived, and bare Abraham a son in his old age, at the set time of which God had spoken to him. And Abraham was an hundred years old, when his son Isaac was born unto him."

God had promised Sarah a son—something that seemed impossible. You may face situations that look impossible too. It might be an illness. It might be a troubled or tangled marriage. It might be the death of a child or spouse. It might be a dilemma that, no matter which way you turn, another obstacle looms. It might be the need to forgive someone who has deeply wounded you. It might be despair caused by debts and financial losses. It might be a disability caused by an accident. No matter what the situation, look to God and His promises. God's promises are like life preservers—they keep a believer from sinking in the sea of trouble.

Faith believes the promise, hope anticipates it, and patience quietly awaits it.

ISAAC'S TRUST
AND SUBMISSION

....

*I beseech you therefore, brethren, by the mercies of God, that
ye present your bodies a living sacrifice, holy, acceptable unto
God, which is your reasonable service. Romans 12:1*

READ GENESIS 22:1-13

Like Isaac, George Mueller of Bristol was a man of faith. Here is a story told by the captain of a ship on which George Mueller was traveling:

We had George of Bristol on board. I had been on the bridge of the ship for twenty-four hours and never left it, and George Mueller came to me and said, "Captain, I have come to tell you I must be in Quebec on Saturday afternoon."

"It is impossible," I said.

"Then very well, if your ship cannot take me, God will find some other way. I have never broken an engagement in fifty-seven years; let us go down into the chart room and pray."

I looked at that man of God and thought to myself, *What lunatic asylum can that man have come from, for I never heard of such a thing as this?* "Mr. Mueller," I said, "do you know how dense this fog is?"

61

"No," he replied, "my eye is not on the dense fog but on the living God who controls every circumstance of my life." He knelt down and prayed one of the most simple prayers. When he had finished, I was going to pray, but he put his hand on my shoulder and told me not to pray. "As you do not believe He will answer, and as I believe He has, there is no need whatever for you to pray about it."

I looked at him and he said, "Captain, I have known my Lord for fifty-seven years, and there has never been a single day when I have failed to get an audience with the King. Get up, Captain, and open the door and you will find the fog has gone."

I got up and the fog indeed was gone, and on that Saturday afternoon George Mueller kept his promised engagement.

The daily reading portrays Abraham's faith. It seems to me that Isaac also showed great trust. He allowed his father to bind and place him on the altar, although he was in his teens or twenties and could have overpowered his aged father. Isaac submitted to being on the altar as a living sacrifice. Perhaps he believed that God would raise him up from the dead, like his father who was "accounting that God was able to raise him up, even from the dead" (Hebrews 11:19).

Isaac demonstrated deep trust. He pleases God best who trusts Him most.

A UNIQUE COURTSHIP

*Trust in the LORD with all thine heart; and lean not
unto thine own understanding. Proverbs 3:5*

READ GENESIS 24:61-67

My uncle, a bachelor who longed to be married, lived in British Columbia in his early fifties. A friend recommended that he date a certain Christian lady. He called her on his phone. Traveling to meet her, he fell asleep at the wheel, smashed his Buick, and hovered between life and death for three weeks. He decided she must not be the one God had for him.

Later, God led him through a series of circumstances to meet Ada, a mission worker from two thousand kilometers away who was traveling through his community. She had car trouble and met him while waiting for its repair. My uncle recognized her name because he had heard her name mentioned years before as a mission worker. He had wanted to meet her ever since. They corresponded and eventually married.

Although the way Isaac acquired a wife was one-of-a-kind, there are some lessons from his experience that can apply to any believer who courts.

First, *marry "in the Lord"* (1 Corinthians 7:3). Abraham's servant Eliezer was sent on a long journey to Abraham's relatives to find a wife rather than seeking one among heathen neighbors.

Second, *some parental involvement is wise.* Although in our culture I'm not in favor of parents arranging marriages, I do think young people should communicate with parents prior to and during courtship.

Third, *trust the Lord to guide.* When Eliezer neared his destination of Nahor, he said, "O LORD God of my master Abraham, I pray thee, send me good speed" (Genesis 24:12).

Eliezer asked the Lord to show him His will by arranging for a prospective bride for Isaac to draw water for his camels (Genesis 24:13-21). After seeing the answer to his prayers, Eliezer prayed, "Blessed be the LORD God of my master Abraham, who hath not left destitute my master of his mercy and his truth: I being in the way, the LORD led me to the house of my master's brethren" (Genesis 24:27). God wants to guide in all of life. "I will instruct thee and teach thee in the way which thou shalt go: I will guide thee with mine eye" (Psalm 32:8).

Fourth, *look at the matter of marriage seriously.* As mentioned in the daily reading, Isaac was outdoors meditating when his bride-to-be, Rebekah, arrived.

HE LOVED HER

And Isaac brought her into his mother Sarah's tent, and took Rebekah, and she became his wife; and he loved her: and Isaac was comforted after his mother's death. Genesis 24:67

READ GENESIS 24:1-14

"He loved her." What a beautiful testimony of how a husband should relate to his wife. That's how Isaac and Rebekah began their marriage. Christian husbands are told specifically to love as Christ loved the church: unselfishly, deeply, sacrificially, and enduringly. "Husbands, love your wives, even as Christ also loved the church, and gave himself for it" (Ephesians 5:25).

What are some ways a husband can show love to his wife? Protect her. Listen to her. Speak well of her to others. Speak kindly to her. Listen intently to her. Thank her for what she does. Promptly make repairs that she requests. Do his part to keep the home tidy. Be gentle with her. Remember her on special days. "Be not bitter against [her]" (Colossians 3:19). Be like the husband of the virtuous woman who "praiseth her" (Proverbs 31:28).

But something seems to have interfered with the love relationship of Isaac and his wife. As shown in the daily reading, there was a lack of cooperation, of confidence, and of communication. Instead of working together, Rebekah was scheming against Isaac. Instead of trusting his judgment, she involved her favorite son in deception. Instead of talking things over, he made his plan and she laid her plot.

A good marriage doesn't just happen. It takes commitment and mutual respect. "Wives, submit yourselves unto your own husbands, as unto the Lord" (Ephesians 5:22). As Martin Luther wrote, "Let the wife make her husband glad to come home, and let him make her sorry to see him leave."

PARENTAL FAVORITISM

Ye fathers, provoke not your children to wrath. Ephesians 6:4.

READ GENESIS 27:30-35, 41-46

There are many ways for fathers to provoke their children to wrath. Examples include anger in discipline, hypocrisy, sarcasm, harsh discipline, failing to listen to a teen, inconsistent discipline, unrealistic expectations, and ridicule. One of the most effectively, damaging ways is to obviously favor one child over another. In Isaac's home, father and mother each had a favorite. "And Isaac loved Esau, because he did eat of his venison: but Rebekah loved Jacob" (Genesis 25:28).

Genesis 27 shows the sad consequences of the favoritism. Because Isaac favored Esau, he ignored the Lord's plan that the elder (Esau) should serve the younger (Genesis 25:23). Because Rebekah favored Jacob, she schemed against her husband and actually planned for Jacob to deceive his father (vv. 5-17). This deception involved Jacob lying repeatedly to his father (vv. 19, 20, 24).

Our daily reading tells of more tragic consequences. When Isaac realized the deception, he "trembled very exceedingly" (v. 33). Also, Esau "cried with a great and exceeding bitter cry" (v. 34). Furthermore, "Esau hated Jacob" (v. 41) and planned to kill his brother after their father died. When this was reported to their mother, she decided it was necessary for Jacob to leave. Rebekah never saw him again, for she died before he returned twenty years later.

Results of partiality in the twenty-first century are likewise very undesirable. The less-favored child often feels bitter. Siblings will likely have interpersonal conflicts. The less-favored child may have a faulty view of the heavenly Father and may not respond with loving obedience to Him.

Parents should make it their aim to be fair to each of their children.

LIVE AT PEACE

If it be possible, as much as lieth in you, live
peaceably with all men. Romans 12:18

READ GENESIS 26:12-28

Years ago, a river divided the farms of two men. The cows of one neighbor crossed the river and ruined about half an acre of beautiful corn. The man who owned the damaged corn put the cows into his barn. He made his neighbor pay for the damaged crop and pay to get the cows back. In the fall the hogs of the man whose corn had been trampled went the other way across the river into his neighbor's potato patch. The neighbor with the ruined potato patch got the hogs back across the river. The owner of the hogs saw him coming, got his gun and hid, intending to harm his neighbor if the hogs were injured. When he saw the neighbor intended no harm to the hogs, he went to meet him, saying, "You have something I don't have. What is it?"

The peaceful neighbor said, "I am a Christian."

Isaac repeatedly showed a peaceable attitude toward those who envied him and made things difficult for him. Time after time, the Philistines filled in the wells that Isaac and his herdsmen needed. Finally, they stopped their mischief instead of stopping the wells.

For his peaceful approach, the Lord blessed Isaac and promised to be with him and give him a host of descendants. The attitude of Isaac foreshadowed the teachings of Christ who said in the Sermon on the Mount, "Blessed are the meek: for they shall inherit the earth. Blessed are the peacemakers: for they shall be called the children of God. Love your enemies, bless them that curse you, do good to them that hate you, and pray for them which despitefully use you, and persecute you" (Matthew 5:5, 9, 44).

When Philistine leaders came to Isaac, he was perplexed until they indicated their desire for a peace treaty. So Isaac made them a feast, and the next morning they departed from him in peace. Proverbs 25:21, 22 says, "If thine enemy be hungry, give him bread to eat; and if he be thirsty, give him water to drink: for thou shalt heap coals of fire upon his head, and the Lord shall reward thee."

Isaac left a very good testimony, for the Philistines said, "Thou art now the blessed of the Lord" (Genesis 26:29). Whether it is at home, at school, at church, or in the neighborhood, "let us therefore follow after the things which make for peace" (Romans 14:19).

ISAAC, A MAN OF FAITH

*Believe in the LORD your God, so shall ye be established; believe
his prophets, so shall ye prosper. 2 Chronicles 20:20*

READ MATTHEW 8:5-13

Charles A. Tindley, a poverty-stricken black pastor, stood at desperation corner. He was serving a tiny struggling church in Cape May, New Jersey, when a blizzard swept down, paralyzing the town. During the cold, dark night his baby died. Dawn brought no sign of relief. There was nothing but stale bread for breakfast. "Set the table like we always do," he urged his wife.

Courageously, he thanked God for his salvation, his health, and his children, confident that their needs would be met. As the family listened in wonder, someone knocked on the door. A brother in the Lord entered with his arms loaded with groceries. The storm had delayed his coming.

Charles Tindley had passed a crucial test of faith by remaining grateful under the darkest circumstances. This ex-slave went on to pastor a church in Philadelphia that reached thousands, including a grandson of the man who once owned him.

This story from the book *Their Finest Hour* by Charles Ludwig illustrates true faith.

Isaac's faith was expressed in various ways. He was a man of prayer. This is implied by his going out into a field in the evening to meditate. As he showed a nonresistant attitude toward the Philistine neighbors, the Lord appeared to him at Beersheba. Isaac "builded an altar there, and called on the name of the Lord, and pitched his tent there" (Genesis 26:25).

Isaac had faith that God's promise to Abraham and to himself would be carried forward by his children having many descendants. "By faith Isaac blessed Jacob and Esau concerning things to come" (Hebrews 11:20).

Isaac is considered a type of Christ in several ways. Like Christ's birth, Isaac's birth was predicted long before it occurred. His birth and Christ's birth caused great joy. The words of Genesis 22:2, "Take now thine son, thine only son Isaac, whom thou lovest," remind us of John 3:16: "For God so loved the world, that he gave his only begotten Son." Isaac's conception was miraculous. He was offered on the altar of sacrifice on Mount Moriah (now also believed to be Mount Calvary). He was submissive to his father's will.

From Canada to China
Jonathan Goforth

by Howard Bean

"Jonathan, how would you like to ride along with your uncle on his wagon?" asked his father.

"Will I get to ride up on the bags of grain?"

"Yes, he will find a good place for you."

Jonathan's uncle found a place for his five-year-old nephew. "All right, here we go. Stay where you are; don't move around."

Jonathan had no plans to hop from one place to another, but suddenly the wagon lurched and he had no choice. The front wheel had sunk deep into a rut.

"Help," Jonathan cried as he was tossed out of his place. Before his uncle could reach him, he fell to the ground. One of the wheels came so close that he felt it pressing against his hip.

"Are you all right, Jonathan?" asked his uncle anxiously. "Here, I'll get you out." But Jonathan was so pinned against the wheel that he could hardly get out. An inch farther and his hip would have been crushed. God spared him, knowing He had great work for Jonathan to do later.

Jonathan Goforth was born in 1859 and grew up near London, Ontario. His father was a farmer, and he taught Jonathan to work. When Jonathan was fifteen, his father put him in charge of a second farm about twenty miles away. His younger brother Joseph helped him. When their father handed over the farm to them, he called special attention to one large field covered with weeds. Father said, "Get that field clean and ready for seeding. At harvest time, I'll return and inspect it."

So Jonathan plowed. He replowed to get the weed roots out into the sunshine to die. He got the best seed he could to plant. He continued to care for the crop. At harvest time, his father arrived as he said he would. Jonathan was thrilled to take his father to a rise where they could see the whole beautiful field of grain. Jonathan was quiet as his father silently looked over the field and inspected it for any weeds. None. He looked at his son and smiled.

"That smile was all the reward I wanted," said Jonathan later. "I knew my father was pleased. So it will be if we are faithful to the trust our heavenly Father gives us."

As a teen he had another close call while helping at a barn raising. They were always alert for danger as the heavy beams were hauled up one by one and placed on the cross bent. Jonathan was standing below these beams in the center of the barn when a sudden cry rang out. "Take care, the cross bent is giving!" Looking up, he saw the beams had already started downward. There was no time to escape by running. There was but one thing to do—stand still and watch the beams as they fell, and dodge between them. This he did, escaping unhurt.

Although his mother taught him to pray and he could recite many verses of Scripture, he didn't become a Christian until he was eighteen. He soon became an active church member. He also wanted to honor the Lord in his home life. He wrote:

"At the time of my conversion I was living with my brother Will. Our parents came on a visit and stayed a month or so. For some time I felt the Lord would have me lead family worship. So one night I said, 'We will have worship tonight, so please don't scatter after supper.' I was afraid what my father would say for we had not been accustomed to saying 'grace' before meals, much less having family worship.

"I read a chapter in Isaiah, and after a few comments, we all knelt in prayer. Much to my relief, father never said a word. Family worship continued as long as I was home. Some months later, my father took a stand for Jesus Christ."

As a school boy Jonathan would stand in front of a map of the world, looking at Asia and Africa. Maybe he was dreaming of visiting such places. Eventually, he did go as a missionary—but first he was a missionary closer to home. While attending Bible college in Toronto, he witnessed in the city slums, some of which were dangerous. One night as he was coming out from a street that had a particularly evil reputation, a policeman met him, "How do you have the courage to go into those places?" he asked. "We never go except in twos or threes."

"Well, I never go alone either," Jonathan answered. "There is always Someone with me."

One summer he visited 960 homes to tell people about Jesus. Sometimes two or three people were converted each day.

He was also involved in a Sunday school. The students tended to be very rowdy. During prayer some of the boys would throw their caps around and say mocking *Amens*. One of the worst behaved was Tim. Here's how Jonathan described one situation.

"One day Tim went over to a trough nearby and filled his mouth with dirty water. Creeping up behind me, he spewed the contents of the water into the faces of the boys. In an instant, the room was in an uproar, and only after great difficulty were the teachers able to get some kind of order again. And then Tim was in another part of the room, knocking the girls' hats onto the floor. He went thus from one thing to another, keeping the school in almost continuous turmoil. For more than a year we could do nothing with him.

One afternoon, when the snow lay deep on the ground, I was walking along Queen Street when I spied Tim dragging a sleigh full of coal across the streetcar tracks. Deep trenches had been dug in the snow to enable the cars to run on the tracks. Tim's sleigh had gotten stuck in one of these trenches. A car was approaching and Tim, seeing it, tugged frantically this way and that, but to no avail. I ran forward to his assistance, and in a moment, the sleigh and Tim were safely out of the trench. He looked up into my face with a smile that spoke louder than words, and in the next instant was gone. I never had any more trouble with Tim. He was on my side ever afterwards.

Jonathan also accepted responsibility to speak in small communities outside Toronto. Often he walked over fifteen miles on a Sunday and preached three times. On one occasion he decided to take a shortcut through a thick forest. As he rounded a bend in the trail, he found a huge black bear sitting ahead of him just on the edge of the path. The bear rose, sat on his haunches, and stared. Jonathan stood and stared back at the bear. He decided that if he were to turn and run, the bear could easily catch up with him. Plus, Jonathan was on a mission for the Lord to share the Gospel. He said to himself, *I'm on the Master's business, and He can keep me safe.*

Praying, Jonathan walked slowly and steadily toward the bear. He almost had to touch the bear to pass it, but the great beast made no sign of moving. When he was some distance beyond the bear, he glanced back and saw it moving slowly into the forest. He went on to church, praising God for protecting him. Jonathan later wrote to his parents that he thought meeting that bear was the most dangerous thing he would ever encounter.

As a boy, he had been told about people who needed to know about Christ. Sometimes when speaking to children, he would tell this story. He said,

"I remember once, when I was but a little boy, someone gave me five cents. I never had so much money before. I felt rich. I thought, *Why, these five cents will buy six sticks of candy!* I raced into the house to ask my mother if I might not go to the store at once and buy that candy. My mother said, 'No, you may not go for it is Saturday evening, and the sun will soon be setting. You must wait until Monday.' I never felt so impatient about Sunday before. It came between me and the candy. Just then something seemed to say to me, 'Well, little boy, do you not think that you ought to give your five cents to the heathen?' At that time I didn't know who put that thought into my heart, but I had heard about a collection for missions announced to be taken on the morrow, and I know now that God's Spirit spoke to me then. He wanted to make me a missionary, but I wasn't willing. The heathen were far away. I didn't know much about them and didn't care. But I knew all about candy, and it was only two miles away at the store. I was very fond of it and decided I must have it. But that didn't end the struggle.

"It was candy and the heathen, and heathen and the candy contending for that five cents. Finally, I went to bed but couldn't sleep. Usually as soon as my head touched the pillow, I was off to sleep, but that night I couldn't get to sleep because of the war going on between the heathen and the candy, or between love and selfishness. At last the heathen got the better of it, and I decided to go to Sunday school the next day and put my five cents into the collection. I felt very happy then and in a moment was asleep. But when I awoke, the sun had arisen and my selfishness had returned. I wanted the candy, and the fight went on, but before Sunday school time, love had gained a final victory. I went to Sunday school, and when the plate was passed around for the mission collection, I dropped my five cents in. And would you believe me, I felt happier than if I had gotten a whole store full of candy! And so will any boy or girl who acts unselfishly for Jesus' sake."

He also spurred a lot of interest in foreign missions among adults. One time when he was being introduced as a speaker at a church in Canada, the moderator said of Jonathan, "This man took an overcoat from me once." Evidently, the moderator had gone to Toronto to buy a new overcoat. Before shopping, he attended a missionary meeting where Jonathan appealed for support for foreign missions. "My precious overcoat money went into the missionary offering, and I returned home wearing my old coat."

Although Jonathan was a gifted speaker and a very effective soul-warrior, people often commented about his humility. Once while the Goforths were attending a mission conference south of Chicago, the chairman introduced him with such generous praise there seemed no room for the glory of God in what was to follow. As Jonathan stepped forward, he stood a moment as if in prayer, then said, "Friends, when I listen to such words as we have just been hearing, I have to remind myself of the woodpecker story: A certain woodpecker flew up to the top of a high pine tree and gave three hard pecks on the side of the tree as woodpeckers are wont to do. At that instant a bolt of lightning struck the tree, knocking it to the ground as a heap of splinters. The woodpecker had flown to a tree nearby where it clung in terror and amazement at what had taken place. There it hung, expecting more to follow, but as all remained quiet it began to chuckle to itself, saying,

Well, well, well! Who would have imagined that just three pecks of my beak could have such power as that?"

Then Jonathan said, "Yes, friends, I laughed too when I first heard this story. But remember, if you or I take glory to ourselves that belongs only to almighty God, we are not only as foolish as this woodpecker, but we commit a very grievous sin, for the Lord hath said, 'My glory will I not give to another.' "

Many times Jonathan Goforth, on returning from a meeting, would say to his wife, "Well, I've had to remind myself of the woodpecker tonight." Early in life he chose as his motto, "Not by might, nor by power, but by my spirit" (Zechariah 4:6).

Sensing God's call to go to China, Jonathan and his wife Rosalind made preparations. They traveled by train to Vancouver on the west coast of Canada and were very excited about sailing to Shanghai. Jonathan wrote, "Let us leave no stone unturned in the effort to move God's people to spread the message to every creature. I know that many eyes are fixed on this movement. It rests with us either to inspire or discourage the host of God forming our church. We have the aid of many prayers. The means sufficient shall certainly not be wanting. Let us win ten thousand Chinese souls. It will please Him, our Lord."

Soon after embarking upon the fourteen-day voyage, their excitement turned to concern. They had good reason for worry. One day they watched several of the crew half carrying their captain down to a lower cabin—dead drunk. Rosalind was the only woman on board. In addition, they learned that the ship had been renamed, repainted, and put in the Pacific rather than the Atlantic because it had such a bad reputation for rolling and pitching that passengers wouldn't ride on her.

Soon after they left sight of land, the ship's carpenter, a Christian, asked Jonathan to pray for the safety of the ship. He was worried about some very heavy machinery on board for the emperor of Japan. One piece, so large it wouldn't fit down into the hold, was fastened to the deck. The carpenter said there was grave danger that the sides of the ship would be pressed outward and the ship would sink.

For fourteen days, Jonathan prayed. On the fifteenth day, after two weeks of sunless, stormy weather, word spread that they were nearing the shores of Japan. The passengers gathered on deck. A dense fog surrounded the ship. But the ship barely slowed; maybe the captain was drunk. Passengers became alarmed. Jonathan and Rosalind prayed earnestly. Suddenly the fog cleared. They saw the ship was headed straight toward the Japanese shoreline, dangerously close to some shoals. Just in time, the ship turned.

When they reached China, other missionaries helped them find a place to live and start learning the Chinese language. Although Jonathan was a gifted English speaker, he had trouble with language studies (this had been a weak spot in his college studies in Toronto). He worked very hard at learning Chinese but made little progress. How could he teach the Chinese about Jesus if he couldn't speak their language? Always using an interpreter would be cumbersome. Time after time when he was trying to preach, the Chinese would point to another missionary, who had reached China a year after he did, and say, "You speak. We don't understand him."

Jonathan refused to be discouraged. "The Lord called me to China," he said, "and I expect His Spirit to perform a miracle and to enable me to master the language." One day he picked up his Chinese Bible and went to a church service. As he began to preach, the miracle happened; he spoke with a fluency and power that amazed the people, and after that, his mastery of the Chinese language was recognized everywhere.

Two months later he received a letter from his old college in Toronto telling of a prayer meeting in which the students prayed "just for Goforth" and in which they sensed God's presence very near. Looking into his diary, Jonathan found that the prayer meeting was at the very time he gained such sudden mastery over the Chinese language.

Jonathan did not have an easy life as a missionary. Soon after getting settled and buying furnishings, their house burned, destroying nearly everything they had. Rosalind was heartbroken, but Jonathan simply said, "My dear, do not grieve so. After all, they're just things." Clearly, Jonathan thought the spiritual was most important.

In their early years in China, their first two children died, causing the parents much sorrow.

Another heartache was the immensity of their task, for sin was everywhere. Jonathan said the word *without* summarized the situation. "Men and women are toiling without a Bible, without a Sunday, without prayer, without songs of praise. They have homes without peace, marriage without sanctity, little children without innocence, young men and girls without ideals, poverty without relief or sympathy, sickness without skillful help or tender care, sorrow and crime without remedy, and death without hope."

After reaching China and being asked to share the Gospel in the province of Honan, Jonathan received a letter from Hudson Taylor. "We as a mission have sought for ten years to enter the province of Honan from the south and have only just succeeded. Brother, if you would enter that province, you must go forward on your knees."

As he went from place to place as an evangelist, he often didn't have comfortable lodgings. For example, he wrote: "One end of the small room I occupied was for the pigs and the donkeys. Besides, we had to contend against other living things not so big as donkeys but a thousand times more troublesome."

But by God's grace and by His Spirit, Jonathan took the challenge. He wrote:

"We crossed the northern boundary into Honan province over the Chang River. The country before us lay rich and fertile with villages as thick as farmsteads in most parts of Ontario. To the west could be seen the beautiful Shansi mountains. I was thrilled with the thought of being at last inside our Promised Land. Walking ahead of the carts, I prayed the Lord to give me that section of North Honan as my own field, and as I prayed, I opened Clark's Scripture Promises, my daily textbook, and found the promise for that day read as follows:

'For as the rain cometh down, and the snow from heaven and watereth the earth and maketh it bring forth and bud, that it may give seed to the sower, and bread to the eater: so shall my word be that goeth forth out of my mouth: it shall not return unto me void, but shall accomplish that which I please, and it shall prosper in the thing whereto I sent it' (Isaiah 55:10,11).

"The promise seemed so wonderful, coming as it did just at that juncture, and as I went on, I kept praying that this promise might be fulfilled to that region."

Jonathan and a few fellow laborers made frequent evangelistic trips into Honan province. It was too dangerous for women, so they were left behind. After returning home, Jonathan often told of narrow escapes from evil mobs.

One day Jonathan and a fellow evangelist came upon a large crowd at a sort of fair. Though both foreigners wore Chinese dress, they could not hide their identity. In a few moments the crowd was upon them, hooting, yelling, and throwing clods of earth. They tried to reach a solid wall, but could not, for again and again the crowd tried and almost succeeded in getting them tripped underfoot. Just when things seemed hopeless, a sudden violent gust of wind blew a tent completely over. In a moment the foreigners were forgotten, and the mob made a rush for the tent. Thus the Lord delivered them, not once, but many times.

Jonathan and Rosalind moved into a new community (they lived in seven different homes in their first seven years), but no one had become a Christian, though Jonathan preached eight hours a day. Part of the reason was that the Chinese believed foreigners were kidnapping Chinese children and using their hearts and eyes to make medicine.

One morning Jonathan said to Rosalind, "Let's kneel down and pray for an evangelist to help us in this work." The next day a man named Wang Fulin appeared at the mission, looking for work. He was a pitiful sight, his face having the ashy hue of an opium user, his form bent from weakness, and his thin frame shaking with a wracking cough. This man became a mighty testimony to the transforming power of Christ and a fervent preacher of the Gospel. In the first five months at Changte, about twenty-five thousand men and women heard the Gospel proclaimed by the Goforths and the converted gambler and opium smoker, Wang Fulin.

Some people came to see Jonathan's home, part Chinese and part Western in style and features. They wanted to see such things as the glass windows, board floors, sewing machine, and organ. The kitchen stove, which sent its smoke up the chimney instead of into people's eyes and all over the house, amazed them. The pump was the talk of the whole countryside—a contraption that could bring water up from the bottom of a well without a bucket! Hundreds of men and women passed through the house on a single day, and all heard the Gospel message.

As Jonathan continued to depend on prayer and God's Spirit, thousands came to believe in Christ. In one city the number of Christians increased from two thousand to eight thousand in a four-year period.

Soon after Jonathan turned seventy, he lost the sight of one eye, and a few years later, he lost sight in his other eye. He still kept on preaching. Finally, he returned to Canada, more for the sake of Rosalind's health than his own.

He died at age seventy-seven. Shortly before his death, he rejoiced with the thought that the next face he would see would be that of his Saviour.

Questions for Review

1. In what way was Goforth a good name for a missionary?

2. In what country did Jonathan grow up?

3. What did Jonathan do when he had the chance of buying candy or giving money for missions?

4. What kind of animal was a danger to Jonathan?

5. How was it that Jonathan suddenly was able to speak the Chinese language?

Questions for Discussion

1. What spiritual lesson did Jonathan glean from his experience at the farm?

2. What do you think you would have done if you had met a bear in the path?

3. How did Jonathan prepare himself for mission work?

4. Did anyone in your family have a close call with danger in childhood?

5. What dangers did Jonathan face and which do you think was the worst one?

Goforth lived from 1859 to 1936. You can read more about his life in Goforth of China, *which was written by his wife Rosalind. I gleaned much of the information for this story from the book. ~Howard*

JACOB

JACOB VALUES
THE BIRTHRIGHT

God is not a man, that he should lie; neither the son of man, that he should repent: hath he said, and shall he not do it? or hath he spoken, and shall he not make it good? Numbers 23:19

READ GENESIS 25:19-34

Two Moravians decided to become missionaries in the West Indies in 1732. They were among the first foreign missionaries to be sent forth from Europe, but they ran into one obstacle after another. They wished to set sail from Copenhagen, Denmark, but no ship would take them. No one in Copenhagen would help them. Their faith was tested, and their morale plummeted. One day they read the verse at the top of this page: "Hath he said, and shall he not do it? or hath he spoken, and shall he not make it good?"

They persevered, and before long, a few people helped them. Then more and more people joined in supporting them and arranging for their travel. Their departure to the West Indies is considered the opening of the modern era of missions.

It's unfortunate that Jacob didn't follow the concept of Numbers 23:19. His desire for the birthright was commendable; his method was ignoble.

God had spoken (verse 23 of the daily reading) that the older would serve the younger. Jacob did not need to take advantage—pottage for privileges—of his twin.

Jacob could have benefited from the insight of the motto, "Faith is living without scheming." Had he had sufficient faith, he wouldn't have schemed and taken advantage of his brother's weakness.

Why was the birthright important? The birthright gave several privileges and responsibilities. First, it gave the right to lead the household. Isaac told Jacob, whom he thought was Esau, "Be lord over thy brethren, and let thy mother's sons bow down to thee."

Second, it included the responsibility of spiritual leadership. This involved building an altar and leading in worship (Genesis 35:1-3). It probably also involved passing on God's Word and His promises.

Third, the oldest son usually received a double inheritance (see Deuteronomy 21:17.) In contrast to Jacob, Esau was not interested in spiritual things. "Lest there be any fornicator, or profane person, as Esau, who for one morsel of meat sold his birthright" (Hebrews 12:16).

Esau was a *profane* person, meaning "godless." He married two heathen wives (Genesis 26:34, 35). He was shortsighted, thinking present food was preferable to future blessing. Take a lesson from Esau—take an interest in the future, for that is where you will spend the rest of your life.

Jacob Lacks
Faith and Integrity

*Lying lips are abomination to the LORD: but they that
deal truly are his delight. Proverbs 12:22*

READ GENESIS 27:15-29

A large business needed a new president. The board was considering
promoting a young man less than forty years old from vice president to president. He had an impressive resumé, and the board
seemed favorable to the proposal to promote him. They decided to leave
the final decision until after lunch.

The young man went to the cafeteria alone. He joined the line to
select food. By chance, he was followed by several men on the board. As
they waited in line behind him, they happened to notice that he placed
a couple of three-cent butter pats on his tray and covered them up with
his napkin. They noticed that when he came to the cashier, he never
revealed the hidden six cents worth of butter.

When the board reassembled after lunch, they decided not to promote
him. Instead they fired him.

Jacob lost a lot because of his lack of integrity. He pretended to be
someone he wasn't. He wore his brother's raiment to deceive his father.

He told his father that he was Esau. He lied when he explained to his dad that the Lord had helped him get the venison quickly.

Jacob's dishonesty earned his father's disapproval and his brother's hatred and intent to kill him. He therefore needed to leave home and never saw his mother again.

Remember: Sin will take you farther than you ever wanted to go, cost you more than you ever wanted to pay, and keep you longer than you ever wanted to stay.

THE STAIRCASE
TO HEAVEN

*And he saith unto him, Verily, verily, I say unto you, Hereafter
ye shall see heaven open, and the angels of God ascending
and descending upon the Son of man. John 1:51*

READ GENESIS 28:10-22

Awesome means "inspiring awe." It is a perfectly good word, but it has been greatly misused and abused. I have heard of awesome pizza, awesome jeans, an awesome hairdo, an awesome game, awesome perfume, and an awesome volleyball serve. Recently, I was with a group of students on an educational excursion. The person in charge of the museum engaged the students in discussion. I noticed that every response of the students, no matter how simple and basic their answer, elicited a one-word reply, "Awesome."

I have seen some things that were truly awesome—the northern lights, a person who has just received Christ as Saviour and found true peace, the Grand Canyon, a newborn baby's cry, and close communion with God.

What Jacob experienced at Bethel was awesome. It filled him with awe, dread, and respect. After seeing the ladder and hearing God speak, he recognized he was at the house of God and gate of Heaven.

The word *ladder* has also been translated *staircase*. It served as a bridge between God and man, foreshadowing Jesus, the Bridge between holy God and sinful man. In John 1:51, Jesus indicated that He was Jacob's Ladder (see the verse above). He is the Way, the Mediator between God and us.

God had spoken to Abraham and Isaac; now He speaks to Jacob. Note God's promises to Jacob. God would give the land in that area to Jacob and his descendants. Jacob's descendants would be many. Jacob and his posterity would expand their land in all four directions. From Jacob's descendants all the nations of the earth would be blessed. This is fulfilled in Jesus, who offers salvation to all people. God promised to be with Jacob. God promised to protect Jacob wherever he went. God would bring him back from Haran. God would be faithful to him.

Sarah F. Adams wrote:

> Though like a wanderer, daylight all gone,
> Darkness be over me, my rest a stone,
> Yet in my dreams I'd be,
> Nearer, my God, to Thee.
>
> There let the way appear, steps up to Heaven;
> All that Thou sendest me in mercy given;
> Angels to beckon me,
> Nearer, my God, to Thee.
>
> Then with my waking thoughts bright with Thy praise,
> Out of my stony griefs Bethel I'll raise;
> So by my woes to be,
> Nearer, my God, to Thee.

FACING FEARS
AND THE FUTURE

*I sought the LORD, and he heard me, and delivered
me from all my fears. Psalm 34:4*

READ GENESIS 32:1-13

An employee in a store in Massachusetts picked up a twenty-dollar bill on a restroom floor and found a note folded inside: "Help. Kidnapped. Call highway patrol." The note also listed two Oklahoma phone numbers and said, "My Ford van, cream and blue, Oklahoma."

According to the Associated Press, the police were notified, who put out a bulletin about a missing older couple. The man and his wife were very embarrassed when they happened to call back to the man's office and heard what was happening. They explained that because his wife felt uneasy about driving back to Oklahoma, a trip she would be making alone, she had written the note and put it into her purse just in case. It had accidentally fallen out at the store.

About thirty-five hundred years earlier, Jacob was "greatly afraid and distressed" when he heard that his estranged brother was coming with four hundred men to meet him. When Jacob had left home two decades earlier, Esau had vowed to kill his deceptive brother.

Jacob had shown courtesy and foresight by informing Esau of his coming, hoping to find grace in his sight. With Esau getting closer, he assumed things didn't look good. He split his company into two groups, thinking that one, at least, could escape death. More wisely, Jacob took his fear to God. Notice his commendable attitudes.

- He had an attitude of prayer rather than resorting to deception or trickery. He had an attitude of trust. He reminded himself and God that God had promised, "I will deal well with thee."

- He had an attitude of humility. He felt unworthy of the blessings and prosperity God had given him.

- He had an attitude of gratitude. He recognized he had left Canaan with only a staff in his hand, and now he was returning with over five hundred animals plus servants.

- He had an attitude of dependency. He pled with God for deliverance for himself and his family members.

- He had an attitude of honesty. Jacob had often been dishonest, but now he was open and honest about his fear of Esau and his need for God's help.

WRESTLING WITH GOD

Peter therefore was kept in prison: but prayer was made without ceasing of the church unto God for him. Acts 12:5

READ GENESIS 32:24-32

A father said that during their family time each person should pray for one person. His son asked God to help his friend Eddie be better at school because he was so bad. The next week the father asked his son if he was going to pray for Eddie again. "No," the son replied, "I prayed for Eddie last week, and he is still bad."

Jacob had a lot of perseverance as he wrestled all night with a divine being. This wrestling is symbolic of prayer. Jacob's experience teaches us valuable lessons. Jacob was alone—we pray to God as individuals even if we are in a group. Jacob persevered in his plea for divine blessing. "Men ought always to pray, and not to faint" (Luke 18:1). Jacob clung to the heavenly being (verse 26). Jacob wanted to know God and the things of God better. He asked, "Tell me, I pray thee, thy name" (verse 29). Therefore, Jacob was blessed (verse 29).

Who was the man? Some people think he was an angel who assumed the form of a man. Hosea 12:3-5 says, "He took his brother by the heel in the womb, and by his strength he had power with God: Yea, he had power over the angel, and prevailed: he wept, and made supplication unto him: he found him in Bethel, and there he spake with us; even the LORD God of hosts; the LORD is his memorial."

Jacob thought he was more than an angel. He said, "I have seen God face to face" (v. 30). He may have been wrestling with the pre-incarnate Christ.

The dislocation of the ball-and-socket joint in the thigh reminded Jacob that God only *allowed* him to prevail, while also reminding him that God had blessed him in this unique encounter and would bless him further.

The Israelites adopted the practice of not eating that particular muscle (probably the portion of the hindquarter containing the sciatic nerve).

A.W. Tozer wrote, "The Lord cannot fully bless a man until He has first conquered him." God showed His strength by weakening Jacob. Jacob was no longer the *supplanter* but the *prevailer*. The name *Israel* means "one who wrestles victoriously with God," or "a prince with power."

Have you "wrestled with God" in prayer?

KEYS TO RECONCILIATION

READ GENESIS 33:1-16

I have seen two children who quarreled be reconciled. I have seen a husband and wife who were at odds with each other be reconciled. I have seen grown men who couldn't be peaceable to each other weep and be reconciled. Each of these was a beautiful occasion. I have read of Jacob and Esau, estranged for seventeen years, being reconciled. It, too, is beautiful.

Conflicts are common in life. Sometimes we disagree. Sometimes we speak before thinking, and offense is taken that is not easily removed. Sometimes our backgrounds contribute to vastly different viewpoints. Sometimes we are carnal instead of kind.

Even very spiritual Christians who are actively serving the Lord have problems in relating to others. In one survey of fifty-five North American mission agencies that had at least one hundred missionaries overseas, the number one problem facing missionaries is "relationships with other missionaries."

Can you imagine the tension Jacob may have felt as Esau and his four hundred men came closer and closer? Jacob wisely bowed himself respectfully seven times to Esau. By bowing, he recognized Esau as ruler of the region.

Then an amazing thing happened. Esau moved to be reconciled. Instead of aiming an arrow at Jacob, he ran to meet him. Instead of hating him as he did before, he hugged Jacob. Instead of felling him with the sword, he fell on his neck. Instead of killing Jacob, he wept with him. Esau had forgiven. They were reconciled.

If there is a breakdown in your relationship with another person, I recommend seven steps.

1. Have a desire to be reconciled.

2. Let the other person know you would like to end the quarrel.

3. Speak carefully and thoughtfully.

4. Accept at least your share of the blame.

5. Ask for forgiveness.

6. Make the wrong right by apologizing, correcting what you have told others, paying up if you have cheated.

7. Leave the quarrel in the past and build a friendship based on kindness and love.

FAITH AND THE FUTURE

By faith Jacob, when he was a dying, blessed both the sons of Joseph;
and worshipped, leaning upon the top of his staff. Hebrews 11:21

READ GENESIS 47:28-31

A mother called Achiamma Yohannan was a godly woman in southern India. She had six sons whom she challenged to listen to God's call and serve Him wholeheartedly. However, the young men had other interests, and it looked as though the oldest five, at least, would look for secular employment.

One morning as she was cooking breakfast over an open fire, she thought about how her time of influence on her boys was short. "Oh, God, let just one of my boys preach," she prayed. Right there she vowed to fast secretly until one of her sons would testify and preach. Every Friday for the next three and one-half years, she fasted and prayed.

By that time only the youngest, a little scrawny boy, was a possible answer to her prayers. Although the boy had made a start in the Christian life, he was timid and showed no leadership skills. But when he was sixteen, he listened to a Gospel team tell about evangelism in northern India. His heart was stirred, and he determined to share the Gospel

99

among unreached Indians in the north. His mother rejoiced in the desire of her son, now known worldwide as K.P. Yohannan.

This mother had faith that God would work in her son's life. Jacob, as shown in the daily reading, had faith that God would fulfill what He had revealed to him as he approached death. "By faith Jacob, when he was a dying, blessed both the sons of Joseph; and worshipped, leaning upon the top of his staff" (Hebrews 11:21). He also predicted the future of his sons and their descendants.

Faith Found in the Early Church
Polycarp, Justin, Symphorian, Maximilian, Justus

by Howard Bean and Cherie Horst

Polycarp

"So you used to listen to the Apostle John tell stories about Jesus," said Irenaeus.

"Oh yes, I distinctly remember listening to John speak about his time with Christ," said Polycarp.

"What did he tell you about Jesus?"

"He told me about miracles Christ did—the feeding of over five thousand men, the raising of Lazarus from the dead, the quieting of the storm on the Sea of Galilee, the gift of sight to blind Bartimaeus," said Polycarp.

"John saw all these miraculous things, didn't he?" asked Iranaeus.

"Yes, he was an eyewitness. And he talked of the stories he heard Jesus tell—the prodigal son, the parable of the sower, the parable of the talents, the story of the Good Samaritan."

"I wish I could have heard John. It must have been very special."

"It was wonderful," said Polycarp. "John also told me about many of the teachings of Christ: how Jesus is the vine, and his followers are the branches; how Jesus is the Light of the world; how we should pray; how we should treat our enemies; how we should give up everything to follow Him; how we should treat others the way we would want to be treated; how to be blessed; how we should humbly wash each others' feet; how we should be ready for Jesus' return."

The things Irenaeus heard from Polycarp left a deep impression on him. Years later, Bishop Irenaeus said, "I can tell the very place in which the blessed Polycarp used to sit when he preached his sermons, how he came in and went out, the manner of his life, what he looked like, the sermons he delivered to the people, how he used to report his association with John and the others who had seen the Lord, how he would relate their words, and the things concerning the Lord he had heard from them, about His miracles and teachings. Polycarp had received all this from eyewitnesses of the Word of life and related all these things in accordance with the Scriptures. I listened eagerly to these things at the time, by God's mercy which was bestowed on me. I made notes of them not on paper, but in my heart. Constantly by the grace of God, I meditate on them faithfully."

It is believed that the Apostle John ordained Polycarp to serve as the bishop in Smyrna, a city in the present country of Turkey. Polycarp also wrote a letter to the Philippians, which you can still read today. In it he often quotes the words of Jesus. One thing he told his readers applied very directly to himself. Polycarp wrote, "Pray for emperors, magistrates, rulers, and for those who persecute and hate you."

When Polycarp was quite old, fierce persecution came to the Christians in Smyrna. Everyone was ordered to worship the Roman emperor. Christians, of course, worshiped only God and refused to offer incense to Caesar.

One day word came to Polycarp that his life was in danger. "We must get you out of Smyrna to a safe place," his friends told him.

"Let me stay here. I am ready to die for my Lord."

"No, that would be foolish. It's not cowardly to go to a safe place."

So he agreed to go to a farm outside the city. He spent his time praying for both persecuted and persecutors. One day after praying, he told his friends, "I have seen a vision of a pillow, blazing with fire. I think that means I will be burned alive."

They took Polycarp to a second farm, but before long, searchers came near his hiding place. They grabbed two youths and ordered them to say where Polycarp was. After being tortured, one of them revealed his hiding place.

When the authorities came for Polycarp, he said, "No doubt you are hungry." He told his friends, "Bring them food and drink. They can help themselves to as much as they want. May I pray undisturbed?"

He prayed for over an hour. Then he said, "I'm ready to go now."

They took him into the city where a crowd had gathered. One officer said to Polycarp, "Please offer some incense and say 'Caesar is lord.' There's no harm in that. Then you don't need to suffer and die."

"I won't do that," replied Polycarp.

Then a higher official spoke to him as he was led into the arena. "Are you Polycarp?"

"I am."

"You are an old man. You don't need to die. All you have to do is swear by Caesar and speak against Christians. Then I'll gladly let you go. Curse Christ."

"Eighty-six years have I served Him, and He never did me wrong," Polycarp testified. "How can I blaspheme my King who saved me?"

"I have wild beasts. I shall throw you to them if you don't change your mind."

"Go ahead," said Polycarp.

"Well then, if you are not afraid of the wild beasts, I'll burn you with fire."

"The fire you threaten me with burns but an hour and goes out. You do not realize there is a fire of coming judgment and everlasting punishment awaiting the ungodly," Polycarp said. "But do what you want."

A fire was kindled, and the executioner prepared to nail him to the wood for burning.

Polycarp requested, "Leave me as I am. He who helps me endure the pain will help me to stay on the wood. You don't need those nails."

Then the gentle bishop lifted up his voice in prayer and praised God that he could die for Jesus. The fire was lit, and Polycarp's spirit ascended to Heaven.

As leader of the church at Smyrna, the words from Revelation 2:10 concerning the church at Smyrna applied directly to this man of faith: "Be thou faithful unto death, and I will give thee a crown of life."

Justin Martyr

"Justin, were you a Christian from childhood?" asked one of his students.

"Oh, no," replied Justin. "I was a heathen. My parents taught me nothing about Jesus. Although, interestingly, I grew up only three days' walk from where Jesus did. When Jesus walked through Samaria on His way to Jerusalem, He likely walked close by where I lived at Flavia Neapolis, called Shechem in the time of Jacob. However, I was born about one hundred years after Christ was born."

"Why did you decide to become a Christian?" the student asked, leaning forward in his eagerness to hear Justin's answer.

"It's a long story," replied Justin. "Most of my friends went to school very little, but my parents had enough money to pay for me to be educated. I really wanted to learn—especially about what is true and what is really important. So I decided to become a philosopher—you know, someone who thinks hard about God, the purpose of living, and how to have a good life."

"Where did you go to school?"

"I decided to wear a special cloak that showed everyone I was a philosopher. I went to a Stoic teacher who told me, 'You don't need to learn about God. All the world is God's body.' This didn't make sense to me. Obviously, he couldn't teach me what I needed to know about God."

"What did you do then?"

"Next I went to a teacher who knew a lot about the teachings of a famous philosopher called Aristotle. This teacher said, 'Let's talk about how much you will pay me, and then I can teach you ideas.' He seemed to be more interested in money than in truth."

"A third teacher said I needed to know about music, the stars, and geometry. When he found out I didn't know much about those subjects, he wouldn't teach me."

"Too bad," his student said. "That must have been pretty frustrating."

"Yes, at the time it was. But I'm glad now, because none of those teachers knew the truth. I didn't give up seeking answers to my heart's longings. For a while I followed Plato's idea about denying the desires of the body, but still my life was empty.

"Then one day when I was about thirty years old, I walked in a field near Ephesus, along the Mediterranean Sea. As I paced, thinking, I saw an old man. I must have been staring at him because he asked, 'Do you know me?'

" 'No.'

" 'Why do you keep staring at me?'

" 'I was not expecting to meet anyone way out here in this quiet spot,' I answered.

"The man explained, 'I have come to look after some of my household. But why are you here?'

" 'I am here to exercise my reason,' I said.

" 'Does philosophy bring you happiness?' the stranger asked.

" 'Yes,' I said, 'I believe so.'

" 'But what is happiness, young man?'

"I answered, 'Happiness is the reward of knowing what's true and being wise.'

" 'But what do you call God?'

" 'The changeless cause of all other things—that is what the philosophers told me.'

" 'But how can one know God without hearing from one who has seen Him? The philosophers have not heard Him nor seen Him. How do they know? I would refer you to teachers more ancient than the philosophers, who spake by the divine Spirit and foretold the future. They proved themselves by their predictions and miracles,' said the old man. 'Pray above all things that the gates of light may be opened to you. These things cannot be perceived or understood by all, but only by the man to whom God and His Christ have imparted wisdom.' "

"I never saw that old man again, but right away a flame was kindled in my soul. And a love of the prophets and of those men who are friends of Christ possessed me; and while revolving his words in my mind, I found this philosophy alone to be safe and profitable. Moreover, I wish that all, making a resolution similar to my own, would not keep themselves away from the words of the Saviour."

"What did you do then?" asked Justin's student.

"I found a group of Christians and met with them to worship and to learn about Jesus Christ. I was baptized and was eager to tell others about the truth and happiness I found."

"Did you ever marry?"

"No, I decided to keep wearing a philosopher's cloak. As I traveled, this gave me opportunities to share the Gospel. I could hardly be married if I wandered over the Roman Empire. I spent some time in Egypt and different parts of Asia before coming to Rome."

"You've also done a lot of writing, haven't you?"

"Yes, I've written to the emperor to show him that Christians are good citizens and shouldn't be persecuted. I've also written to Jews to show them that Jesus is the fulfillment of the Old Testament prophecies."

Later, Justin and five students from his school at Rome, including one woman, were arrested and brought before a judge named Rusticus.

"Obey the gods at once, and submit to the authorities," Rusticus commanded.

"We do no wrong by obeying Christ," said Justin.

"I order you to sacrifice to the gods," said Rusticus.

"But no right-thinking person falls away from godly living to doing wrong."

"What do you believe?" asked Rusticus.

"We believe in one God, and in Jesus Christ His Son," Justin respectfully replied.

"Where is your gathering planned?"

"We meet where each one chooses. Our meetings are open to all. The God of Christians is not limited by space. If anyone wants to talk to me at any time, I share with him the Gospel."

"Are you a Christian?"

"Yes," said Justin, and his five friends said the same.

"If you are beheaded, do you believe you will ascend into Heaven?" the judge asked.

"I know and am fully persuaded of it."

"Unless you obey, you will be mercilessly killed," the judge threatened.

"Do what you will," Justin and his friends answered. "We are Christians and do not sacrifice to idols."

Rusticus pronounced the formal sentence of scourging and beheading. Justin and the faithful Christians were led away to die. Afterwards, Christians gave him the name of Justin Martyr.

Maximilian

"Thank You, Lord, for saving me from sin," prayed twenty-one-year-old Maximilian. "Thank You for the teaching and example of Jesus. Help me to love as Jesus loved."

Maximilian lived in northern Africa in modern-day Algeria. This was a part of the Roman Empire that needed thousands and thousands of soldiers to maintain its power.

In the spring of 295, a recruiting officer came to find strong young men for the Roman army. Soon Maximilian was forced to appear before Dion, a government official called a proconsul.

Dion said, "What is your name?"

Maximilian said, "Why do you want to know my name? I am a Christian; I cannot serve in the army."

Dion said, "Get him ready to be measured."

Maximilian said again, "I cannot serve in the army. I dare not commit sin. I am a Christian."

"Measure him," ordered Dion.

"He is five feet, ten inches tall."

Dion commanded, "Give him the military seal to wear."

"I won't wear it. I cannot serve in the army. I serve Christ," insisted Maximilian.

When told he must become a soldier or die, Maximilian said, "You may cut off my hands, but I cannot serve. My army is the army of God, and I cannot fight in this world."

"But there are Roman soldiers who claim to be Christian."

"That is their business; but I know what Christ wants me to do," Maximilian said firmly.

Dion told him again, "Agree to serve and receive the military seal."

Maximilian replied, "I already have the seal of Christ, my God. I will not accept the seal of this world. If you give it to me, I will tear it off. I cannot wear a piece of lead around my neck after I have received the saving sign of Jesus Christ, my Lord, the Son of the living God. You do not know Him; yet He suffered for our salvation. God let Him die for our sins. He is the One whom all Christians serve—we follow Him as the Prince of life and Author of salvation."

Dion asked, "What wrong do soldiers do?"

"You know very well what they do," answered Maximilian. "I am ready to die. Really, I won't die. When I am put to death, I shall live with Christ, my Lord."

Just before his execution, Maximilian further showed his nonresistance and love by telling his father, "Give my clothes—they are new—to the executioner."

Symphorian

"Young man, don't you see the goddess Cybele on the wagon? She must be worshiped; she is the mother of the gods that we here in France worship."

Symphorian answered, "I will not worship a carving. It is not alive."

"Don't despise the gods, or else I will place you under arrest."

He was arrested and brought before the judge. "What is your name?"

"Symphorian."

"What is your religion?"

"I am a Christian, and I was born into a Christian family."

The judge said, "Why didn't you honor the mother of the gods and worship her image?"

Symphorian answered, "Because I am a Christian and call only upon the living God, who reigns in Heaven. But as to the image of Satan, I not only refuse to worship it, but if you will let me, I will break it in pieces with a hammer."

The judge said, "This man is not only sacrilegious at heart, but also stubborn and a rebel; but perhaps he does not know what the Emperor has ordered."

So the judge read the Roman laws to him. Then Symphorian said, "Notwithstanding, I shall never confess that this image is anything but a worthless idol of Satan, by which he persuades men that he is a god; while it is a proof of their eternal destruction for all those who put their trust in it."

The judge declared, "Scourge him and throw him into prison. We'll let him think things over till another day."

A few days later, the judge called for him again and spoke kindly to him. "Please sacrifice to the gods. I will promote you to a position of great honor in the court. Otherwise, you will be tortured and killed."

Symphorian explained, "It doesn't make sense to deny Christ who bought me. I am greatly indebted to Him. Your gifts are like honey mixed with poison. The Christian's rewards in Christ are forever, and they satisfy now and always. Even though it looks like you have wealth, possessions, and honor, in the long run, you have nothing. The earthly things you now enjoy are like an expensive, beautiful glass that crashes and breaks in two. Only God brings true and lasting joy."

After this, the judge sentenced him to be killed with the sword.

Symphorian's godly mother was able to get near him as he was led out of the city. She called down to him from the walls of the city. "Symphorian, my son! My son! Remember the living God; let your heart be steadfast and brave. We can surely not fear death, which beyond doubt leads us into the true life. Lift up your heart to Heaven, my son, and behold Him who reigns in Heaven! Today your life will not be taken from you, but be changed into a better one. If you remain steadfast today, you shall make a happy exchange; leaving this earthly house, you shall go to dwell in the tabernacle not made with hands."

"Thank You, God, for my godly mother, for her words of encouragement that have strengthened me," prayed Symphorian.

Justus

The cave was clammy and slightly cool. Justus had never imagined in all of his fourteen years that he would be hunted like a criminal. But he and his brother and father were all being hunted because they were Christians.

His older brother Justinian snored quietly in the far corner of the cave. Nearby their father Mattheus sat studying a sermon for the next Sunday. It was midnight. Only hours earlier a close friend had warned Justus that the soldiers of Emperor Diocletian were on their trail, having been alerted by some spies among the church. It was the year 303 A.D., and the Emperor was determined to stamp out Christianity.

Justus huddled just outside the cave, keeping watch. He thought the authorities might have pity on a youth and give up their pursuit, or if they killed him, they might give up looking for his father and brother. An hour passed. Justus peeked into the cave; both his father and brother were sleeping.

Justus settled himself back against a rock and gazed at the stars. Then he heard hoofbeats far in the distance. His heart leaped and he felt his knees grow weak, but in a second his decision was made. He crept back into the cave and took the quill gently from his father's limp fingers. By the light of the full moon, he wrote a quick note to his father and brother.

Father, Justinian, I'm going to meet the horsemen. I will be back with you as soon as possible. Love, your son and brother, Justus.

At the bottom of the page, he penned his favorite verse: *For me to live is Christ, to die is gain.*

Justus knew well he might never see his father and brother again. A lump rose in his throat, and he turned to the mouth of the cave. He looked back once and then ran toward the thunder of hoofbeats.

As soon as Justus saw the swords reflecting the bright moonlight, he slowed to a steady walk. As he expected, the soldiers soon saw him. The captain spurred his horse into a gallop towards Justus. "Halt!"

Justus took a deep breath and, breathing a prayer, stopped walking. The horse stopped only a few feet from Justus.

"Surround him!" the captain ordered. The other four horsemen brought their mounts in a ring around Justus.

"What's your name, and where are your companions?" the captain barked.

"My name is Justus, and I freely confess that I am also a Christian. But since I know that you are persecutors of the Christians, I cannot and will not betray my companions."

The captain looked rather taken aback, but he quickly regained his confidence. "Yes, you can. Who were you traveling with?"

Silence.

"Young man! I expect an answer."

"Sir, I cannot say." Justus felt unexpectedly calm and sensed God's presence.

"Tell us, or we will kill you," said the captain.

Justus wavered inwardly but remembered God's promises of a great reward in Heaven for the persecuted. "I would be happy if I am permitted to suffer and die for Christ. I feel just as the Apostle Paul said, 'For me to live is Christ, to die is gain.' "

The captain gave Justus a disgusted look. "Hopeless."

"My life is very hopeful," Justus corrected. "I know I will go to Heaven when I die. That is hope. I am ready to lose my life here on earth to keep my life in Heaven."

"You are hopeless," the captain repeated. "I am giving you one more chance to answer. Who were your companions?"

"I cannot say, sir."

Time seemed to stand still as the captain glared at Justus. Then his sword blade slashed forward, cleanly striking Justus' neck. The blow ended Justus' earthly life, but began his life in Heaven.

"We got one," said the captain. "The Emperor should be pleased. Now back to our camp."

Just as the first rays of sun appeared, Justinian and Mattheus found Justus' body. Justinian drew in a sharp breath, sickened by the sight. "How could he die for us?"

Mattheus took Justus' note out of his cloak and wordlessly handed it to his only remaining son. Justinian read softly, "For me to live is Christ, to die is gain."

Questions for Review

1. In what way was Polycarp kind to his enemies who came to arrest him?

2. To what did the Roman judge order Justin Martyr to sacrifice?

3. What did a Roman official want Maximilian to become?

4. Who encouraged Symphorian to be faithful to Christ?

5. Where did the father and brother of Justus hide?

Questions for Discussion

1. What do you admire about Polycarp?

2. An older man influenced Justin to become a believer; what or who influenced one of your family members to become a believer?

3. In what ways did Maximilian follow Jesus' teaching about nonresistance?

4. Do you think Symphorian was too bold in speaking to the judge about the idol?

5. In what way is it true that "to die is gain" for a Christian?

Much of the information about Polycarp, Symphorian, and Justus I acquired from Martyrs Mirror on pages 112, 113, 143, and 179 respectively. As Cherie Horst turned the account of Justus into a story, she added some fictional details. More about Justin Martyr and Maximilian can be learned from history books about the early church.

~Howard

JOSEPH

JOSEPH AND JESUS:
RELATING TO SIBLINGS

Is not this the carpenter, the son of Mary, the brother of James,
and Joses, and of Juda, and Simon? and are not his sisters here
with us? And they were offended at him. Mark 6:3

READ GENESIS 37:1-11

Who are you like? A friend, your uncle, or a person at church? Joseph was like Jesus in a remarkable number of ways.

Joseph had a lot of brothers (actually half brothers except Benjamin). Jesus had brothers also—actually half brothers. See the verse above to find out how many brothers He had.

Joseph's brothers were offended by his dreams that he would rule over them. Jesus' brothers were offended at Him too. They challenged Him to go to Judea before His time had come, "for neither did his brethren believe in him" (John 7:5).

Joseph's brothers hated him partly because he brought a report of wrongdoing about his brothers to his father. Jesus' brethren in a broad sense—the Jews—hated Him because He rebuked them for their evil and told them the truth. Joseph wasn't a talebearer; he was a truth bearer. Joseph was hated "for his words" (v. 8). The Jews at Nazareth hated Jesus and planned to cast Him over a cliff because "when they heard these things, [they] were filled with wrath" (Luke 4:28).

Although Joseph's brothers didn't realize it at first, they ultimately realized he saved their lives. He told them after their father's death, "Ye thought evil against me; but God meant it unto good, to bring to pass, as it is this day, to save much people alive" (Genesis 50:20). Jesus' brothers believed Him after His resurrection as they waited for Pentecost (Acts 1:14). His brother James became the leader of the church at Jerusalem and wrote the Epistle of James.

How do you get along with your siblings? It's a happy family where the only scraps are those brushed off the dining room table.

Is Jesus your Elder Brother and your Saviour?

Joseph and Jesus:
Relating to Parents

And he went down with them, and came to Nazareth, and was subject unto them: but his mother kept all these sayings in her heart. Luke 2:51

Read Genesis 37:12-28

A fourteen-year-old boy once wrote a letter to advice columnist Ann Landers to tell her about his "problem." He explained his situation. He had an understanding mother and a caring father who didn't drink. His parents met his needs, supplying him with a comfortable home and clothes to wear.

Yes, he was expected to follow the rules of the home, but his parents gave him great privileges too. He told Ann that when he broke the rules, he was punished, and when he obeyed them, he was praised.

He ended his letter this way: "With a problem like that, who needs a solution?" He signed his name as *Just Plain Happy*.

Joseph was a son who appreciated, respected, and obeyed his father. As indicated in the daily reading, Joseph responded well to his father's instruction to find out how his brothers were doing. As a youth, Jesus also obeyed his parents.

Joseph was like Jesus in that he was sent on a mission by his father. Jesus also was sent on a mission. "Herein is love, not that we loved God, but that he loved us, and sent his Son to be the propitiation for our sins" (1 John 4:10).

Joseph sought the welfare of his brethren. He was told, "See whether it be well with thy brethren" (Genesis 37:14). Jesus was sent into the world for the eternal welfare of the human family. "For God sent not his Son into the world to condemn the world; but that the world through him might be saved" (John 3:17).

Children and young people, do you respect, appreciate, and obey your parents?

JOSEPH AND JESUS: PURITY

For such an high priest became us, who is holy, harmless, undefiled, separate from sinners, and made higher than the heavens. Hebrews 7:26

READ GENESIS 39:1-12

A large number of tuna were feeding about thirty miles off Nantucket in the fall of 1999, according to the Associated Press. There hadn't been so many around Cape Cod for close to fifty years, so a lot of people were heading out in relatively small pleasure craft. Besides the thrill of catching a 700-pound fish, ordinary tuna could bring about $3,000 and a nice fat bluefin close to $50,000.

The lure of tuna fishing brought some danger. A Coast Guard commander said, "You'll have two or three people in a boat, and they'll catch a tuna, and all go to the same side of the boat with the fish—then over they go."

One 28-foot boat was swamped and sank after catching a 600-pound tuna. The next day two more boats capsized. They weren't prepared for the strength of the large fish.

Joseph faced the lure of a powerful temptation, but he was alert to its strength. He had a healthy fear of the Lord and of sin. He said to

Potiphar's wife. "How then can I do this great wickedness, and sin against God?" (v. 9). Joseph was aware of God being with him (vv. 2, 3, 21, 23). Jesus was certainly aware that His Father was with Him. He said, "He that sent me is with me: the Father hath not left me alone; for I do always those things that please him" (John 8:29).

Furthermore, Joseph's life demonstrates the value of taking preventive measures to safeguard purity. He tried to avoid the seductress, and when he couldn't, he didn't listen to her invitation to sin. When faced with temptation, Jesus said, "Get thee hence, Satan" (Matthew 4:10).

Ultimately, Joseph needed to flee when Potiphar's wife became physical and insistent. First Corinthians 10:13 says, "There hath no temptation taken you but such as is common to man: but God is faithful, who will not suffer you to be tempted above that ye are able; but will with the temptation also make a way to escape, that ye may be able to bear it." Jesus lived a totally pure life. He was holy, undefiled, and separate from sinners.

JOSEPH AND JESUS: FALSELY ACCUSED

*And when he was accused of the chief priests and
elders, he answered nothing. Matthew 27:12*

READ GENESIS 39:13-20

In 2012 I read the story of a twenty-six-year-old father in a local city who was accused of having a gun in the house that his children could access. It all started when his four-year-old drew a picture of a gun at school. The kindergarten teacher at Forest Hill Public School concluded that the gun was likely a threat to the four small children in the home. She reported it to the principal who called Children and Family Services who contacted Waterloo Regional Police. They arrested the father as he was picking up his children from school, handcuffed him, and hauled him to the police station.

After a few hours, the father was released and allowed police to search his home. They found a plastic toy gun that had been left behind by a brother-in-law who had lived with the family. The father, a counselor who was scheduled to speak to high school students about violence and bullying, was dismayed by the false accusation against him.

When Joseph refused to engage in evil with Potiphar's wife, she falsely accused him of attacking her. She misrepresented him to the other servants and then to her husband. Potiphar then put him into prison. Jesus was also falsely accused by those in authority. "Now the chief priests, and elders, and all the council, sought false witness against Jesus, to put him to death" (Matthew 26:59).

We don't read of any self-defense on Joseph's part. Jesus, "when he was reviled, reviled not again" (1 Peter 2:23). In fact, his silence amazed the judge. "When he was accused of the chief priests and elders, he answered nothing. Then said Pilate unto him, Hearest thou not how many things they witness against thee? And he answered him to never a word; insomuch that the governor marvelled greatly" (Matthew 27:12-14).

Joseph was sentenced unjustly. He had committed no crime. Jesus was also sentenced unjustly. Pilate said repeatedly, "I find no fault in him" (John 19:4, 6).

Joseph suffered at the hands of the Gentiles—the Egyptians. Jesus suffered not only from the Jews, but also the Gentiles—Pilate, Herod, and the soldiers.

When you are falsely accused, how do you respond? Christian love bears and forebears; it gives and forgives.

JOSEPH AND JESUS: FAITHFUL

*Wherefore, holy brethren, partakers of the heavenly calling, consider
the Apostle and High Priest of our profession, Christ Jesus; who
was faithful to him that appointed him. Hebrews 3:1, 2*

READ GENESIS 39:21-23; 40:1-8

As a Canadian under the official rule of the monarchy of Britain (and Canada), I admire the fortitude and faithfulness of the king and queen of Britain during World War II. They received the same ration coupons as did their subjects. The queen saved her meat coupons for a Sunday dinner. When part of Buckingham Palace was bombed by the Nazis, the king waited his turn to have the windows of the palace repaired. Their bathtub had a blue line around it to show how much water could be used for a bath—the same as their fellow Londoners. The king sent his horses for agricultural work.

When Eleanor Roosevelt stayed at Buckingham Palace in 1942, she reported on the rationing of food at dinner and noted that hot bath water was rationed as well. The king and queen walked among the rubble of bombed homes. A citizen in London said, "They share the same dangers and privations I do. Their home was bombed just like mine."

125

Jesus, the King of Heaven and earth, was faithful in all of His responsibilities (see verse above). He also could honestly say, "I do always those things that please [God]" (John 8:29).

Joseph was like Jesus in the area of faithfulness. Potiphar made him an overseer and entrusted everything he had into Joseph's hand. He didn't concern himself at all about things, because he knew Joseph was a faithful servant.

In prison Joseph quickly gained the favor of the keeper of the prison, who soon put him in charge of the prison activities because he was so trustworthy.

Are you faithful? It is far more important to be faithful than to be famous.

JOSEPH AND JESUS:
EXALTED

*So then after the Lord had spoken unto them, he was received up
into heaven, and sat on the right hand of God. Mark 16:19*

READ GENESIS 41:37-46

Prior to being exalted, Joseph was seen as a revealer of the future. Through God's revelation, Joseph predicted what would happen to the butler and the baker, his fellow prisoners. The butler was restored to his position by Pharaoh, and when Pharaoh had a perplexing dream, the butler remembered how Joseph accurately interpreted his dream. Like Joseph, Jesus accurately foretold the future—for example, his crucifixion and resurrection as well as the destruction of Jerusalem.

After interpreting Pharaoh's dream as an indication of famine, Joseph warned others of upcoming danger and urged his hearers to prepare. Jesus likewise warned His listeners to prepare as He told of the rich man and Lazarus, of the unjust steward, and of the king who made a wedding feast for his son.

Prior to his promotion, Joseph was a wonderful counselor as he advised Pharaoh to stockpile food in preparation for seven years of famine. One of Christ's names was "Counsellor" (Isaiah 9:6), "in whom are hid all the treasures of wisdom and knowledge" (Colossians 2:3).

Joseph's wisdom impressed others. Concerning Jesus, "When he was come into his own country, he taught them in their synagogue, insomuch that they were astonished, and said, Whence hath this man this wisdom?" (Matthew 13:54).

Joseph was exalted from the prison to the palace. His word became law. Pharaoh set him over all the land of Egypt. Jesus suffered the humiliation of the cross. "Wherefore God also hath highly exalted him, and given him a name which is above every name" (Philippians 2:9).

As Joseph traveled through Egypt in his chariot, "they cried before him, Bow the knee" (Genesis 41:43). Philippians 2:10, 11 says about Jesus, "That at the name of Jesus every knee should bow, of things in heaven, and things in earth, and things under the earth; and that every tongue should confess that Jesus Christ is Lord, to the glory of God the Father."

Have you knelt before Jesus as your Ruler? Have you confessed Him as Lord?

JOSEPH AND JESUS:
FORGIVENESS

*Then said Jesus, Father, forgive them; for they
know not what they do. Luke 23:34*

READ GENESIS 50:15-21

A remarkable example of forgiveness was demonstrated by an elderly woman in South Africa. According to an article in the *Canadian Mennonite* by Stanley W. Green, she listened to a white police officer acknowledge the atrocities he had committed under apartheid. Officer van de Broek admitted he had shot her son and then partied while his group burned the body to destroy any evidence. He also acknowledged coming to her house eight years later to get her husband. She had been forced to watch as they burned her husband to ashes. Her husband's last words were "Forgive them."

South Africa's Truth and Reconciliation Commission of the late 1990s then asked what she wanted. (This was a government-appointed body, somewhat like a court, that heard the crimes. An officer who voluntarily faced his victims, confessed his crimes, and admitted his guilt couldn't be tried.)

"I want three things," the elderly lady said. "I want Mr. van de Broek to take me to the place where they burned my husband's body. I would like to gather up the dust and give him a decent burial.

"Second, Mr. van de Broek took all my family away from me, and I still have a lot of love to give. Twice a month, I would like for him to come to the ghetto and spend a day with me so I can be a mother to him.

"Third, I would like Mr. van de Broek to know that he is forgiven by God and that I forgive him too. I would like someone to lead me to where he is seated so I can embrace him, so that he can know my forgiveness is real."

As the elderly woman was led across the courtroom, the guilty officer fainted. Someone began singing "Amazing Grace," and others joined in.

Joseph's attitude toward his brothers is another amazing example of forgiveness. They hated him, envied him, put him into a pit, ignored his pleas for mercy, sold him to slave traders en route to Egypt, and lied about him to his father. Then when they were totally at his mercy, he wholeheartedly forgave.

Jesus is the supreme model of forgiveness. "If we confess our sins, he is faithful and just to forgive us our sins" (1 John 1:9). When the Lord forgives, He assigns the wrong to be forever forgotten. We are to forgive others as God forgives us.

Faith Facing Danger and Death
Stephan Gingerich

by Brenda Gingerich

Beneath the tall swaying palm trees stood the Tree of Life Christian School. Almost one hundred students studied there—not only math and language and social studies, but the Bible. For many of the students, this school in El Chal, Guatemala, was the only place they learned about God and how to obey Him. Their parents didn't take them to church, nor did they have Bible stories and songs at home.

Stephan Gingerich, director of the school and pastor of the church in El Chal, sat at a picnic table for a meeting with Aron, a teacher, and Oswaldo, the father of several students. After the meeting he would go home for lunch and then travel with his family to Guatemala City in the afternoon.

Partway into the meeting, his cell phone rang. The caller ID said *Private Number.* Stephan excused himself and answered, thinking it was an international call.

An unfamiliar male voice responded. "Look, I need to do a deal with you, Stephan. There is a man who wants me to kill you. He will pay me 50,000 quetzales (over 7,000 dollars) to kill you. But look, I am a good man, and I know you're a good man, so let's strike a deal. You pay me 25,000 quetzales today yet, and I won't kill you."

Stephan put the phone on speaker so Aron and Oswaldo could hear the conversation. They were both Christians, and it might be wise to have them listening in. Maybe they would recognize the caller's voice. "Look, I don't do business like this," Stephan said. "I'm in a meeting, and I really don't have time to talk with you."

The man didn't like that answer. "Look, man. You choose. Pay me nothing, and I'll have to kill you. Pay me 25,000 quetzales, and you keep on living."

"Well," Stephan responded, "I'm going to have to pray about this. I always pray when I have big decisions in my life."

"Stephan," snarled the man. "I'm calling you back in thirty minutes, and you better have your mind made up. Got it?"

"Okay," responded Stephan, and hung up. There was stunned silence around the picnic table. Stephan laughed shakily. "I guess we better get back to our meeting," he said. "That guy is going to be calling back before long."

But nobody could concentrate on the task at hand, so they talked about the phone call. No one recognized the man's voice. Tracing the number was practically impossible. It would do no good to call the police—sometimes they themselves were the extortionists!

But there was Someone whom he could rely on for wisdom and direction. Stephan talked to His heavenly Father, just as if he were sitting at the picnic table with Him. He asked for wisdom and for safety and most of all for God's will to be done. Then he called his wife Brenda, his parents who lived in Guatemala City, and the director of the mission. Each one had the same advice—do not pay any money. It would only lead to more extortion threats in years to come.

Half an hour later, the phone rang again. "What's your decision, Stephan?" the man challenged.

Stephan told him he would not pay. The man became upset. "I'm telling you, man, you better pay me that money today, or you're a dead man! I know where you are. You're at the Tree of Life school. I know all about you. I know where you live. You need to cooperate or you die!"

Stephan repeated that he would not pay. "I like to help people," stated Stephan. "But there is no way I'm able to help you in this way."

"Then you better get ready to die!" shouted the man. "I'm on my way! I'm on my way with eight other guys in three pickups." The call ended. Stephan packed his papers and planner and prepared to go home. Normally, he would have taken his motorcycle, but that day he had walked to school. He felt vulnerable as he walked the five blocks to his house. Did the men really know where he was? Were they watching him? Would they act on their threats? He called his wife as he walked. Brenda had been strong and confident on the phone earlier, but he knew she would be worried. This wasn't the first extortion threat he had received—a year and a half ago they had received one in the form of a letter. Nothing had ever come of it, and they hadn't paid anything.

He relaxed a bit as he walked in their gate. *Safely home.* Then the phone rang again. It was the same man. "Look, Stephan, the conditions have changed. We will kill your entire family too. And we're on our way."

Stephan courageously repeated that he would not be able to pay them anything. Then he hung up the phone, determined not to answer it again.

Brenda met him at the door. "I'm so glad you're home safely," she whispered. They had been married seven years and were expecting their first baby in December. They had six Guatemalan boys living with them, ranging in age from seven years to fifteen years. In just a few days, they would reach their five-year milestone of serving in El Chal.

They ate a quick lunch, along with their visitors who would travel to the city with them that afternoon. "Isn't it a blessing that we've had this trip planned for several days already?" commented Brenda as she refilled water glasses. "We don't have to decide whether or not to stay in El Chal."

Seventeen people piled into the fifteen-passenger van around 2:30, ready for the nearly eight-hour trip to the city. They arrived at Mennonite Air Missions' headquarters safely, with no more threatening phone calls, and they could relax.

The next morning Stephan's cell phone rang. Feeling sure it was the extortionists, he let the call go to voice mail. Sure enough, the message was from the same man he had talked to the day before. He said the deal was the same, but they would give Stephan more time to come up with the money. Stephan had talked with both the American and Canadian embassies since he was a citizen of both countries, and they advised him not to pay. The Canadian embassy was especially helpful, saying that extortionists are looking for quick money. If someone had actually been kidnapped, their advice might be different.

Stephan and Brenda emailed an update to those on their newsletter list, and many people emailed back, assuring them of their prayers. Several churches put it on their church's prayer chains. A children's summer Bible school class had special prayer for the Gingerich family. Stephan and Brenda felt tremendous support from the church in other countries as well as from their fellow missionaries. A missionary friend wrote, "We're praying for your protection and are standing with you. Live bravely in God's peace, but don't be foolhardy. Be sensitive to the Holy Spirit and if you feel uneasy, don't hesitate to act. We care about you."

The Gingerich's van was having trouble, and on Saturday evening while in heavy traffic in the city, the gearshift broke. Because the van couldn't be driven well in that condition, they stayed several extra days in the city while it was repaired. They were grateful for the extra time with Stephan's parents and their fellow missionaries. They received no more phone calls from the extortionists, and once the van was working again, Stephan and Brenda decided it was time to return to El Chal. The church needed them, the school relied heavily on Stephan, and the boys were getting bored in the city.

They felt a deep peace about going back home, but it was still a bit unnerving as they prepared for the trip back. They took great comfort in God's Word, and Psalm 37 and Psalm 91 were especially meaningful. It was also a blessing they hadn't heard from the extortionists for several days.

They arrived in El Chal late at night. The porch lights glowed warmly, but their property was covered in dark shadows. Was anyone lurking there? They quickly unpacked a few essentials and went to bed. After praying for protection and claiming God's comforting promises, they soon fell asleep.

The Canadian Embassy had encouraged them not to follow the same routine every day. Stephan didn't have to worry—his days were so unpredictable that nobody could really guess where he might be at any given time. They moved with caution and tried not to go anywhere alone. As the days passed with no more calls, they became more relaxed.

About two weeks after they returned to El Chal, as Stephan read his Bible one morning, the Lord impressed upon him that the extortionists were taken care of and that he would not be bothered any longer. Later that day a newspaper headline caught his eye: "Extortionists who worked between Poptun and Santa Elena were killed." Incredulous,

Stephan remembered the strong feeling he had that morning as he communed with the Lord and realized that El Chal was exactly in the middle between Poptun and Santa Elena. Was it the same group that had been calling him?

Several days later Stephan was talking to Wilmer, a twelve-year-old neighbor. Wilmer brought up the extortion case. The Gingerich family hadn't told many people about it, though their congregation and fellow missionaries and several of the teachers had been informed. But word like that tends to spread quickly.

"Stephan," Wilmer asked, "what happened that night when all those men were in the field in front of your place?"

"What men?" asked Stephan.

"You know, all those armed men! Surely you saw them! They were swarming all over the place with guns."

"I don't know anything about it," replied Stephan.

Wilmer looked shocked. "How could you not see them? Were they good guys or bad guys?"

"Wilmer," Stephan said, "I have no idea who they were. I did not see them. But I have no doubt in my mind that God has been protecting us, and He knows exactly who they were."

"Stephan? Do angels wear guns?"

Stephan's brother James was going to be married to Silvia in just a few days, and the Gingerich family was busily preparing for the outdoor event. There were no churches or community buildings large enough to host the 400 guests invited, so they planned to have both the ceremony and reception under the tall palm trees behind the mission house and beside the Tree of Life Christian School.

Mark and Norma Gingerich, Stephan's parents, had lived in Guatemala for most of their married life. Now James, their oldest, was getting married to a lovely Christian girl from El Chal.

Several family members from Canada had traveled to El Chal to witness the special event and to help. They had exchanged their warm jackets and boots for summery cottons and sandals. It was March—the peak of dry season in El Chal.

That morning Mark and his two teenage children, Sarah and Mark Andrew, tackled the job of mowing grass, raking, and cutting down the huge clusters of *corrozo* nuts so that they wouldn't fall on some unsuspecting victim during the wedding. *Corrozo* palms are giants, with massive palm leaves that dance with the slightest breeze. As the tree grows, the bottom leaves become dry and brittle and hang down. Mark and Mark Andrew whacked those leaves off with machetes, and Sarah raked up the mess they made.

The pile of leaves and clippings grew larger and larger. They made a fire and carefully tended to it. In the dry weather, a fire could soon get out of control.

Up on the second-story porch, Norma was going over wedding reception plans with Stephan and Brenda. "The servers will pick up the prepared plates of food in the school," she told them, "and will bring them out to the guests. We're serving fried chicken, rice, Russian salad, and tortillas, with cake for dessert." As parents of the groom, it was customary for them to put on the wedding. "We're going to put red hibiscus flowers on each table," she continued. "That will give a splash of color to the white tables."

The warm afternoon sun made Brenda sleepy. She stretched and said, "I'm heading down for a glass of water. Do you want me to bring you each some?" She stood and then stopped, transfixed by what she saw.

A ball of fire was in the tree at her eye level, about twenty meters away from where she stood. Evidently, the work crew down on the lawn hadn't noticed it yet. The reception discussion stopped abruptly as Norma and Stephan saw the fire.

Stephan sprang into action, racing down the stairs. The ladies followed, "Fire! There's a fire in the tree!"

They stopped long enough to grab buckets of water from the *pila* on the back porch, and raced through the gate to the school property, water sloshing. Someone unraveled the garden hose and tried to extinguish the spreading fire. But the water pressure was low, and it wasn't very effective. Normally, the water was pumped up to a tank, and it entered the house with gravity flow. The fire in the tree was higher than the tank, so it was impossible to get a good stream of water up to the fire.

All around the yard stood the tall palms—perhaps fifteen of them—their leafy branches intertwined as if they were holding hands. With a sickening feeling, Stephan realized that the fire could spread rapidly from one tree to another, and the whole property could be destroyed—including the mission house, the little two-room school, and the clinic. The dry leaves burned quickly, but the green leaves were even more combustible—with their shiny, oily finish, they burned faster than the dry leaves did.

Curious neighbors streamed through the gate to watch the frenzy and help fight the fire. The crackling fire had now spread to another tree, and it looked certain that it would keep spreading if they couldn't get the fire under control.

On the other side of the school gate was a little spring where the ladies would gather to wash their clothes by hand and children would bathe. A bucket brigade commenced, with helpful neighbors and children dipping a bucket into the spring, passing the bucket along a row of more than twenty people until it reached Stephan on the ladder. He would try to douse the shooting flames with each bucket of water. Sparks stung his face and hands and made holes in his shirt. Doggedly he kept on, ignoring the intense heat.

Every Christian there was praying. With no fire department close by, they had to fight the fire themselves. But they had God on their side, and they called on Him to work a miracle, to give them strength, to give them wisdom, to grant them safety.

The flames kept climbing and climbing. The men decided to cut down one of the burning trees, hoping to keep the fire from spreading. The wood was fibrous and very difficult to saw through, and the chainsaw blade soon jammed. Everyone was grateful when they got it out and began again. With much care, they kept sawing until the tree fell with a thunderous crash. Now they could get the flames of that tree extinguished easily. The bucket brigade continued, with kind neighbors passing bucket after bucket of water along the line and little boys running back to the spring with the empty buckets.

A young man passed by on his way home from working all day in the fields. When he saw the commotion, he stopped to help. On his back he carried a plastic jug-like apparatus with a handheld sprayer. The field workers fill these with herbicides to spray their fields. Now empty, the jug could be filled with water, and the sprayer would be perfect for getting into some of the hard-to-reach areas where there were still sparks. He clambered up the ladder and started to spray.

Gradually the tide turned, and it seemed like the fires would not spread. There were still sparks, but the huge flames had died down. The lawn was a mess, littered with blackened palm fronds and ashes and wood chips. The once noble tree now lay blackened and scarred on the ground.

The bucket brigade continued until they were sure that all the fires were extinguished. Mark expressed their heartfelt appreciation to the neighbors who had helped. As the action decreased, the neighbors trickled home, no doubt to tell of the excitement and teamwork that afternoon. Norma pressed a *quetzal* into the hands of each of the children as they left—a small token of appreciation for their help. Black eyes shining, they politely said "*Gracias,*" and then raced down the dirt street, perhaps to spend their *quetzal* at the corner store.

Charlotte, the oldest daughter and nurse at the Good Samaritan Clinic, bandaged Stephan's sore hands and applied ointment to the burns. Sarah and Brenda brought out pitchers of cold water, and everyone quenched their thirst. Mark and Stephan and Mark Andrew looked comical, their faces raccoon-like from the soot.

James and Silvia with some cousins had been over at the house James was building. What a shock when they returned to the mission property and saw the once beautiful yard. It wasn't exactly what they had anticipated when they pictured their wedding taking place there.

"How did the fire get up in the tree?" was the foremost question.

It seemed like a spark had been carried up into the tree, smoldered for a while (perhaps when everyone was at lunch), and then eventually burst into flame.

"How do we know it's not going to do it again?" questioned someone else.

"Someone is going to have to keep vigil out here all night," Mark said.

"I think we should pray specifically that God sends rain," remarked Norma. "We need a gentle soaker rain that would put out any sparks that may still be smoldering." Not a cloud was in sight.

"That's gonna take a miracle, Mom," piped up Mark Andrew. "It's dry season—and it sure doesn't look like it's going to rain any time soon."

"We've seen miracles before," she replied. "Who's going to join me in prayer?"

They all gathered around the old stone bench in the middle of the yard. One by one, they talked to God and asked Him to send rain.

It looked impossible. It was the middle of dry season—like Pennsylvanians asking for snow in July. But they served a God who cared for His children and loved to answer prayer in wonderful ways.

After prayer, they trooped into the house for a simple meal. Making supper that afternoon just hadn't happened, so it would be leftovers and fresh hot tortillas from Irma the neighbor.

The doors were propped open to let in a bit of breeze. It was after six—now dark, but still so hot outside.

The overwhelming theme that night at supper was gratefulness. Gratefulness that the fire hadn't continued its reckless path. Gratefulness that nobody was badly hurt. Gratefulness for willing neighbors, and for the boy with the sprayer. Gratefulness that God protected their wooden home from the fire. Gratefulness that even though the lawn was a mess, they could clean it up and the wedding could continue as planned.

And while they still sat at the table, everyone looked up expectantly. A breeze at that hour sometimes signaled rain.

The tall palm branches started to wave in cadence with the breeze. The first drops of rain began to fall. Dishes forgotten, the family raced out to the thirsty lawn, arms outstretched. Rain mingled on their faces along with tears of joy. An informal praise and thanksgiving service began right there.

The rain came down as the praise went up. And it rained all night—a nice soaker rain—just what they needed. No more fires started, and everyone could go to bed. God was on vigil, and He had sent his special firefighting team—millions of drops of rain.

Just a few days later the wedding day arrived. Traditionally, at special events in Guatemala, pine needles are scattered about. This time, the pine needles covered the blackened earth and grass and created a lovely floor for the outdoor ceremony. The rest of the yard looked nice as well—the neighbors had cut up the tree and had hauled the wood away, and the white tables and chairs looked fresh and clean against the backdrop of green foliage. It was hard to believe that just a few days before there had been fire and panic and frantic prayers.

Yes, it is a miracle that the fire didn't spread more, thought Norma as she surveyed the happy mingling of guests. Her eyes took in the charred trunks of several trees, the proximity of the mission house and school, as well as neighbors' houses. *That rain was such a gift from the Lord.*

Gratefully, she joined the rest of the family as they prepared to enter the outdoor sanctuary.

Questions for Review

1. Whom did Stephan ask for wisdom about the demand to pay money or else be shot?

2. What was Stephan doing when he felt sure that he wouldn't be bothered anymore by the extortionist?

3. What is it called when a person threatens someone with harm or death if money is not paid?

4. Why was the Gingerich family burning leaves?

5. What "firefighters" did God send in the evening?

Questions for Discussion

1. Which countries touch Guatemala? Check on a map.

2. How would you have felt concerning the extortion threat if you had been Brenda?

3. Do you think a mission family should pay when there is an extortion attempt?

4. What are some dangers missionaries may face?

5. Has your family ever helped a bucket brigade or something similar?

Brenda is my daughter. She and Stephan were married in 2001 and have lived in Guatemala most of the time since, serving under Mennonite Air Missions. Brenda wrote about the extortion threat that happened in 2008 and about the wedding excitement.

~Howard

MOSES

MOSES THE BABY

By faith Moses, when he was born, was hid three months of his parents, because they saw he was a proper child; and they were not afraid of the king's commandment. Hebrews 11:23

READ EXODUS 2:1-10

In Dallas, Texas, a four-week-old child was dragged from her crib and killed by the family dog, a big Rottweiler named Byron. The authorities asked the mother's permission to destroy the dog. She refused, using this strange logic, "I can always have another baby, but I can't replace Byron."

These words reflect a growing attitude in our society, an ungodly attitude further reflected in the killing of more than a million unborn babies in America each year.

Thankfully, Moses' mother Jochebed showed an altogether different attitude toward her baby. In the daily reading, we can observe the love and care shown to Moses by both his earthly parents and his heavenly Father.

With good reason, Moses' mother hid her third child. Pharaoh had commanded that all male babies be drowned in the Nile River. She had a creative approach, no doubt directed by the Lord: first hiding, then constructing, then supervising through Miriam. Moses' parents, like the Israelite midwives who "feared God, and did not as the king of Egypt commanded them, but saved the men children alive" (Exodus 1:17), had the same outlook as Peter, who said, "We ought to obey God rather than men" (Acts 5:29). Moses' parents acted by faith.

Pharaoh's daughter came, walked, saw, sent, opened, cared, identified, instructed, and paid. But really it was God who was acting and who was responsible for Moses' salvation.

We don't know exactly how old Moses was when he left his parental home, but it was long enough for his mother to teach him lifelong convictions about God and His eternal reward.

Jochebed hid Moses in a literal way to keep him from danger. How can parents "hide" their children to avoid dangers from the world? Parents can hide children from dangerous influences like television and ungodly media. Parents can set a good example and hide children from partaking of alcohol, tobacco, and harmful drugs. Parents can regulate music matters and guard children from developing an appetite for ungodly music. Parents can guard against some unwholesome influences by sending their children to a Christian school or by homeschooling. Parents can provide some protection by supervision of play activities among neighborhood children and worldly cousins.

MOSES THE PRINCE

. . . .

By faith Moses, when he was come to years, refused to be
called the son of Pharaoh's daughter. Hebrews 11:24

READ EXODUS 2:11-15

Choices made when young make a big difference. As a man preached in a prison, he saw a familiar face in the audience. At the close of the message, he went to the convict. The prisoner said, "I remember you very well. We were boys in the same neighborhood and went to the same school. At the age of fourteen, you made the choice to become a Christian. I refused to come to Christ. I chose the ways of sin. Now you are a happy servant of God. And me? I have served ten years in this penitentiary and am to be a prisoner here for life!"

Even more serious than being sentenced to life in prison is death imprisonment in hell. Our most important decision is to choose Christ and identify with the people of God.

Moses in his younger years surely faced many choices. Hebrews 11:25, 26 tells us about his most important choice. Instead of remaining a prince, Moses chose "rather to suffer affliction with the people of God, than to enjoy the pleasures of sin for a season; esteeming the reproach of Christ greater riches than the treasures in Egypt: for he had respect unto the recompence of the reward."

Although Moses' technique in correcting the mistreatment of the Israelite was impulsive, unwise, and ineffective, the incident did reveal some admirable things about Moses. For one thing, we can appreciate Moses' readiness to identify with and assist the people of God.

Second, he was ready to turn his back on his position as the son of Pharaoh's daughter and possibly in line for being the next Pharaoh. God's work in his heart and his home training prior to his education "in all the wisdom of the Egyptians" (Acts 7:22) were so powerful that worldly opportunities were less attractive to him than the riches of Christ.

Third, Moses wanted to defend an innocent sufferer. Acts 7:24 says, "Seeing one of them suffer wrong, he defended him, and avenged him that was oppressed, and smote the Egyptian."

He quickly realized his life was in danger and fled to Midian. The Midianites were descendants of Abraham through his second wife, Keturah. They lived in the desert, so Moses could scarcely have had a better education for the wilderness journeys God would later ask him to lead.

MOSES THE SHEPHERD

And God said unto Moses, I AM THAT I AM: and he said, Thus shalt thou say unto the children of Israel, I AM hath sent me unto you. Exodus 3:14

READ EXODUS 3:1-12

Moses spent forty years in Egypt learning to be a somebody; forty years in the backside of the desert learning to be a nobody; and forty years in the wilderness learning how God can make a somebody out of a nobody. The Bible reading tells about Moses' encounter with God near the end of the "nobody" stage as a shepherd. God had a special method of giving Moses a special message.

What lessons can we learn about Moses receiving God's communication?

1. Moses was *busy*. God may call you to a special sphere of service, but you should be diligent and faithful in your present duties even as Moses was as a shepherd.

2. Moses was *content*. Though he grew up in a palace, mastered the learning of the Egyptians, and was mighty in word and deed

149

(Acts 7:22), yet he was satisfied to herd sheep and be enrolled in God's school.

3. Moses was *attentive.* God spoke when He saw that Moses turned aside to see the bush. Do you turn aside from your regular work and activities to behold wondrous things out of God's law and hear God's message?

4. Moses was *responsive.* He answered, "Here am I." Are you available to do God's bidding?

5. Moses was *reverent.* He humbly hid his face and took off his shoes, for his feet were on holy ground. Are you reverent when God is speaking in a time of worship?

God gave Moses a difficult assignment that he was very reluctant to accept. Are you ready to go where the Lord commissions you to go? A missionary who was home on furlough was asked, "Do you expect to return to India again?" She replied, "I dislike India with its dirt and filth, its fevers and dreadful diseases. I dislike the perpetual fight with mosquitoes, the snakes in our bathroom, the scorpions in our shoes. I dislike its poverty and its hardships, its demon-possessed priests, its sin and shame, its anxieties and discouragements. But the voice of God is calling day and night, calling me back to India. I can be happy only in the center of God's will, and His place for me is over in hot, dusty India, telling the simple message of God's love to a multitude of dark-skinned people, whose souls I love with my whole being."

MOSES THE LEADER

And Israel saw that great work which the LORD did upon the Egyptians: and the people feared the LORD, and believed the LORD, and his servant Moses. Exodus 14:31

READ EXODUS 14:10-18

A man visiting a shepherd, who was watching over hundreds of sheep, spent the night with him on the prairies in Texas. During the night the cry of coyotes began. The shepherd's dogs growled and stared into the darkness. The sheep awoke and began bleating. The shepherd threw logs onto the fire. As the flames shot up, the visitor saw the reflection of the fire in the eyes of the sheep. It dawned on him that the sheep, instead of looking in the direction of the coyotes, were looking toward the shepherd.

In times of danger, distress, and despair, we should look to our heavenly Shepherd. The Israelites faced danger. Moses told them not to fear but to look for the salvation of the Lord.

You probably know what it's like to be cornered in a game of chess, checkers, or tag. But a person may also feel trapped in real life.

Think of Moses' dilemma. Ahead was the Red Sea. On either side was rugged terrain. Advancing behind Israel were the pursuing Egyptians. It looked as if there was no escape.

But there was a Deliverer from their predicament. And there is a Deliverer in every dilemma you face—a Deliverer from sin's grip, from unrest and worry in times of uncertainty, and from the fear of death.

Moses revealed his strength as a leader and his faith in the Lord by his meekness and restraint in the face of Israel's foolish questions and charges.

What a dramatic demonstration of God's power! All Israel needed to do was to take courage, stand still, observe God's salvation, hold their peace, and then go forward once the sea divided.

All Moses needed to do was to obey God's instructions to stretch his rod over the sea and command the Israelites to move forward.

All honor and praise belongs to the Lord today for saving us, for opening the way out of tight spots, and for providing victory over our enemies of sin and death.

MOSES THE TEACHER

*And he said unto them, Take heed, and beware of
covetousness: for a man's life consisteth not in the abundance
of the things which he possesseth. Luke 12:15*

READ DEUTERONOMY 6:5-15

Spiritually speaking, possessions could be considered in the category
of hazardous materials. As Moses taught, we need to beware of
material things capturing our love and devotion, and causing us
to exclude God.

As a husband and wife began their marriage, they dedicated themselves
to God and His church. For some time they served Him faithfully. Then
prosperity came. They lived in affluence and forgot God. They stopped
going to church.

One Sunday in Chicago, the husband said to his wife, "Business
demands that I stay in the city for several days. I want you to return by
train to our home in New York."

A fearful train wreck occurred. Many passengers were killed outright.
Others were pinned helplessly beneath overturned coaches and twisted
steel. Among them was the homeward-bound wife. Piteously she pled

with a doctor who came to administer morphine to her, "Please save my life. Don't let me die!"

"I regret very much that I am unable to do what you ask," said the doctor.

Then the dying woman said remorsefully, "If I had only known this would happen, I would have given myself fully to Jesus Christ!" Soon she was gone.

Have you ever been told, "Watch out!" Maybe a ball was whizzing toward you. Or a tree was falling. Or a car was approaching you on your bicycle. The Israelites were to "watch out" as they enjoyed the blessings of the promised land. Why should you watch out also?

1. Lest you forget the Lord (v. 12). A person who lacks food, clothing, and shelter likely senses his need of God more acutely than a person to whom God has already given these things. Israel was also warned of forgetting the great deliverance from Egypt. How soon we, too, may forget God's great help and blessings of the past.

2. Lest you follow false gods (v. 14). The gods of money, fashion, possessions, finery, and pleasure vie for our allegiance. These are some of the "gods of the people which are round about you."

3. Lest you be destroyed by God's anger (v. 15). Turning from God brings God's anger upon you.

Instead of a love of possessions, we should have a supreme love of God.

MOSES THE INTERCESSOR

*Who is he that condemneth? It is Christ that died, yea
rather, that is risen again, who is even at the right hand of
God, who also maketh intercession for us. Romans 8:34*

READ NUMBERS 14:11-21

S. C. Todd made quite a discovery as he looked through the records of the work of the China Inland Mission. He was struck by the fact that one of the mission station's number of converts and Christian growth was much greater than the others. It wasn't the consecration of the missionaries at that particular place, for equally dedicated men had been in charge of similar places with fewer results.

The cause of the effectiveness of the one station was a mystery until Hudson Taylor, the leader of the missions, discovered the reason on a visit to England. At the end of one of his messages, a man came forward to get acquainted. Hudson Taylor was amazed at all the gentleman knew about one particular mission station.

"How is it that you are so conversant with the conditions of that work?" Hudson Taylor asked.

"Oh, the missionary and I are old friends and schoolmates, and for four years we have regularly corresponded. He sends me the names of inquirers and converts, and then I have daily taken them to God in prayer."

Then Hudson Taylor knew why that particular mission station had been so successful. The intercessory prayers, daily and fervently, had made the difference.

Moses' intercession for the Israelites was effective also. The Israelites were in deep trouble. The Bible reading tells us of their sin and unbelief (v. 1), murmuring against leaders (v. 2), finding fault with the Lord (v. 3), plans to return to Egypt (v. 4), rebellion (v. 9), and intentions to stone the two faithful spies (v. 10). God pronounced judgement—intercession was desperately needed.

Because Moses interceded, God pardoned. Intercession was and is effective.

E. M. Bounds wrote: "Talking to men for God is a great thing, but talking to God for men is greater still. One will never talk well and with real success to men for God who has not learned well how to talk for men."

Moses the Deceased

And there appeared unto them Elias with Moses: and they were talking with Jesus. Mark 9:4

Read Deuteronomy 34:1-10

Some people have especially unusual ways. Take Emily Carr, for instance. This famous Canadian painter from Victoria, British Columbia, would take her groceries home in an old-fashioned baby buggy. Her pet monkey went along for the ride.

Hans Langseth of Iowa had a unique appearance. At one point his beard reached a record-breaking length of seventeen and one-half feet (5.2 meters).

Moses was a unique individual (v. 10). But he was not extraordinary because he was eccentric, but because of God's influence in his life. The Lord knew him face to face.

After Moses' birth, God was his Protector as he floated on the river. At his death, God was his Undertaker.

How Moses longed to enter the promised land! He begged God for the privilege (Deuteronomy 3:23-27). But the Lord said, "No!" and that settled it. However, God let him see the land from the top of the mountain. What a view it was! Had it not been that "his eye was not dim," he wouldn't have been able to see the vast panorama.

Because Moses had not perfectly obeyed the Lord's instructions at Meribah (Numbers 20:1-13), he was not permitted to enter the promised land. But God had a better "promised land" prepared for Moses, Heaven itself.

Moses had an appointed time to die according to the word of the Lord. You also have an appointed time to die.

Moses was ready to die. He was the servant of the Lord. Are you prepared to die? Are you a servant of the Lord?

There was no viewing of his dead body nor a funeral. No one knows exactly where Moses is buried. If it were known, there would probably be a shrine located there with pilgrimages and worship given to Moses.

Moses was remembered as a wise man. He showed his wisdom by preparing a man to lead Israel after his death. He was remembered as a prophet. He told the people God's will and he foretold the Prophet (Deuteronomy 18:15-18). Through his intimate fellowship with God and the mighty works God did by him, Moses was unparalleled.

Two Kinds of Faith
John Troyer and Gary Miller

by Howard Bean

"Where's the rest of my class?" asked Kent as the junior class entered the Sunday school room. "Will I only have two students? Somebody sick?"

"Nigel is sick, his dad told me," said Brandon.

"What about the twins?" asked Kent.

"Kendra and Carter are visiting their grandparents in Michigan," replied Kaylin.

"Well, we can still have a good class with only two if you answer and ask questions a lot," stated Kent. "Let me introduce the lesson with a story. This story comes from the book *By Their Blood.*

"A young pastor by the name of Arseny lived in Ukraine during the time of the Soviet dictator Stalin who had sent millions of political prisoners to Siberia. The pastor believed God was calling him to share the Gospel in Siberia.

"When he arrived in a city in central Siberia, he learned that atheists had arranged a series of anti-Christian debates. Immediately he decided, 'I will go and defend the faith.'

"For three nights he spoke with such eloquence that he was frequently interrupted by applause. At the end of the debates, he was given an ovation.

"The next day an atheist visited his landlady. 'Tell Arseny not to come anymore to our debates. Otherwise something will happen to him.'

"Arseny listened gravely to the warning, then he said, 'Whatever may happen, I will go to the debates and will fulfill my duty.'

"Eyewitnesses reported that he spoke with special power, and his face shone like that of an angel. The audience gave him a resounding ovation as the debates closed. When the applause died down, three young men came and took him away.

"The next morning Christian brothers found him dead in the snow near the railway station. They noted that he was in a half-kneeling position with his New Testament in his hands. He had been shot while praying."

"Arseny's faith was a lot like the faith of a man called Stephen who was the first Christian martyr. Had you ever heard of Stephen and his death before you studied this lesson?" asked Kent.

"Lots of times," said Kaylin.

"Ever since I was a preschooler," added Brandon.

"Good," said Kent. "To make this lesson more challenging for you, I want Brandon to tell the story of Stephen up to the time that he had the face of an angel. That's in Acts 6. Then Kaylin, you tell about what happened in Acts 7. You may look at the lesson verses."

"I'll give it a try," said Brandon. "Here goes. Stephen was part of the church at Jerusalem. The church made him one of the seven deacons that they chose to help widows who weren't getting their fair share. It seems he did a bunch of miracles—I don't think the Bible says what they were. He also told people about Jesus. This made some people mad, so they hired some men to tell lies about him. A bunch of people believed the lies and got all excited and hauled him off to the Jewish leaders—sort of like a court, I guess. There the lies about Stephen were repeated. Then people who were watching Stephen mentioned that his face was like an angel's. What does that mean, Kent?"

"I don't know for sure. I've always assumed it meant his face was shining. Did you notice that in the story about Arseny, the observer said his face shone like an angel's? What do *you* think it means?"

"I've never seen an angel," replied Brandon. "Maybe it was a very kind face."

"Brandon, you told that part of the story very well," Kent commended him. "Now it's your turn, Kaylin."

"Well," Kaylin began, "they gave Stephen the chance to defend himself, so he started talking. He referred to a lot of Bible stories in the Old Testament and said some things that got them all upset, and they made ugly faces at him. It says something about their teeth; that reminds me of a dog showing its teeth and snarling. Anyway, he just stood there looking up. Then he said that he could see into Heaven and could see Jesus standing up there beside God. That really got them worked up, and they started throwing rocks at him to kill him. Before he died, Stephen asked God to forgive them. That's how he died."

Kent complimented her. "You also did a good job of telling the story, Kaylin. Thanks to both of you. Next, I'd like to have a little contest.

Here's the question: What do you admire about Stephen? In other words, what was good about him? We'll alternate between the two of you and see who can think of the most. I'll be part of the contest too, because after you're done, I'll tell you if I can think of any you haven't mentioned. All right, ladies first—or I guess I should say *lady* first."

"He was brave."

"He had faith," suggested Brandon.

"Good, keep going back and forth," said their teacher.

"He was willing to be a deacon."

"He told people about Jesus."

"He forgave the people killing him."

"He did miracles."

Then there was silence. "Your turn, Kaylin."

"I can't think of any more."

"He looked like an angel," put in Brandon.

"I know another one," blurted Kaylin. "He saw Jesus."

"Any more?" asked Kent, after a pause. "No? You both got four ways. That's pretty impressive. I'm not sure I can think of four more."

The students looked expectantly at their teacher to see if he would win the contest. "For one thing, the Bible says the deacons needed to be honest, full of the Holy Ghost, and wisdom; so Stephen must have had these qualities. Secondly, he knew his Bible well to summarize what happened in the Old Testament." Kent paused. "I think that's all I have to add. Anyway, that makes ten admirable things about Stephen. He certainly deserves to be called a hero of faith."

"My teacher's guide suggested that I tell about some modern-day people who have been persecuted or killed for their faith in Jesus. So in the last half of our class period, I'd like to tell you about a friend of mine who died for Christ."

"Really? You actually knew someone like that?" exclaimed Brandon.

"Who was it?" asked Kaylin.

"John Troyer. He lived in Michigan and I lived in Ontario, but our church youth groups would visit back and forth. John was a fine young man and very dedicated.

"As he grew up, he helped his dad in his butcher shop. Later he became a missionary in Guatemala. There he courted a young lady named Marie, whom he had met at Bible school. She is a remarkable woman—I'll tell you more about her later. After a couple of years, they got married. By 1981, they had five children."

"What did he do in Guatemala, and why was he killed?" asked Kaylin. "Did he mistreat people?"

"No, no, just the opposite," replied Kent. "He had a heart for people and spent his time helping them. The people around them, the Mayans, were very poor. He helped them with agricultural projects, such as raising chickens. He gave them interest-free loans that often didn't get paid back. He taught them to use better methods of farming. He helped to distribute quilts and clothing from North America. He took sick people over rough roads to the hospital. But most importantly, he told the people about Jesus and how to be saved."

"Then why did they want to kill him?"

"Most of the people *were* John's friends," explained Kent. "But there was a civil war going on, and Communist guerillas were killing those who opposed them. The guerillas assumed that all Americans were against them.

"John and Marie knew there was danger but felt they were where God wanted them to be. On the evening this story happened, John had devotions at church from Philippians 1:21, which says, "For to me to live is Christ, and to die is gain." At midnight John and Marie were awakened by somebody smashing something against the front door. Then they heard voices ordering them out of the house. Peering through the curtain, they saw masked men, some with guns and others with machetes hacking on the door."

"That would be so scary," said Kaylin.

"It was," agreed Kent. "A young man named Gary Miller lived with John and Marie. He joined them, and they quietly prayed together. By that time, the guerillas were breaking down the door and commanding them to come out with their hands in the air. They gathered the children together. When they got outside, they saw lots of guns pointing at them. There was a bright moon."

"Some of the men began stealing things from the house, while the leader made some wild accusations about the missionaries. They said the Americans were teaching the natives lies and taking advantage of them.

"Then the leaders ordered John and Gary to move away from John's family. The leader told a gunman to shoot.

"The gunman shot, but the bullet missed. John was still standing. Another bullet came. Missed again. During this time John pled for mercy while Marie begged them to spare her husband for the sake of their five children.

"Another bullet. Another miss. I'm pretty sure the gunman was missing John on purpose. I don't think he wanted John to be killed. So the leader raised *his* gun and fired. John fell to the ground dead."

"That poor mother and children watching all that," said Kaylin, shaking her head sympathetically.

"What about the other man?" asked Brandon. "Did he stay alive?"

"Yes," Kent went on. "After the leader shot John, he pointed his gun at Gary. The bullet hit Gary in his chest and threw his body backwards. He lay on the grass without moving, hoping the gunmen would think he was dead and wouldn't shoot him again.

"After playing dead for a while, he whispered, 'Are they gone?' Gary was able to sit up. One of the native Christians ran through the darkness and got to the mission headquarters the next morning. Other missionaries were able to reach the native hut where Gary had spent the night. They took him to the hospital."

"So that's the story of a Mennonite martyr. John died for Christ. There is a book in the church library called *Awaiting the Dawn* that will tell you many more details."

"He was a brave man. How old was he when he died?" asked Brandon.

"Twenty-eight."

"He sure had a lot of courage and faith," remarked Kaylin. "To stay in a dangerous area, then to stand there, waiting for the bullet to come."

"That's true. But you know, it takes faith to live for Christ as well as die for Christ. Can you imagine what his widow went through? The memories of that night. The grief. The funeral. The care of five young children. The huge adjustments."

"What happened to Marie?" asked Brandon. "Is she still alive?"

"Oh, yes. You know, some Christians, when faced with something hard, give up their faith in God. They say God must not care. But Marie has remained faithful. Whenever I meet her and her husband, I'm always impressed with her attitude."

"Her husband, did you say? So she got married again?" asked Kaylin.

"Yes," said Kent. "Guess who she married?"

"How do you expect us to know?" asked Brandon.

"Oh, I think I can guess," interrupted Kaylin. "Was it Gary?"

"That's right. Gary and Marie got married a few years after John's death."

"That's pretty neat," said Kaylin. "Do they live in Guatemala?"

"No, in North Carolina where he grew up. Some children were born to them also—two, I think. They had many good years together, but in recent years Gary's health has tested their faith." Their teacher held up the book *Shaking Hands With Mr. Parkinson.* "Guess who wrote it?" he asked, covering the author's name.

"I have no clue," said Brandon, "but I'll guess it was Mr. Parkinson."

"No," said Kent. "Try again."

"Well, I guessed right last time," said Kaylin, "so I'll guess Gary again."

"Right on," said Kent. "The same Gary Miller we've been talking about." He showed them the author's name on the cover of the book.

"What's this about Mr. Parkinson?" Brandon inquired.

"Well, have you heard of Parkinson's disease?"

"Yes, I have," said Kaylin. "My friend Erica's grandma has it. Old people sometimes get it. Your hands start shaking and you can't stop it, isn't that right, Kent?"

"You've got the right idea. It's a disease in which the connections in the brain don't work properly. So a person can't control the movements of his body like he used to. It affects walking, speaking, and, as you mentioned, the hands."

"Gary and Marie still need to trust in God. Gary was diagnosed with Parkinson's several years ago. It's been very hard on them, especially since Gary was young when it started. Let me read a bit to you. This part talks about how he began to lose the normal function of his hands. He's writing about a softball game at a school picnic.

Now thirty-eight, I lacked the speed and strength of youth, but I still looked forward to the game. To my satisfaction, the team captain assigned me to pitch. But pitching did not go well for me that day. I was not able to deliver the ball with precision and control. Frustrated, I felt the problem had more to do with picky hitters than my own poor pitching. To my disappointment, the captain replaced me after a few innings.

I taught in our school from 1999 to 2002. During that time, I enjoyed many fine ball games at recess with my students. But more and more I avoided pitching. I increasingly recognized that I lacked coordination and control, especially under pressure in a close game.

The all-time low spot in my softball experience happened when I substituted for one of our schoolteachers for a day in 2006. The students wanted me to pitch, and I reluctantly agreed. It was a disaster. My pitches went everywhere but over the plate. I gave up in disgrace when one of my wobbly pitches struck a student.

"I can't do this," I lamented, embarrassed.

"Don't feel bad," comforted fourth-grade Anna. "I'm an even worse pitcher than you are."

I chuckled at the irony of it all, even as my heart warmed at her sincere effort to make me feel better. She had put my ability in better perspective than she knew.

"That must have been really hard," said Brandon, who loved softball.

"That's for sure," said Kent.

"Then the next year, he was diagnosed with Parkinson's. The evening of his diagnosis, as Gary and Marie went for a walk, he asked, 'How are you feeling, dear?' "

"Let me read a bit more. *Beside me walked a woman who had faced many battles… She had survived the devastation of the 1976 earthquake in Guatemala. In 1981 she had watched in anguish as terrorists murdered her husband. To have her second husband stricken would perhaps be the toughest battle of all.*

She clasped my hand in her own as we walked, our way illuminated by the glimmer of stars. "We still have each other," she replied. "God will be with us, and perhaps He will heal you. If not, you will still be here to give us advice and counsel."

Kent stopped. "You see how it takes a lot of faith for both of them."

"Couldn't God heal him?" asked Kaylin.

"Yes, He could," said Kent. "Gary asked his church leaders to anoint him with oil like James 5 says. Let me read about that experience. *As Gary was giving his testimony, he said, "God has no less power today. But I trust Him to do what is best for us, whether He chooses to let me have Parkinson's or to heal me."*

Kneeling, we cried out in fervent prayer that God's will might be done.

After prayer Marie and I again knelt together. From a small bottle, Pastor Solomon poured olive oil onto my head. As the droplets trickled through my hair, the elders laid hands on me and prayed for healing.

God spoke distinctly to me in that sacred moment. "My son, I will take care of you."

"I'd like to read that book," said Brandon. "May I borrow it?"

"Sure," said Kent.

"I hate to interrupt you, Kent, but the second bell sounded a minute or two ago for Sunday school to end," said Kaylin.

"Oh, I'm sorry. I got so involved in the story. You are excused now."

Questions for Review

1. Who was the Sunday school lesson about?

2. Who were two men whose faces shone like an angel?

3. How did John Troyer help the native people in Guatemala?

4. How did Gary keep from being killed?

5. Whom did John's widow Marie marry?

Questions for Discussion

1. What kind of faith was shown by John Troyer, and what kind of faith was shown by Gary Miller?

2. What do you admire about John Troyer?

3. In what way does Gary need as much or more grace and strength than John did?

4. Does your family know anyone with Parkinson's disease?

5. Would you be able to tell a Bible story like Brandon and Kaylin did? Try it.

I visited John Troyer several times in my youth, and he and Marie visited Barbara and me soon after their marriage. I have been privileged to get to know Gary Miller at various school meetings. He gave me permission to quote from his very enlightening book Shaking Hands With Mr. Parkinson. *He and Marie also confirmed the accuracy of the information about them. They live in North Carolina.*

~Howard

RAHAB

RAHAB'S FAITH

By faith the harlot Rahab perished not with them that believed not, when she had received the spies with peace. Hebrews 11:31

READ JOSHUA 2:1-13

Faith is like a toothbrush: every person should have one and use it regularly, but should not try to use someone else's. Rahab's faith was personal, powerful, and practical. Note six aspects of her faith.

- *Faith's expression.* Rahab said, "I know" (v. 9). Godly faith has been defined as the profound knowing that comes before reality confirms it. The believer knows, for example, that Christ is coming, but reality has not yet confirmed it.

- *Faith's basis.* Rahab said, "We have heard how the LORD..." (v. 10). She mentions how God made a path for Israel through the Red Sea, and how Israel defeated the military power of Sihon and Og. It is important that the knowledge of God's power to deliver be made known so faith can germinate and grow. "Faith cometh by hearing, and hearing by the word of God" (Romans 10:17).

- *Faith's object.* Rahab believed in God. She said, "The LORD your God, he is God in heaven above, and in earth beneath" (v. 11). While the rest of her people put their faith in the city walls, Rahab put her faith in something that could never fall.

- *Faith's concern.* Rahab pled with the Israelite spies, "Deliver our lives from death" (v. 13). Through faith in Christ, a person is delivered from eternal death. "He that believeth on the Son hath everlasting life: and he that believeth not the Son shall not see life; but the wrath of God abideth on him" (John 3:36).

- *Faith's link.* James 2:17 shows faith's link to works. "Even so faith, if it hath not works, is dead, being alone." Faith moves a believer to action. Someone gave this advice: "Pray not for faith to move mountains; rather pray for faith to move you." Faith needs to be exercised. Faith is not like diesel fuel that runs out as you use it, but it is like a muscle that becomes larger and stronger as you exercise it.

- *Faith's reward.* Today's verse includes Rahab among the heroes and heroines of faith. It points out that Rahab was delivered from destruction, unlike her neighbors who believed not and perished. Her faith saved her life and won her a place among God's people.

THE SCARLET CORD

In that day there shall be a fountain opened to the house of David and to the inhabitants of Jerusalem for sin and for uncleanness. Zechariah 13:1

READ JOSHUA 2:14-22

Why was the cord that Rahab hung from her window a scarlet color? Did it just happen to be red? Was it red to be more noticeable? I don't know, but I find it interesting that it was the same color as blood.

Some Bible students have pointed out the scarlet line that runs through the Bible—from the killing of an animal to clothe Adam and Eve and the sacrifice of a lamb by Abel through the various blood sacrifices of Israel to Isaiah 53 and Zechariah 13:1 (see today's verse). The scarlet line finds its fulfillment in Christ shedding His blood on the cross, and the importance of Christ's blood is explained in the epistles.

The safety of Rahab and her family depended on being inside the house marked by scarlet. This has some similarities to the blood that marked the doors of the believing Israelites at the time of the first Passover. Exodus 12:22 says, "And ye shall take a bunch of hyssop, and dip it in the blood that is in the bason, and strike the lintel and the two side posts with the blood that is in the bason; and none of you shall go out at the door of his house until the morning."

Compare that with Joshua 2:18, 19, which reads, "Behold, when we come into the land, thou shalt bind this line of scarlet thread in the window which thou didst let us down by: and thou shalt bring thy father, and thy mother, and thy brethren, and all thy father's household, home unto thee. And it shall be, that whosoever shall go out of the doors of thy house into the street, his blood shall be upon his head, and we will be guiltless: and whosoever shall be with thee in the house, his blood shall be on our head, if any hand be upon him."

At the Passover, the angel of death saw the red blood on the door and spared the inhabitants. At the capture of Jericho, Joshua and the two spies saw the house with the scarlet cord and spared the inhabitants.

What is the application for us today? We must be in the house of God, covered by the blood of Christ, to experience divine deliverance.

Salvation is by atonement, not by attainment.

GOD'S MERCY

* *

It is of the LORD'S mercies that we are not consumed, because
his compassions fail not. Lamentations 3:22

READ JOHN 8:1-11

Police brought a woman to the emergency room of a large hospital. The doctor checked out her condition and said, "There is nothing more to do. She'll die." Her condition physically (and spiritually) appeared to be hopeless. A Christian nurse sat by the bedside of the dying woman, waiting for an opportunity to tell her about the love and mercy of God. As they talked, the woman asked, "Does God care about a person like me?"

The nurse replied, "He loves you, and Christ died for you."

The sinful woman said, "I've been such a bad girl. Tell me the truth—does God care for a bad girl like me?"

The nurse assured her with the words of John 3:16. "Yes, God loves you and wants to save you." As she continued to speak words of salvation and assurance to the woman who was rapidly slipping toward death, a smile broke out on the dying woman's face as she realized the mercy and forgiveness of God.

The Lord showed mercy on Rahab, whom the Bible calls a harlot. She evidently had an immoral past. But she heard of the wonder-working God and sought mercy from His representatives, the two spies from Israel. Where there is a seeking soul, there is a seeking God. The Lord delights in mercy. Micah 7:18 says, "Who is a God like unto thee, that pardoneth iniquity, and passeth by the transgression of the remnant of his heritage? he retaineth not his anger for ever, because he delighteth in mercy." Someone said, "God's throne is mercy, not marble."

Salvation is closely tied to God's mercy. "God, who is rich in mercy, for his great love wherewith he loved us, even when we were dead in sins, hath quickened us together with Christ, (by grace ye are saved)" (Ephesians 2:4, 5). Law condemns the best person; grace saves the worst person.

We all need God's mercy. According to a story, a woman from a high class of society hired a professional photographer to take her picture. When he showed her the proofs, she said angrily, "This picture does not do me justice."

The photographer said, "Ma'am, with a face like yours, you don't need justice, you need mercy." With a heart like ours, we all need mercy.

God's grace is immeasurable; His mercy is inexhaustible; and His peace is incomprehensible.

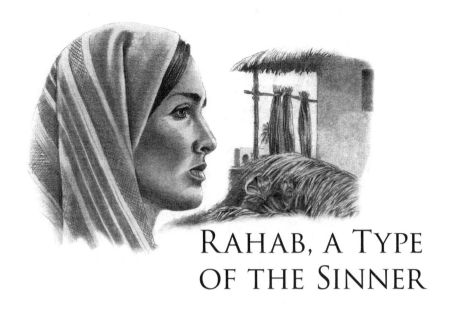

RAHAB, A TYPE OF THE SINNER

....

This is a faithful saying, and worthy of all acceptation, that Christ Jesus came into the world to save sinners; of whom I am chief. 1 Timothy 1:15

READ JOSHUA 6:1-5, 20-23

Rahab typifies sinners in several ways.

- Rahab and her fellow citizens of Jericho were "strictly shut up" (v. 1). They couldn't get out and away from their captors. As sinners, we have been bound by sin. "For all have have sinned, and come short of the glory of God" (Romans 3:23). The sinner is enslaved by sin. Jesus said, "Whosoever committeth sin is the servant of sin" (John 8:34).

- Because of sin, Rahab and Jericho were under God's judgment (v. 21). Apart from God's mercy, the sinner is doomed to hellfire.

- Rahab believed God and was saved. Paul told the Philippian jailer, "Believe on the Lord Jesus Christ, and thou shalt be saved" (Acts 16:31).

- Rahab accepted God's message and obeyed Him. "But God be thanked, that ye were the servants of sin, but ye have obeyed from the heart that form of doctrine which was delivered you" (Romans 6:17).

- Rahab the sinner was saved. "And Joshua saved Rahab the harlot alive, and her father's household, and all that she had; and she dwelleth in Israel even unto this day; because she hid the messengers, which Joshua sent to spy out Jericho" (Joshua 6:25).

The following story may be apocryphal, but I like the account of Mr. Kline, a sinner in despair. He walked by a church one Sunday evening as the service was in progress. As the congregation sang, he caught these strains of a hymn: "Saved by grace alone, this is all my plea. Jesus died for all mankind, and Jesus died for me."

His hearing, however, was not very good, so when the congregation came to the words, "Jesus died for all mankind," he thought they sang, "Jesus died for ol' man Kline."

"Why," he said, "that's me!" Stopping in his tracks, he turned and entered the small auditorium. There he heard of salvation through Christ and received Him as his Saviour and Lord.

FAITH THAT WORKS

*Now there was at Joppa a certain disciple named Tabitha,
which by interpretation is called Dorcas: this woman was full
of good works and almsdeeds which she did. Acts 9:36*

READ JAMES 2:14-26

Years ago a godly man in Scotland operated a little rowboat to transport passengers. One day a passenger was curious why the oarsman had carved the word *Faith* on one oar and on the other *Works*, and asked the old man about it. The oarsman said, "I will show you."

He dropped one oar and plied the other called *Works*, and they just went around in circles. Then he dropped that oar and began to ply the oar called *Faith*, and the little boat just went around in circles again—this time the other way around, but still in a circle.

After this demonstration, the old man picked up *Faith* and *Works*, and plying both oars together, moved the boat steadily over the water, explaining to his inquiring passenger, "You see, that is the way it is in the Christian life. Works without faith are useless, and 'faith without works is dead' also, getting you nowhere. But faith and works pulling together make for safety, progress, and blessing."

Rahab not only had faith, she acted. She hid the spies, and then let them down from Jericho's wall in a basket. She didn't just say, "Well, I hope you get out of Jericho and back to camp safely."

We are not saved by faith and works, but by faith that works.

To bring the analogy of faith and works into the twenty-first century, faith without works is like a car without gasoline.

HALL OF SHAME

The Son of man came eating and drinking, and they
say, Behold a man gluttonous, and a winebibber, a
friend of publicans and sinners. Matthew 11:19

READ MATTHEW 1:1-6, 18-21

Not only does faith work (as yesterday's devotional showed), it also has a long-term impact. Future generations can be powerfully impacted by one person's decision to follow the ways and words of God. Rahab is mentioned in the Old Testament Hall of Fame (Hebrews 11) but also in the Old Testament Hall of Shame (Matthew 1).

The genealogy of Joseph in Matthew 1 mentions four women of doubtful reputation: Tamar, Rahab, Ruth, and Bathsheba. This shows that Jesus was born into a family of sinners. This listing could be called the "Hall of Shame." Christ came to save people from their sins (v. 21).

- *Tamar* (Thamar, v. 3) was a widow pretending to be a harlot who committed adultery with Judah, her father-in-law, who himself had failed to follow God's law. As a result, Tamar had a child called Perez (Phares) who was in the Messianic line. This shameful story, found in

Genesis 38, is an illustration of the sinfulness of the human family and of God's grace.

- *Rahab* (Rachab, v. 5) came from the Canaanites, who were steeped in idolatry and immorality and were destined for God's destruction through the military campaigns of Israel. She also was a harlot—not the kind of ancestor you would want to publicize in your genealogy.

- *Ruth* (v. 5) was a Moabite. The Moabites were idol worshipers, particularly of Chemosh, to whom they offered children in burnt sacrifices. The Moabites could not become Israelites fully for ten generations (Deuteronomy 23:3), yet Ruth was the great-grandmother of David.

- *Bathsheba* (v. 6) committed adultery with David and later became David's wife.

So of the four women mentioned in the genealogy of Joseph, two were harlots, one was a Moabitess and one was an adulteress—truly a Hall of Shame. And the men were really no better. Each one needed his sins covered by sacrifice.

Jesus came to earth, identified with sinners, and died to save them from their sins.

LESSONS FROM RAHAB

And ye shall seek me, and find me, when ye shall search for me with all your heart. Jeremiah 29:13

READ 1 CORINTHIANS 6:9-11, 19, 20

Rahab's life illustrates several Bible teachings. First, God knows the sincere seeker who fears Him. Rahab and her family were saved out of thousands in Jericho. She emerged from an evil environment where idolatry was normal. The Canaanites worshiped the gods of fertility, Baal and Ashtaroth, whose worship encouraged immorality. God honored Rahab's seeking and her courage to leave such a wicked environment.

Second, salvation is conditional. She would be saved *if* the scarlet cord was in the window (Joshua 2:18), *if* she and her family stayed in the house (Joshua 2:19), and *if* she kept the mission of the spies a secret (Joshua 2:20).

Third, a person's extended family can be greatly helped by one's faith and commitment. Joshua 6:23 indicates that quite a number were delivered from death due to Rahab's influence. In terms of a family's response to imminent judgement, the harlot of Jericho was far more influential than "just Lot" in Sodom.

Fourth, an immoral life prior to conversion does not restrict one from salvation. Rahab was a harlot. According to the Law given to the children of Israel nearly forty years before Rahab's conversion, the penalty for prostitution was death by stoning. But Rahab desired something better than her previous life of sin, and God met her on that basis.

Fifth, it is good to look after the welfare of guests. The spies recognized her kindness and made sure that it was rewarded. Wherever there is a human being, there is an opportunity for kindness.

Trust and a Steamboat
George Grenfell

by Howard Bean

"Look at the size of that crocodile!" shouted one of the sailors. George Grenfell, captain of the steamboat *Peace,* glanced at it as it hastily plunged into the river, alarmed by this noisy river monster. George was more interested in figuring out whether the people in the large village they were approaching were friendly or not. Sometimes the Congo natives ran pell-mell into the jungle; other times they swarmed out in their canoes to fight with spears and arrows.

"Slow down," shouted George. "I want to go ashore." He saw signs that the villagers, although curious and uncertain, were friendly.

George climbed down into the ship's canoe, and several of his men paddled the canoe to land. As George began to talk, they gathered closer to see the man with white skin.

"I've come to bring you good news! God loves you. He is light and has told us how to live in the light. You don't need to stay in darkness."

"What do you mean?" asked the chief. "Do you mean to say that we are living in darkness?"

Just then the missionary heard the sound of sobbing. Making his way through the crowd, he found two little girls bound with cords and tied to a tree.

"What does this mean?" he asked.

With no evidence of shame, the chief told how he and his warriors had gone far up the river in their canoes on a raiding expedition against another tribe. "And these girls," continued the chief, "are part of what we captured. They are my slaves and are tied here until somebody buys them."

His heart touched by the sight of the trembling, sobbing girls, George said, "I'll buy them from you." He handed over some beads and cloth, took the girls down to the river, and told them to get into the canoe. As they were paddled out to the *Peace*, they must have wondered who this white man was and whether he would be cruel or kind.

Soon the ship started upstream again, and the girls were astonished at how swiftly they traveled. After several hours, the *Peace* rounded a bend in the river to the sight of a fleet of canoes filled with fierce-looking warriors. Some held spears; others had bows in their hands with poisoned arrows aimed at the steamboat.

These men of the Congo were very angry because, just a few days earlier, people from down the river had raided their town, burned their huts, killed many of the villagers, and stolen some of their children. Since the *Peace* had also come from downriver, they thought the people on board must also be enemies.

The chief signaled, the men gave a fierce battle cry, and a shower of spears and arrows struck the steamer. One of them almost hit George.

Suddenly, one of the little slave girls began to shout and wave.

"What is it?" asked George.

"See!" She pointed to one of the warriors. "That is my brother. We've come back to my town!"

"Call to him!" said George.

The little girl shouted loudly, but the African warriors were making a great deal of noise and did not hear her. The only answer was another rain of spears and arrows. Hastily George ordered the ship's engineer to sound the whistle, and in a moment its wild, piercing shriek rent the air. The warriors ceased their yelling and stood as if turned to stone. They had never heard the whistle of a steamer.

"Shout again—quickly!"

Instantly, the girl called her brother's name. The astonished warrior dropped his spear, seized his oar, and quickly paddled to the steamer. The girl told her brother how the white man in "the big canoe that smokes" had found her and the other girl with their enemies. "This white man offered our captors some cloth and beads and bought us from them. Then he and his men took us to this big canoe that smokes. Now he has brought us home."

"What does he want to do with you?"

"He bought us to set us free. He doesn't believe slavery is right. We are back to stay."

The story passed quickly from one canoe to another, and the two girls were taken ashore. All the warriors, who only a few minutes before had tried to kill him, gazed wonderingly at the white friend who had brought back the girls they thought were lost forever. Now they were ready to listen to his story of the great Father God who sent His Son to be the Light of the world in order to set people free from sin.

As George and his men sailed on to another village, he began to count his blessings. He was thankful that he and his men had not been killed.

He was thankful for God's wonderful gift of salvation. He had been saved at the age of fifteen back in England, just five years after the great revival of 1859. He was glad for the writings of David Livingstone, who sparked his interest in being an explorer of Africa to open up the dark continent to mission work.

George also gave thanks for his friend Robert Arthington, who had dedicated his fortune to Christ. Robert had saved money in every way he could so that he could give more money to missions. George smiled at the memory of Robert wearing the same coat for seventeen years and hardly using any candles to light his house in order to save money. Robert had had a vision of a steamer to carry the Gospel, saying, "I believe the time is come when we should place a steamer on the Congo River, where we can sail northeastward into the heart of Africa for many hundred miles uninterruptedly. We can bring the glad tidings of the everlasting Gospel to thousands of human beings who now are ignorant of the way of life and of immortality." Robert had given tens of thousands of dollars to build and maintain the steamer.

It had taken a lot of faith and hope to get the steamer to Africa. In England, George had supervised its construction and tested it on the River Thames. Then he took it apart and packed it in eight hundred parcels weighing sixty-five pounds each. Once the parts reached the Congo, it took one thousand men to carry them many miles upstream around some rapids.

Even the next problems George faced had not stopped the steamer from being assembled. The young missionary engineer who was to put the ship together and operate it had become sick and died. Two others came from England but they died too, leaving George to finish putting the boat together. He said the ship was "prayed together."

He smiled as he remembered the first time the steam was up and the *Peace* began to move. The excited Africans shouted, "She lives, Master, she lives."

Traveling on this steamer was so much easier and safer than other means of travel. Before, he and his workers had splashed through swamps, tramped through grass that was often fifteen feet high, and faced dozens of dangers from natives intent on killing them. True, they sometimes had traveled by canoe, but canoes could easily be upset by hippopotamuses, after which the canoers would be attacked by crocodiles. George thanked God again for his many escapes from death. He remembered how David Livingstone had nearly been killed by a lion.

David had been living in an African village to share the Gospel. There were lions in that area killing the cattle and sheep and terrifying the villagers. David had been told that if one lion would be killed, the others would flee. So one day he set out on a lion hunt, he with his gun and some villagers with spears. When he saw a large lion behind a bush, he aimed his gun and fired both barrels. As he was reloading, the wounded lion suddenly sprang toward him and grabbed him by the shoulder. As the lion shook David in fury, several natives attacked with their spears. The lion left David to attack them, biting several before the bullets finally took effect, and he fell dead.

Livingstone had about a dozen tooth marks as scars and a badly splintered bone in his arm. But the lion was dead, and he was still alive.

No white man had ever traveled the Congo River—second largest in the world—before.

Once a European traveler asked a native, who was said to have traveled extensively, about the river. "Do you know where this river goes?"

"It flows north and east."

"And then?"

"It keeps on flowing north and east."

"And then?"

"*Allah yallim*—God knows."

Until George's explorations, that was the sum of human knowledge on the subject—"Allah yallim."

David Livingstone, George's missionary hero who died two years before George came to Africa, had found a branch of the Congo called the Lualaba, but didn't have the supplies or strength to explore further.

On the first voyage of the *Peace* up the Congo River and some of its tributaries, George traveled twelve hundred miles. Besides opening the way for other missionaries to take the Gospel into inland Africa, he himself also shared the story of Jesus, the Light of the world. He said, "It was a wondrous joy to take, for the first time, the light of life into those regions of darkness, cruelty, and death."

George believed that God's power and the teachings of the Bible could transform the evil and darkness he encountered. For example, belief in witchcraft was very prevalent. People believed that sickness was caused by witchcraft; when someone became ill, he sent for a witch doctor to figure out who was guilty of causing the sickness. The witch doctor then gave poison to the accused person. If the accused managed to vomit the poison, he was declared innocent; but if he died of the poison, which usually happened, he was declared guilty. Sometimes the accused person was simply killed and then cut open to see if he had a gallbladder. If he did, they thought it proved he was guilty. All normal people, of course, have a gallbladder. Hardly anyone in central Africa died a natural death in old age.

As George began to translate the Bible, he found out that these people had no word for forgiveness. They didn't know what it was to forgive or to be forgiven. George longed for them to experience God's forgiveness and express this love by forgiving others.

George also had faith that the darkness of the slave trade could be changed. Villagers captured slaves, both to replenish the work force that was reduced by warfare and poison ordeals, and to sell to traders who in turn sold the slaves to other parts of the world.

Many of the tribes were also cannibals, and George had heard many terrible stories. On one occasion, a chief who was used to having many wives said to George, "See this beautiful woman? You may have her for another wife. In exchange, I would like to have that plump boatman of yours. He would be so good to eat."

George was burdened by all the sin and darkness. In a letter, he wrote, "I cannot write you a tithe of the woes that have come unto my notice and have made my heart bleed as I have voyaged along. Cruelty, sin, and slavery are as millstones around the necks of the people, dragging them down into a sea of sorrows. I pray that God will speedily make manifest to these poor brethren of ours that light, which is the light of life, even Jesus Christ, our living Lord."

George trusted in the living God rather than idols. He recalled the experiences of a fellow missionary, Thomas Comber. Thomas was shown an image of wood that the natives considered to be a god. "Could this image hurt me?" asked Thomas.

"Oh, yes, it could strike you dead!" they exclaimed in alarm.

"May I try?" he asked.

"Oh, it will kill white man," they asserted. But at last they agreed. So in breathless silence Thomas drew his knife from his pocket and slowly cut off part of the idol. Piece after piece fell from the image, but still it made no sign. "Behold," he exclaimed, "your god has no power. See what I have done, and yet I am not hurt. It is but a senseless piece of carved wood." Thomas then went on to explain the difference between such gods and the God he believed in.

George needed lots of faith during the approximately thirty years he lived in Africa. He needed faith in times of danger. At the end of one voyage, he wrote, "Thank God, we are safely back. It might have been otherwise, for we have encountered perils not a few. But the winds that were sometimes simply terrific, and the rocks that knocked holes in the steamer when we were fleeing from cannibals, have not wrecked us. We have been attacked by natives about twenty different times; we have been stoned and shot at with arrows, and have been the mark for spears more than we can count."

Sometimes when they asked for food, George said, "All they gave us was poisoned arrows sent our way."

George needed faith in times of sorrow and death. He buried his first wife and four of his children. From 1883 to 1887, over a dozen of his fellow missionaries died. Africa became known as the White Man's Grave. Missionary death was especially common in the Congo, sometimes called "the shortcut to Heaven." But George had an anchor. He wrote to a friend, "I know John 3:16 and that's good enough holding ground for my anchor."

George's faith in God was rewarded by seeing some people turn to Jesus, the Light of the world. Concerning one place, he wrote, "Just twenty years have elapsed since I first landed at the foot of this cliff and was driven off at the point of native spears. The reception this time was very different. The teacher and a little crowd of schoolchildren stood on the beach to welcome us."

In 1905 he said of another place, "It was here that, twenty-one years ago, we first came into view of the burning villages of the big Arab slave raid of 1884. This time, as we were looking for a good camping place, we suddenly heard strike up, 'All Hail the Power,' from on board one of the big fishing canoes hidden among the reeds so that we had not observed it. What a glorious welcome! Whose heart would not be moved to hear 'Crown Him Lord of all' under such circumstances? I little thought to live to see so blessed a change, and my heart went forth in praise."

At the age of fifty-seven, George fell ill with a fever. His native helpers were with him as they sailed along on the *Peace*. His last words were "Jesus is mine."

Questions for Review

1. What was the name of the country in Africa in which George was a missionary?

2. What was the name of the ship that he used to travel on the Congo River?

3. How did George get the natives who were yelling and trying to kill him to be quiet so the kidnapped girl could talk to her brother?

4. Who was George's missionary hero?

5. Who is the Light of the world?

Questions for Discussion

1. If you had been with George Grenfell, what do you think could have frightened you the most?

2. What are some things you admire about George Grenfell?

3. How was the *Peace* a big help to George?

4. What are some uses of technology that help missionaries today?

5. George had many things that he was thankful for. What are things your family has been grateful for recently?

George Grenfell lived from 1849 to 1906. A good summary of his life is found in Giants of the Missionary Trail, *which provided a lot of information for this story.*

~Howard

GIDEON

A Brave Coward

Be strong and of a good courage, fear not, nor be afraid of them: for the Lord thy God, he it is that doth go with thee; he will not fail thee, nor forsake thee. Deuteronomy 31:6

Read Judges 6:1-14

Courage is fear that has said its prayers. So it was with Gideon. He experienced courage—the victory of faith over fear.

The angel of the Lord called Gideon, "Thou mighty man of valour." Gideon didn't seem to be a brave man. He was threshing wheat by a winepress. Normally wheat threshing was done in an open place, preferably on a hilltop where the wind could help separate the chaff from the kernels.

God saw what Gideon would become, not what he was. In this way Gideon was like Peter of whom Jesus said, "Thou art Simon... thou shalt be called Cephas, which is by interpretation, A stone" (John 1:42). God sees the potential of each person.

Israel's spiritual level was low, and so was Gideon's outlook. In the daily reading, Israel had been *rebellious* (v. 1). The *results* included fearful hiding (v. 2), disappearing food (v. 4), and great poverty (v. 6). Therefore, they needed *rebuke* (v. 8).

The children of Israel cried unto the Lord (v. 6), and the Lord called a deliverer who lacked courage and trust. Words like "if," "why," "where," and "but" are not exactly the language of faith. But God gave a series of promises, and Gideon's faith began to develop: "The LORD is with thee" (v. 12); "Thou shalt save Israel" (v. 14); and "Have not I sent thee?" (v. 14). Gideon listened. "Faith cometh by hearing, and hearing by the word of God" (Romans 10:17).

We can learn from Gideon. The Bible says that, "Whatsoever things were written aforetime were written for our learning, that we through patience and comfort of the scriptures might have hope" (Romans 15:4).

Here are a few lessons:

- Sin brings trouble, loss, fear, and bondage.

- God hears our sincere cries for help.

- God uses the weak to confound the mighty.

- We can move from fear to faith by accepting the Word of God.

GIDEON FINDS PEACE

These things I have spoken unto you, that in me ye might have peace. In the world ye shall have tribulation: but be of good cheer; I have overcome the world. John 16:33

READ JUDGES 6:15-24

Augustus, the Roman ruler when the Prince of Peace was born, heard of a man in Rome who faced difficulties and great debt. In spite of the troubles this man faced, he reportedly slept easily and peacefully. Augustus decided to buy the bed that the gentleman slept upon, but the purchase didn't bring the emperor ease of sleep or peace of mind. True peace didn't come from a couch, but from Christ; not from a mattress, but from the Messiah.

Gideon did not enjoy peace internally or externally. He had to be on the outlook for Midianite marauders if he was to retain any wheat. Internally, he was wrestling with the angel's message that he would be the conqueror of the Midianites. He didn't see how he could save Israel. He was from a poor family and felt that he was the least important member of it (v. 15).

The Lord reassured Gideon of His presence and of the victory (v. 16). Gideon still wanted a sign that the Lord graciously gave him in a spectacular way. Gideon was in awe and was assured of God's presence and power. This meeting with God was a turning point in Gideon's life (v. 22).

He proceeded to build an altar to the Lord. An altar stands for the place where one meets God. Gideon's altar stood for his turning to God in faith, his turning away from the false gods, and his worshiping of the true God.

Gideon gave the altar a name—a name that means "Jehovah is my peace." Just prior to building the altar, the Lord said to him, "Peace be unto thee; fear not" (v. 23).

It is wonderful to meet God and experience peace. I love the reality of Romans 5:1, "Therefore being justified by faith, we have peace with God through our Lord Jesus Christ."

FAITH IN ACTION

Even so faith, if it hath not works, is dead, being alone. James 2:17

READ JUDGES 6:25-35

After Gideon's "conversion," the Lord had work for him to do—and dangerous work it was. After Gideon tore down the altar of Baal and replaced it with an altar to God, the men of the city came in the morning to his father's house to kill Gideon. (Perhaps Gideon did it at night because he was fearful, or maybe God had told him to do it at night. By doing it at night, he was able to accomplish the task without interference.) Joash, Gideon's father, basically told the Baal worshipers, "Let Baal defend himself if he is a god."

Here are some conclusions I've drawn from the daily reading:

- True faith is demonstrated by obedient actions (v. 25).

- The right kind of worship is important (v. 26).

- Sometimes we need to stand up to relatives (v. 27).

- God uses saints who are willing to live openly for Him to win great battles (v. 27).

- A young person who takes a stand for God can positively influence older ones (v. 31).

- Common sense tells us that worshiping objects like cars, money, and medals is foolish (v. 31).

- Faith can be infectious (v. 31).

- We need the Holy Spirit for victory (v. 34).

- It is valuable to have the help of others to win battles (v. 35).

Phillip Brooks, author of *O Little Town of Bethlehem* said, "When you are so devoted to doing what is right that you press straight on and disregard what men are saying about you, there is the triumph of moral courage."

Once Gideon heard God's call and command, he didn't get cold feet but acted promptly. Remember you are your own doctor when it comes to curing cold feet.

FAITH AND THE FLEECE

Ye shall not tempt the LORD your God, as ye tempted
him in Massah. Deuteronomy 6:16

READ JUDGES 6:36-40

The story is told that when John Wesley, age thirty-two, was living in Georgia, he fell in love with a Christian young lady. But some of his friends said that the Lord would be more pleased if he stayed single. One of them suggested using the lot to discern God's will. Wesley agreed.

They prepared three slips of paper. On one was written, "Marry." On a second was written, "Think not on it this year." On the other was written, "Think of it no more." Wesley placed them in a container and closed his eyes. Then he drew one out. It said, "Think of it no more." Although he was heartbroken, he ended the courtship. After fifteen years he married a wealthy widow who didn't make a good wife and who hindered his ministry. After twenty years, she left him.

Should a Christian "put out the fleece" like Wesley did? This expression comes from the daily reading. Gideon asked for a miraculous sign. In fact, he asked for a second one, and God honored both requests.

Whether or not a person should put out the fleece seems to depend on circumstances. In the case of King Ahaz, God invited him to ask for a sign—any sign (Isaiah 7:10-12). God honored the request for a sign from Eliezer who went seeking a bride for his master's son (Genesis 24:14, 15). King Hezekiah also received a sign that he would be healed (2 Kings 20:10, 11). But when Jesus was tempted, He said, "Thou shalt not tempt the Lord thy God" (Matthew 4:7).

So when it is permissible to seek God's will through the fleece? Do not use it for a sign when the Bible has already given clear direction. For example, don't use the fleece to determine if you should marry an unbeliever (1 Corinthians 7:39), honor your parents (Ephesians 6:2), or engage in twenty-first century forms of witchcraft (Galatians 5:20).

However, a fleece in the form of a sign and not necessarily miraculous, could be used where the Lord's will is indefinite or unclear. For example, if I am considering doing mission work in Ghana, a requested sign could be that either a member of my church or a mission agency in Ghana mention the need for a missionary in Ghana.

I have never used this method of seeking God's will. But I would consider asking the Lord for a sign depending on the circumstances.

GIDEON
CONQUERS HIS FEARS

* *

The LORD is my light and my salvation; whom shall I fear? the LORD
is the strength of my life; of whom shall I be afraid? Psalm 27:1

READ JUDGES 7:1-15

Foster Walker unwittingly strolled into the middle of a holdup at a store. The gunman ordered him to surrender his money or be shot.

"You just go ahead and shoot," Walker said. "I just got through reading my Bible, and I've already said my prayers."

The robber was dumbfounded, and Walker was able to walk away.

Through God's promises and his prayers, Gideon fought his fears by faith and overcame them.

Why did the Lord reduce the size of Israel's army from thirty-two thousand to three hundred? The daily reading gives the answer—mainly to avoid Israel taking the credit to themselves, saying, "Mine own hand hath saved me" (v. 2). Also, twenty-two thousand may have been paralyzed by fear. It may have had something to do with Deuteronomy 20:8, which mentions how fear spreads from person to person. Furthermore, the men who put their heads right down to the water to drink weren't being very vigilant.

After decimating Gideon's army, the Lord kindly bolstered his courage and faith by telling him to pay a nocturnal visit to the enemy camp. He even offered that Gideon's servant, Phurah, could accompany him. So Gideon and Phurah went to the immense Midianite camp.

Gideon overheard a conversation in which a dream was recounted and its interpretation given. The barley, the poorest kind of grain, represented Gideon.

Here are a few lessons from the daily reading:

- Our human tendency is to take the credit when the Lord helps (v. 2).

- God is not bound by normal methods of achieving His purposes (v. 7).

- Spiritual victory is not dependent on numbers but on the Spirit of the Lord (v. 8).

- God fans the flame of faith (vv. 9-11).

- Victory is won through faith (v. 15). "This is the victory that overcometh the world, even our faith" (1 John 5:4).

- Napoleon was wrong when he said, "God is on the side of large battalions."

FAITH CONQUERS

And what shall I more say? for the time would fail me to tell of Gedeon, and of Barak, and of Samson, and of Jephthae; of David also, and Samuel, and of the prophets: who through faith subdued kingdoms ... escaped the edge of the sword, out of weakness were made strong, waxed valiant in fight, turned to flight the armies of the aliens. Hebrews 11:32–34

READ JUDGES 7:16-25

I often sing this children's song about Gideon:

> Brave Gideon had three hundred men;
> The Midianites had a host.
> But Gideon had the Lord with him
> And so he had the most.
>
> So if you'd be a soldier true
> And win a full reward,
> Be brave and strong in all you do
> And always trust the Lord.*

Someone said that Gideon used psychological warfare, but I would say it was spiritual warfare. Gideon's weapons of torches, trumpets, and pitchers were hardly typical weapons of warfare. They remind Christians that "the weapons of our warfare are not carnal, but mighty through God to the pulling down of strong holds" (2 Corinthians 10:4).

What are some lessons?

- As vessels we must be broken in God's service.

- We must let our lights shine.

- We must trumpet out the message of the Lord.

- We must have an obedient faith.

D. L. Moody was an effective evangelist. Yet his speech contained poor grammar, his voice was high-pitched, and it had a bit of a nasal tone. Many of his letters are preserved, and they are full of grammatical errors.

A reporter was sent to cover a Moody evangelistic campaign in Britain and observe what made him so effective with all classes of people. After careful observation and studious thought, the reporter wrote, "I can see nothing whatever in Moody to account for his marvelous work."

After reading the report, Moody chuckled. "Why, that is the very secret of the movement. There is nothing in it that can explain it but the power of God. The work is God's, not mine."

THE GOOD AND THE BAD

. . . .

Take heed unto thyself, and unto the doctrine; continue in them: for in doing this thou shalt both save thyself, and them that hear thee. 1 Timothy 4:16

READ JUDGES 8:1-3, 22-35

Many of the heroes of faith listed in Hebrews 11 have failures recorded in the Bible in addition to accounts of their faith. So it is with Gideon.

On the good side, I like the way he responded to the unreasonable criticism of the men of Ephraim recorded in the first three verses of the daily reading. Gideon could have "told them off" with a sharp retort, but instead he used the defensive method of Proverbs 15:1: "A soft answer turneth away wrath: but grievous words stir up anger."

Godly leaders need to control their emotions. "He that is slow to anger is better than the mighty; and he that ruleth his spirit than he that taketh a city" (Proverbs 16:32). Gideon was wise enough to be conciliatory rather than offensive to his critics, who felt left out and marginalized. He understood that "a brother offended is harder to be won than a strong city: and their contentions are like the bars of a castle" (Proverbs 18:19).

Another good thing about Gideon was his decision to decline to be ruler with a lineage, in effect, becoming a king. Gideon rightly said that the Lord should be their ruler.

But I find the request of Gideon (v. 24) to be puzzling. The ephod that he made of the golden earrings became an idol. What the Midianites could not accomplish with weapons, Satan achieved with earrings.

A few lessons:

- Watch out personally after great victories. "Let him that thinketh he standeth take heed lest he fall" (1 Corinthians 10:12). The same tendency to fall after memorable success can be seen in other heroes of faith—David, Noah, and Joshua, for example.

- "Keep yourselves from idols" (1 John 5:21). Idols are things that have more importance than God. Idols in the twenty-first century include vehicles, sports, business, and entertainment.

- How disappointing when saints fall into sin and backsliding after years of victory! How encouraging when saints live godly lives until they cross the river of death!

Greater Than Guerrilla Guns
José Benito

by Dorcas Hoover

*T*hey plan to kill me, José realized. *They are tormenting me like a jaguar teases a monkey before sinking its teeth into the neck.* But this Guatemalan village had no jungle for the "monkey" to hide in. He was surrounded by enemies. *When they tire of teasing me, they will shoot me,*

211

the young pastor knew. *And my body will be dumped over the side of the mountain. My family will never know why I didn't come home.*

He had seen the mangled bodies sprawled at the bottom of cliffs. He had helped to bury mutilated corpses in the crowded graveyard back at San Bartolomé after the terrorists finished torturing their victims. Many who disappeared were never seen again. Their families never knew if their loved ones were dead or alive. And, sometimes, that was worse than death.

"¡Ayúdame *Señor!* Help me, Lord!" José cried. No one would know how the Quiché merchant had pretended to argue about the money for the plumbing supplies José had purchased to bring running water to his village, luring José into what he claimed was a lawyer's office. It had made no sense to José because everyone knew the project engineer was dependable and had promised to pay the bill very soon. It made no sense until he realized he had walked into a trap: this businessman was actually a terrorist.

A quick glance around the dark room had sent chills up the young pastor's spine. This was no law office. The dispute about the payment was only an excuse to lure him into this building, away from any sympathizer who might defend him or report his murder.

José thought of his wife Tiburcia back at San Bartolomé, likely patting out tortillas right now while black beans bubbled in the kettle over the fire. The baby would be in the sling on her back, the older children playing nearby. Tiburcia knew he had traveled to Quiché for business, but she would never know where to look or whom to ask. Who would harvest the corn for his wife and tell Bible stories to his children? Who would care for the precious little church and buy rice and beans for all the widows who had no one else to help them?

Maybe I should pretend to agree with the guerrillas, and then they would leave me alone. The fleeting thought was tempting—*then I could protect and provide for my family... No! Never! I cannot live a lie, nor can I turn my back on my Jesus and support these corrupt murderers!*

"I know all about you deceitful evangelicals... I won't stand for you deceiving the people with that Bible of yours!" his captor snarled. "I hate that Book!"

José tried to think of how to answer the captors. The guerrilla terrorists had been influenced by the Communists spreading their half-truths and outright lies in the colleges and communities. The Communists taught that the government was corrupt, and that they needed to rise up to take back the lands and wealth that rightly belonged to them. But much of their warfare actually ended up being against the village people. The terrorists intimidated them into joining their army and killed any who refused or whom they felt were standing in their way. That put pastors like José, who taught nonresistance, at the top of the guerrillas' hit list.

"We want to help people learn about God and to live better and happier lives," José tried desperately to explain. "You know about our project to bring running water into San Bartolomé so the women won't need to carry water from the river, and the children won't die of diseases from the polluted water... "

José's explanations only made the terrorists angrier. They hated José for discouraging his church members from joining their army. In desperation, José pulled the Bible from the satchel he always carried. He tried to show them Jesus' teachings of bringing hope to the poor and the hurting. He pulled several tracts from his bag as further proof of his beliefs, but the captor snatched his Bible, tossed it to the floor, and ripped the tracts to pieces.

Any second, they would begin shooting, and that would be the end. As José tensed for the bullets, scenes from his past flashed through his mind like the flipping pages of the Bible storybook his daughter liked to look through.

In his memory he could still hear the droning of the airplane as it floated out of the sky like a monstrous insect, landing in the pasture along the cornfield. He could see missionary Harold Kauffman's gentle smile as he stepped out of the plane and told them about Jesus' love. He recalled Pastor Victor's wise explanations of the teachings of God's Word as José sat at the dinner table in the missionary's little adobe house. He remembered how the chains of sin and addiction fell away when he asked Jesus into his heart. José remembered the cool droplets of water over his head at his baptism and the joy in his heart. He remembered clearly the ordination service where God had called him to lead the growing Mount of Olives church. And he remembered Harold and Victor's words of encouragement.

But Harold had left. And so had Victor. Both had been warned that they were on the guerrillas' hit list. If they did not leave, they would disappear like thousands of other men in Guatemala. Across the mountains, another American missionary, John Troyer, had been shot and killed, leaving his wife and five small children behind. Harold or Victor would be next, the church brothers warned. They must leave. So Brother Harold had flown the little plane to Texas until it was safe to return. Other missionaries across Guatemala moved back to their homes in the United States to wait out the warfare. At the urging of the church, Pastor Victor had moved his family to the mission headquarters in Guatemala City. He would lead the mission churches from that slightly more secure and central location and return when the terrorist activity had settled down.

Men in the community who did not join the guerrilla forces continued to vanish into the night. Before Victor left, José had been appointed to guide the church at San Bartolomé. Mount of Olives Mennonite Church was now known as "the church of the widows." The church was full of women whose husbands, fathers, and sons had been killed because they refused to join the Communist guerrilla warfare against the "wealthy" who were ruling the government.

Surrounded by gunmen in the building in Quiché, José knew the men holding him hostage wanted to kill him so they could more easily influence others from his village to join them. He had often been warned that the guerrillas wanted to kill him. But he never thought they would grab him in daylight, in the middle of a city. Someone had been following him and waiting to distract him and lure him away. Why had he listened to the man who had tried to quarrel with him and had led him into this trap?

This is how Pedrito must have felt when they came after him, José thought, recalling how his friend was pursued in broad daylight. The rebels had come to San Bartolomé, shouting, "Pedrito! Give us Pedrito!" There were no police in the remote village, and the townsfolk were frightened and unarmed, unable to even protect themselves. Pedrito fled to his hut and hid in the loft under the drying corn.

"Where is your husband, woman?" the terrorists yelled at Teresa. They kicked in the door, threw the table against the wall, and stabbed a pile of corn with their machetes, frightening the baby with their shouts. And then they had left. But they would return. The guerrillas knew this was Pedrito's house. He could not stay where he was sure to be found and shot. It would be better to run and try to find a safer hiding place.

Hearing the shouts grow closer once again, Pedrito leaped down from the rafters and ran out of the house. As Pedrito dashed down the street pursued by screaming men, shots rang out, and he fell in front of the Mount of Olives Chapel. José could never forget the sight of Teresa with her baby, kneeling in the pool of blood by her husband's body in the shadow of the church house where they had been married a short time before.

José had helped to bury Pedrito in the crude graveyard filled with the bodies of the village men. Teresa and her toddler still came to church. The bodies of her father and brother lay in graves next to her husband. Who would look after Teresa and her child if José died? Who would make sure they had money to buy rice and beans?

As the rebels ranted, José thought of his friend Bartolo, the deacon who had been wounded by terrorist guns. The guerrillas had surrounded his house in the night, demanding that he come out. The neighbors fled into the cornfields, leaving Bartolo to face the gunmen alone. As the terrorists fired at him, Bartolo said he had seen Jesus standing nearby, blowing the bullets so that they missed him, dropping harmlessly to the ground. Only dried beans in the hand-packed bullets had hit Bartolo's head. For some reason that no one could explain, the gunmen suddenly fled into the night as if something had frightened them.

Bartolo's terrified wife huddled in their tiny house with the children. She heard the shots and knew her husband must be dead. Later she heard a noise outside, and a familiar voice calling out to her to open the door. Cautiously she peered out and saw her husband lying in front of their hut.

"How did you get here?" she asked.

"Jesus carried me," Bartolo had said.

Jesus' presence had been with José and Bartolo and their Christian brothers so often in those terrifying times. There had been no soldiers or policemen in the village to protect them, but God had been there.

Now José knelt in the adobe building in Quiché with the guns aimed at his head. But God was still there. A gentle peace wrapped his pounding heart in a quiet calm. The God who had blown away the bullets aimed for Bartolo was in the room with José.

"We know all about you deceitful evangelicals!" One man grabbed José by the shoulders, shaking him until his teeth rattled. "I won't put up with you lying to our people!" he spat.

José, on his knees, began to softly sing his dying prayer:

I am trusting Lord in Thee,
Thou art faithful Lord,
Oh, so faithful to me.
Ne'er hast thou forsaken me.

With a crash, a violent wind slammed through the building. The windows and adobe walls rattled as if shaken by a mighty, unseen hand, while hailstones pelted the roof. The evil smirks slid from the faces of the gunmen as they shrieked in terror, scrambling frantically over each other to reach the door.

Then as suddenly and mysteriously as it had come, the wind and violent shaking stopped, and all was still. And José was alone in the empty room.

The pastor lifted his radiant face toward the ceiling, raising his hands in awe. "Thank You, Jesus! Thank You, Jesus!" he whispered rapturously. Then, picking up his Bible, he walked out the door and down the street toward to the cattle truck that would take him home to San Bartolomé. Back to the village where the terrorists still stalked him in the night, but where God and His angels were more powerful than the enemies' guns.

Questions for Review

1. In what country did this story take place?

2. What project was José working on to help the women and children of his village?

3. What did one of the terrorists do with José's Bible?

4. Who was the American missionary that had been shot and killed?

5. What did God send to scare the terrorists away and save José's life?

Questions for Discussion

1. How was José (Spanish for Joseph) like Joseph in the Old Testament?

2. Why were the Communist guerillas so much against the missionaries?

3. How had God protected Bartolo when the guerillas shot at him?

4. If you were to visit Guatemala and talk to José, what questions would you want to ask him?

5. What do you especially admire about one or more of the missionaries in the story?

I have met José Benito a number of times in Guatemala. I admire his humble, faithful life. You can read more about the dangerous times for nonresistant Christians in Guatemala during the civil war in the book Under His Wings *by Dorcas Hoover, who kindly agreed to write this story. The book tells more about José, who was born in 1953, and at the time of publication, continues to serve as a bishop in the church.*

~ Howard

JEPHTHAH

GETTING PAST THE PAST

· ·

Brethren, I count not myself to have apprehended: but this one thing I do, forgetting those things which are behind, and reaching forth unto those things which are before. Philippians 3:13

READ JUDGES 11:1-11

Many people can't get past the past. They have difficulty following the testimony of the Apostle Paul given in the verse above. They cling to past injuries and injustices. Perhaps their parents treated them unfairly. Perhaps someone took advantage of their innocence. Perhaps they were cheated in a business deal. Perhaps they were rejected by a special friend. Perhaps a teacher unjustly disciplined them.

Rather than mentally rehearsing the wrong things that have happened to us, it is better to focus on the right. Philippians 4:8 tells us to think on things that are true, honest, just, lovely, of good report, virtuous, and praiseworthy.

Jephthah had a lot of strikes against him, as mentioned in the daily reading. He was an illegitimate child (v. 1). He had an immoral father as a parental example. His half brothers rejected him and made him leave

(v. 2). He had to establish himself in a new geographical setting in the land of Tob (v. 3). His associates there didn't have the best reputation (v. 3).

Evidently he overcame the problems of the past and became a successful leader in his new community. When Israel was attacked, the leaders asked Jephthah to lead their army. Jephthah reminded them of their rejection and hatred of him in the past. They assured him that they would accept his leadership. So he became their head and captain, calling upon the Lord.

Like Joseph, Jephthah was hated and rejected by his brothers. Like Joseph, he was forced to go to another land. And like Joseph, he was forgiving. Like Joseph, Jephthah was the means of deliverance. Jephthah was approached by his half brothers in their distress. Jephthah was acknowledged as their leader, and they promised to serve him.

Jephthah also reminds us of Jesus, who was rejected and mistreated by his brothers, and who forgave others.

Take a lesson from Jephthah, who didn't let his past prevent him from becoming useful. Take a lesson too from New Testament characters—Levi, a disreputable tax collector, the unnamed woman who was an adulteress, Peter who denied Jesus three times, and Zacchaeus who was evidently a dishonest civil servant. These all were restored by the Lord.

The Hebrew writer said, "Let us go on" (Hebrews 6:1). Don't let your past be a prison.

MAKE PEACE
BY PERSUASION

*But the wisdom that is from above is first
pure, then peaceable, gentle, and easy to be
intreated, full of mercy and good fruits, without
partiality, and without hypocrisy. James 3:17*

READ JUDGES 11:12-15

In Judges, we read some unconventional names of leaders and unusual
things about them. Shamgar used a cattle prod (an ox goad) as a
weapon. Deborah's "capitol building" was a palm tree. Gideon had
seventy sons. Tola was the grandson of a Dodo, and Jair had thirty sons
who rode on thirty donkeys.

Jephthah fits right in as an unconventional leader, and he had some
admirable qualities. One thing I appreciate about Jephthah was his
attempt to make peace through speaking and reasoning. He sent messengers to Israel's enemies (v. 12), but the king of Ammon was more
interested in arguing than in peacemaking.

The parents of the famous English poet, Elizabeth Barrett Browning,
so greatly disapproved of her marriage to Robert that they disowned her.
Elizabeth repeatedly wrote letters to her parents, expressing her love for

them and her desire for reconciliation. They never replied. She wrote almost weekly for about ten years.

One day she received a large box in the mail. To her dismay, she opened it to find all of her letters to them, still unopened.

Those letters, still available today, are written beautifully. If only her parents would have read them, reconciliation might have taken place.

God has written a letter of reconciliation to us. We should open it and read it thoroughly and frequently.

APPRECIATE
GOD'S PROVIDENCE

As the mountains are round about Jerusalem, so the LORD is round about his people from henceforth even for ever. Psalm 125:2

READ JUDGES 11:16-28

According to a popular legend, Robert Bruce of Scotland was persecuted and pursued by authorities. While fleeing for his life, he spied a small cave and darted into it. Immediately, a spider appeared and spun a web over the opening. Bruce's pursuers spread over the landscape, knowing Bruce must be in the area. Two of them approached the cave, and one of them was about to enter it. The other man stopped him saying, "He could never have gotten in there without breaking the spider's web."

Bruce prayed, "O God, thank You that in the tiny bowels of a spider, you can place for me a shelter."

I think Jephthah would have made a good student in history class. His reply to the king of Ammon revealed an accurate grasp and breadth of historical fact. He organized his thoughts well. He deserved an A plus.

First he corrected the king's interpretation of history, explaining how Israel wanted to pass through the land of the Edomites, Moabites, and

Amorites, but none of these groups would permit passage. In fact, Sihon, king of the Amorites, engaged in hostilities with Israel, but God enabled Israel to defeat the Amorites, and so they took possession of that area.

Clearly, Jephthah appreciated God's help to Israel in the past and looked to Him for His aid in the future. So should we.

HAVE FAITH

For whatsoever is born of God overcometh the world: and this is the victory that overcometh the world, even our faith. 1 John 5:4

READ JUDGES 11:29-33

Faith sees the invisible, believes the incredible, and receives the impossible.

Jephthah needed faith for the future. He faced a strong army. Yet he believed that "whomsoever the LORD our God shall drive out from before us, them will we possess" (Judges 11:24). In the catalog of heroes, Hebrews 11 identifies Jephthah among those "who through faith subdued kingdoms... waxed valiant in fight, turned to flight the armies of the aliens" (Hebrews 11:33, 34).

Today we need faith for the future. Someone testified, "I do not see my way, but I know He sees the way, and that I see Him."

We also need faith when perplexed. When James M. Gray, former president of Moody Bible Institute, was recovering from a severe illness, his doctor suggested an ocean voyage to help him convalesce. After Mr. Gray made arrangements to sail, he had a physical setback. He was deeply disappointed that he couldn't go after all and wondered why God had permitted this to happen. About a week later, he read in a newspaper the account of a ship that had sunk after hitting a reef in the St. John's harbor and discovered it was the ship he had planned to be on. There were no survivors. His setback had delivered him from death. "Though He slay me, yet will I trust in Him" (Job 13:15).

We should trust God in times of trouble. The psalmist prayed, "Hide not thy face from me in the day when I am in trouble" (Psalm 102:2). This includes the afflictions that commonly come with advancing years. A. D. Martin wrote this poem called "Hide Not Thy Face":

A wee voice from the nighttime called,
  "Tell me, Daddy, are you there?
Is your face still looking my way?
  If it is, I will not care
That the night is dark and fearsome—
  I will go to sleep again."
And the voice trailed off in slumber
  With never a care or pain.
And we who are growing older
  As we face life's greatest tests
With minds that are sore distracted
  And our hearts with cares oppressed;
We can still be brave in darkness
  When we know our Father's near;
With His face turned ever toward us,
  We can sleep without a fear.

DON'T BE RASH

Seest thou a man that is hasty in his words? there is more hope of a fool than of him. Proverbs 29:20

READ ACTS 19:35-41

Jephthah is best known for his rashness. Before the battle with the Ammonites, Jephthah vowed to offer to the Lord whatever came out the doors of his house upon his return, if the Lord gave him the victory. Jephthah, by God's help, won a great victory. When he returned, his only child, a daughter, came out to meet him. When Jephthah saw her, he greatly regretted his rash words. Too bad he couldn't have heard the town clerk's advice, mentioned in the daily reading, "Do nothing rashly."

Harsh, hasty words are sometimes spoken in a home. "I'll never bring you flowers again—you are so unappreciative," or "I'll never make you a pie again." Praise on a tombstone does not erase harsh words spoken in life.

Some people hastily say, "I'll never set foot inside that church house again." An adolescent may say, "I'll never go to school again." A young woman may say, "Yes, I'll marry you." A widow may say, "I promise never to marry again." A farmer may say, "I won't ever do business with that company again." Proverbs 21:5 says, "The thoughts of the diligent tend only to plenteousness; but of every one that is hasty only to want."

Act rashly; repent at leisure. Moses impetuously slew an Egyptian and soon needed to flee. Joshua quickly accepted the fictional story that the Gibeonites fed him about moldy bread. They led him down the path of deception about worn-out shoes. Joshua and the other leaders "asked not counsel at the mouth of the LORD" (Joshua 9:14). Herod rashly promised a damsel whatever she wanted, but regretted his statement after realizing John the Baptist would lose his head. Fortunately for Naaman, he listened to reason from his servants that he dip into the Jordan waters after declaring he would not.

Even those under divine authority can make serious errors when neglecting sober reflection. They may follow their heart without consulting their head. They may act with zeal without knowledge. "Be not rash with thy mouth, and let not thine heart be hasty to utter any thing before God: for God is in heaven, and thou upon earth: therefore let thy words be few" (Ecclesiastes 5:2).

A LIVING SACRIFICE

. . . .

I beseech you therefore, brethren, by the mercies of God, that
ye present your bodies a living sacrifice, holy, acceptable unto
God, which is your reasonable service. Romans 12:1

READ JUDGES 11:34-40

Jephthah knew he needed to keep his vow to God. And his daughter bravely echoed that sentiment. How do you feel about those solemn promises known as vows? If you've been baptized, are you keeping your vows to renounce the world, the flesh, and the devil? If you are married, are you keeping your vow to love and cherish your spouse in health and sickness, to exercise patience, kindness, and forbearance, and live in peace?

If you've been ordained, are you keeping your solemn promises to be loyal to God's Word and to do the work of the ministry faithfully? "When thou vowest a vow unto God, defer not to pay it" (Ecclesiastes 5:4).

What did Jephthah do with his daughter? I know of two interpretations of verse 31. First, Jephthah offered his daughter as a burnt offering, perhaps being ignorant of God's law against human sacrifice and being influenced by pagan culture.

A second interpretation is based on a marginal reading of verse 31, "... shall surely be the Lord's or I will offer it as a burnt offering if it was a thing, or give it to the Lord if it was a person." If this is the correct interpretation, then Jephthah's daughter would have lived a life of singlehood, being consecrated to God as a living sacrifice. Jephthah would have been humiliated by having no grandchild, and in terms of his descendants, his name would perish off the earth (considered a tragedy in Israel). This interpretation avoids the problem of how Jephthah could offer a sacrifice *to the Lord* in direct contradiction of what God would accept (Leviticus 18:21).

I tend to think that Jephthah gave his daughter as a living sacrifice to God. This would be similar to the Levites. "And thou shalt set the Levites before Aaron, and before his sons, and offer them for an offering unto the LORD. Thus shalt thou separate the Levites from among the children of Israel: and the Levites shall be mine" (Numbers 8:13, 14). It also explains why she would bewail her virginity for two months in view of her willingness to remain single. Her gentle submission reminds me of the attitude of another virgin in Israel who said, "Be it unto me according to thy word" (Luke 1:38).

No matter which interpretation you take, the account reminds us that we are to be a living sacrifice to God with no rights of our own, but have a total desire to please God.

ID'D BY ONE'S SPEECH

For by thy words thou shalt be justified, and by thy words thou shalt be condemned. Matthew 12:37

READ JUDGES 12:1-6

There are various ways of identifying a person—fingerprinting, iris scanning, DNA testing. But in terms of testing for spirituality, a good method is listening to a person talk.

For years I thought that Martin Luther went to the Diet (a special council) of Worms (pronounced like *earthworm*). In recent years, I've learned the city is pronounced *Verms*. Conversely, in German, the *v* is pronounced like a *w*. Thus, those of German descent may say *The vine is made of grapes from the winyard.*

The daily reading records that the Ephraimites couldn't make the *sh* sound. Instead of saying *Shibboleth*, as they were asked to do, they said *Sibboleth*. This simple feature of speech identified them as enemies.

I have a friend from the Waterloo County area of Ontario who spoke the Pennsylvania Dutch dialect as his first language. When he called to book a motel in his nation's capital, Ottawa, the motel keeper asked if he came from Germany and spoke German. My friend asked, "How could you tell I spoke German?" (only he pronounced it *Cherman*). His speech identified him as being associated with Germany.

Our speech patterns identify us too. Our words should identify us with Christ. "Hereby know ye the Spirit of God: Every spirit that confesseth that Jesus Christ is come in the flesh is of God" (1 John 4:2).

Not only should our speech confess Christ, but it should also reflect that we are followers of Him.

> Thy Speech Betrayeth Thee
> Oh, that my tongue might so possess
> The accent of His tenderness
> That every word I breathe should bless!
> For those who mourn, a word of cheer;
> A word of hope for those who fear;
> And love to all men, far or near.
> Oh, that it might be said of me,
> "Surely thy speech betrayeth thee
> As friend of Christ of Galilee!"
> —Thomas R. Robinson, adapted

Jesus said, "Out of the abundance of the heart the mouth speaketh" (Matthew 12:34). The Christian's walk and talk must go together.

Fearless Woman of Faith
Mary Slessor

by Juliann Good

Come with me to the western coast of Africa in the year 1876 to the country today called Nigeria. A rusty ship is steaming toward the mouth of the Calabar River. This part of Africa is wild, unexplored territory. Killer elephants, lions, leopards, swarms of insects, witch doctors, and cannibals live here. For a white person, entering that land is risking life itself.

But when the ship drops anchor at a rough village called Duke Town, a white woman steps off and looks around. Her name is Mary Slessor, and she has come all the way from Scotland to serve God here.

Mary came from a poor family. Her father died when she was eleven, and she worked in a weaving factory to support her family—morning till night, six days a week. As she worked, Mary propped books up on her machines and educated herself by reading a few sentences at a time.

One of Mary's heroes was David Livingstone, missionary to the jungles of Africa. She thrilled to read about his adventures. When her mother read stories to the family about missionaries in Nigeria, Mary envisioned a steaming river with alligators sunning on its muddy banks, savage chiefs who could order scores of men to be beheaded for a cannibal feast, witch doctors chanting their charms, wives strangled or buried alive so they could go to be with their dead husbands in the spirit land, multitudes of black people chained and sold into slavery. And Mary made up her mind to take the Gospel of Jesus Christ into the heathen darkness of Africa.

And so, when she was twenty-nine years old, she stepped off that rusty ship on the shore of the Calabar River. Very soon Mary saw the enormity of the work ahead of her. Satan's grip on these people was powerful.

Mary learned the language quickly. Soon she was able to talk to the people and teach them about Jesus. She began visiting the women in their homes. There she found filth and sickness. More than half of the babies died before they were a year old because mothers did not keep them clean and properly fed. They listened to her teaching on cleanliness and the Gospel but made little effort to change their ways. They feared their witch doctors too much.

One of their most terrible practices was the poison ordeal. They believed that sickness and accidents were caused by an evil spirit or an enemy. When someone was sick or injured, the witch doctor would take bits of bones from his bag of charms and toss them around. Then he would pounce on the person he decided was guilty and force him to drink poison made from the Calabar bean. If the person vomited the poison, he was considered innocent; if not, he died in dreadful pain with everyone thinking him guilty. Mary begged the people to stop this awful practice, but they told her it was their custom and kept on doing it.

Perhaps the heathen practice that Mary hated the most was the killing of twin babies. The people of Nigeria believed twins were children of the devil. As soon as they were born, they were thrown into the forest to die, and the mother was driven from home. Mary rescued many twin babies and raised them as her own.

After twelve years, Mary grew restless. Sometimes at night she would lie awake. "Oh, Lord," she prayed, "I thank Thee that I can bring these people Thy Word. But, Lord, there are other villages back in the jungle where no white man has gone. They need Jesus too. Help me reach them!" But whenever she asked a missionary or a native about going to these villages, the answer was always the same: "No. You would be killed. They cannot be reached."

Yet Mary felt a strong urging to take the Gospel to the terrible tribe called the Okoyong. "It's a gunboat they need, not a missionary," some English traders warned. "Remember, they obey no laws, and there will be no one to rescue you if you get into trouble." Her fellow missionaries said, "Not a woman's job at all." Calabar chiefs told her, "We'll never see you again. You'll be murdered."

"I'm going!" Mary said.

She made the journey in a dugout canoe with five native children she had rescued, the oldest a boy of eleven, the youngest a baby in her arms. All day long it rained. Night had fallen when they pulled the canoe in to the riverbank. The village of Ekenge lay four miles back in the forest. Taking the baby in her arms and leading the other children, who were terrified by the darkness and the knowledge that snakes and leopards abounded, Mary struck out along the forest path, leaving the men to follow with the bundles of food and clothing. Wet, hungry, and exhausted, they waited for their belongings to arrive. After a while, news reached her that the men were tired and had gone to sleep in the boat. Exhausted as she was, Mary trudged the four miles back through the forest, aroused the sleeping men in the canoe, and brought them all on to Ekenge by midnight.

Chief Edem liked her brave spirit and gave her permission to stay in the village. She soon made herself at home among the people. With her own hands she helped build a mud-walled house. She went about on bare feet, lived on native food, drank the bad water, and slept on the ground.

She began a teaching program at once, opening a school at Ekenge and another two miles away. People of all ages came, mostly out of curiosity at first, wanting to see what this white Ma was doing. When teaching them to write, she used the sand or boards for a blackboard. She taught them Bible verses and told them to recite these to others at home.

Little by little Mary won the people's respect. They began sending for her when they were sick. Always, at any hour of the day or night, she went. Even Chief Edem began asking her for advice.

One day she learned of a coming fight between two Okoyong villages. Chief Edem was to lead Ekenge's warriors. Mary visited Chief Edem and kept talking to him, hoping to keep him at home. He wanted her to leave. Finally, she told him she knew his plans to fight that night and added, "You promised me that you would not fight. That is why I must stay here, to see that you keep your word."

Silently Edem left her. Mary called the chief's sister and said, "I shall sleep here. But if Chief Edem makes any move, wake me at once."

During the night his sister wakened Mary. Mary hurried outside and found Edem with his sword. She felt sure armed men waited in the bush for him to lead them. She asked, "Where are you going, Chief?"

"For a walk," he replied.

"Good. I'll go with you."

They walked and walked. When at last they turned back to the compound, she relaxed, knowing there would be no fight that night.

Mary watched Edem day and night for a whole week. Finally, he laid his sword at her feet and said, "I am willing, Ma." The missionary had won the warrior.

This was not the only time Mary stopped a war. When she heard of trouble, she would rush to the place where men were preparing for war. Covered in war paint, they passed around liquor, danced, and yelled threats. Spears and shields glimmered in the sun. The skulls and scalps of earlier victims waved from poles.

Just as the two sides were ready to rush together, they would see a small woman standing on a log between them. "Out of the way, Ma. We fight!"

She ignored the shouts.

"Out of the way. You die too, white Ma. Move on!"

"Throw if you dare!" she called back.

When men from both sides came to remove her, Mary knew that she had won. She would scold them as children, plead with them to forgive each other, or suggest they move to the shade of a tree to talk. Mary knitted while they talked, and she got a lot of knitting done. After hours of talking, the men were calmer. They went home without bloodshed.

After a while the natives helped this white Ma put up a two room house for herself and her African children. They made it like their own, of mud-covered bamboo walls and mat roof. Then they built a larger building in the village two miles away where she had her other school. They called this *The House of the Book* during the week and *The House of the Lord* on Sunday.

After Mary had been at Okoyong about a year, the mission at Calabar sent a carpenter to build her a better house. This meant they saw the value of her work and wanted to make Okoyong a mission station.

The carpenter arrived on a Monday and found Mary in the midst of a church service. She asked him, "Why are you traveling on Sunday?"

"Today is Monday," he told her.

"I've lost track of the days," she admitted. "Well, the people here think it's Sunday, so you'll just have to have two Sundays this week!"

Next day he began the new building, a mission house with doors and windows, porch, and medicine room.

Years passed. Mary Slessor's name was known in all the villages for miles around. She was, to them, the white Ma who was brave and wise and kind. They admired her wisdom, her skill in healing, and her courage, which was more heroic than that of their bravest warriors. She would wrench weapons from the hands of drunken native men three times as strong as she was. They thought her notions very strange, but many of them began to realize that her brave and loving spirit came from the great God of whom she spoke so much.

Many times Mary was stricken with fever, diarrhea, and diseases, but she toiled tirelessly on. Her house was always filled with orphans, whom she loved dearly. She had a string running from her cot to the hammock of each of her twenty-five or thirty little children, so that whenever one of them began to cry in the night, she could pull the right string and swing the youngster to sleep.

During a smallpox epidemic, Chief Edem got the disease. Everyone who had not yet died fled in fear. In a letter describing her experiences, Mary wrote: "It is not easy. But Christ is here and I am always satisfied and happy in His love." Mary alone stayed by Chief Edem's side until he died. Then she made a simple coffin, dug a grave, and buried him.

By now Mary's strenuous life had affected her health, and she suffered pain much of the time. But the light of the Gospel had changed

Okoyong like nothing else could have. She wrote: "All the children within reach are sent to the school. Raiding, plundering, the stealing of slaves have almost entirely ceased. Any person from any place can come now for trade or pleasure, and stay wherever they choose... as safe as in Calabara."

At the age of fifty, she said, "I would like to go farther inland and make a home among a tribe of cannibals."

The Christians in Okoyong protested, "We love you. They will kill you. Do not go." Mary loved the Okoyong people, but her call was, "Onward! I dare not look back."

More than a hundred miles farther up the Cross River, the fierce Aro people lived, fought, and captured slaves to sell. She had learned about them from runaway slaves who came to her for protection. The Aros' center was the grove of their god Chuku. Here Chuku's priests pretended to offer human sacrifices that they coaxed from people as payment for answers to prayers. Instead of sacrificing their victims, however, they sold them as slaves.

In 1903 Mary rode a government boat that was sailing inland to the Aros. Here she visited Aro chiefs, many of whom had heard of her work in Okoyong. They begged her, "Come and make your home with us. We will build you a house, a school, a church—anything you want."

So Mary moved on, leaving her established work in the hands of helpers. Again she built churches and schools. The local people began to live "in God's fashion." Even the head chief, who had been in control of the slave trade, told the other chiefs he was going to start ruling in God's ways. He offered to build a house for any missionary who would come.

A government officer gave Mary a bicycle, which saved her many miles on foot. Her new friends excitedly called it the iron cow.

Later, with the opening of roads, the government often sent an automobile with an African driver to her door, making it possible for her to easily visit schools and churches miles away.

Sometimes when she walked home late at night, a leopard would stand in her path. She would break a stick from the bush, shoo it away, and go on. Once while on a journey by canoe, her paddlers shouted in alarm, "Ma! Look, a hippopotamus!" She hurled a bamboo pole at the beast's head, shouting, "Go away, you!" The amazed paddlers watched it dive and disappear.

Pain and weariness plagued the worn missionary more and more. The government car could take her only where there were roads, and the roads were few. Many forest villages could be reached only by bicycle or on foot. She kept on taking in twin babies and orphans. People from farther inland kept asking Mary to come work among them, and she tried to answer their calls. The mission at Duke Town would then place workers at stations she started, while she moved farther on to open new ones.

Overwork and neglect of proper food and rest aged Mary's body early and, at sixty-four, she could no longer walk the trails. Determined to keep on, however, she had her boys push her in a basket-chair on wheels.

"You'll kill yourself working so hard," the Duke Town missionaries warned. "Besides, we don't have enough workers to place on the stations you start."

If only there were two of me! Mary thought.

Mary spent much time with her Bible. Each morning she rose at daybreak and studied, jotting down her thoughts in the margins.

The more mission work she did, the more she still saw to do. But at the age of sixty-five, she knew she was worn-out. She approached Christmas of 1914 very tired and very weak. Soon after New Year's Day, she became ill with fever. Her African family called the doctor and missionary friends. They watched over her lovingly until early dawn on January 13, 1915, when she quietly left for her home in Heaven.

On a hill outside Duke Town, Mary's body was laid to rest. But her work goes on in the churches, schools, and hospitals she started.

"Mine has been such a famous service," she wrote shortly before her death. "God has been good to me, letting me serve Him in this humble way. I cannot thank Him enough for the honor He conferred upon me when He sent me to the Dark Continent."

Questions for Review

1. What is the modern day name for the country in Africa where Mary lived?

2. Who was a missionary hero of Mary's?

3. What happened to twins that were born in Calabar?

4. How did Mary keep villagers from fighting each other?

5. What did the Africans call a bicycle?

Questions for Discussion

1. What were some dangers that Mary faced in her missionary work?

2. How did life change for the better in villages where Mary lived?

3. Why did Mary wish that there would be two of her?

4. What is an example of Mary's courage?

5. Do you know anyone who resembles Mary in some way?

Mary Slessor lived from 1848 to 1915. My thanks to Juliann Good who put this story together from various sources. ~Howard

SAMSON

SAMSON'S STRENGTH

*Finally, my brethren, be strong in the Lord, and in
the power of his might. Ephesians 6:10*

READ JUDGES 13:24—14:9

Gregg Ernst is a strong dairy farmer from Nova Scotia. In 1993 he lifted 5,340 pounds, which is the world record. At that time he weighed 315 pounds and ate a couple of pounds of meat each day as well as a gallon of yogurt and huge helpings of an oat and raisin combination. By his first birthday, he weighed 35 pounds and at age twelve, he lifted a ton of sheet metal. He liked to lay a 200-pound rock on his chest and then do situps. In 1992 he carried a 480-pound rock 225 feet (70 meters) in Iceland, breaking a record that had stood for 1,000 years. (Interestingly, he and his wife, along with eight of their children sing a cappella music. They also homeschool their children.)

The Bible tells us of a stronger man. He killed a lion with his bare hands. Later he caught three hundred foxes. On another occasion, he broke two new ropes with which he had been tied. I would have liked to watch him carry the entire city gate structure to the top of a hill.

Why was Samson so strong? The basic reason was the influence of the Holy Spirit on his life. Verse 6 of the daily reading says, "The Spirit of the LORD came mightily upon him." There were conditions that he needed to keep. He was a Nazarite and as such he abstained from wine—even raisins—and any unclean thing, and from contact with death. Also he abstained from cutting his hair. The main part of the Nazarite vow to keep him strong was the uncut hair.

The word *Nazarite* means "separated one." The Nazarite vow was a promise of living a life of separation. His mark of separation couldn't be concealed.

The New Testament commands the Christian to be separate from sin and the world. Romans 12:2 says, "Be not conformed to this world; but be ye transformed by the renewing of your mind, that ye may prove what is that good, and acceptable, and perfect, will of God."

In order to have spiritual power and be an effective witness, the believer needs to live a life of separation. People around us may not accept our faith; but they do expect professing Christians to be different.

A STRONG WEAK MAN

Dearly beloved, I beseech you as strangers and pilgrims, abstain from fleshly lusts, which war against the soul. 1 Peter 2:11

READ JUDGES 16:1-9

When Oliver Cromwell, leader of England in the 1600s, sat for his official portrait, the artist proposed that Cromwell would cover up a disfiguring wart by resting his head in his hands. Cromwell said, "No, paint me as I am, warts and all."

The Bible paints a portrait of Samson as he was—with his strengths but also with his weaknesses.

Part of Samson's weakness was his desire for self-gratification. Pleasure trumped purity. Sin was more important to him than separation. Harlots appealed to him more than holiness. He had a lust for immorality, and he developed a lust for revenge. Both lusts led directly to his imprisonment.

A second reason for his weakness was hypocrisy. He carried some outward marks of the separated life of a Nazarite but failed to live completely like one. For example, he was to have no contact with death, but he ate honey from a lion's carcass.

A third reason for his weakness was presumption. He evidently thought he could play with sin, and God would overlook it. He presumed on God's mercy. He found out that going into a sinful atmosphere to indulge his appetites inevitably brought sad results.

A fourth reason was his outright disobedience. Samson was disrespectful to his parents, and he disregarded the requirements of the Nazarite vow.

Matthew Henry wrote, "Let all take warning by his fall carefully to preserve their purity and to watch against all fleshly lusts for all our glory has gone and our defense departed from us when the covenant of our separation to God as spiritual Nazarites is profaned."

COMPROMISE CAN KILL

Be not deceived: evil communications corrupt
good manners. 1 Corinthians 15:33

READ JUDGES 16:10-20

The collapse of character often begins on compromise corner. Samson's character had a colossal collapse due to a series of compromises. For one thing, he entered into an unequal yoke in marriage. He saw a Philistine woman that pleased him, and he ordered his dad to arrange for the marriage. His father and mother protested, saying, "Isn't there a suitable woman among the Israelites?" Although "marriage is honourable" (Hebrews 13:4), a Christian should marry "only in the Lord" (1 Corinthians 7:39). Though Samson wasn't a Christian, he would have been much better off marrying an Israelite woman who worshiped God.

In addition, Samson began to trifle with the secret of his strength. He told Delilah that if she were to weave the seven locks of his head with the web and pin, he would be powerless. Although he didn't lose his strength because he still kept the Nazarite vow of uncut hair, he came close to disclosing the secret of his strength by mentioning that it related to his hair.

251

Samson knew Delilah was surrounded by bad company, and so was he when he was with her. Yet he continued to associate with her. Ultimately, it was neither Delilah nor Samson who cut his locks. Daily, Delilah pressured him to tell her the secret of his strength. Finally and foolishly, he gave her the answer. At this point, he was asleep spiritually as she caused him to sleep physically on her knees while a Philistine shaved his head.

Samson's repeated compromise caused him to become powerless and imprisoned. He had not realized the Lord had departed. Gradually his adherence to principle went downhill until he went down to Gaza and down into prison. Sin deceives, then defiles, then deadens.

WHAT SAMSON LOST

The integrity of the upright shall guide them: but the perverseness of transgressors shall destroy them. Proverbs 11:3

READ JUDGES 16:21-30

Years ago a man was in prison doing the menial labor of mending burlap bags. A visitor said to him, "Sewing, are you?"

"No," said the sorry inmate, "reaping." In Judges 16 we notice aspects of Samson's reaping what he had sown. Samson lost eight things.

1. He lost his *hair*. Delilah "called for a man, and she caused him to shave off the seven locks of his head" (Judges 16:19). Though Samson's strength didn't lie in his long hair, it was the external evidence of obedience to God and the Nazarite vow.

2. He lost his *strength*. When Samson awoke from his physical sleep, he said, "I will go out as at other times before, and shake myself" (v. 20). He didn't realize at first that the Lord had departed from him. When he lost the Lord, he lost his power.

3. He lost his *sight*. "The Philistines took him, and put out his eyes" (v. 21). But Samson's spiritual vision had become dim long before this.

253

4. He lost his *liberty*. The Philistines "brought him down to Gaza, and bound him with fetters of brass" (v. 21). He had become a slave to sin earlier; now he was a slave physically.

5. He lost his *usefulness* for God. "He did grind in the prison house" (v. 21). Day after day, he faced the same old grind, literally. Instead of leading Israel, he was working for the enemy. In Samson's life we see the blinding, binding, grinding results of sin.

6. He lost his *testimony*. Israel's leader had become a laughingstock, and the Philistines exalted their god Dagon. "Then the lords of the Philistines gathered them together for to offer a great sacrifice unto Dagon their god, and to rejoice: for they said, Our god hath delivered Samson our enemy into our hand" (v. 23). Sin in one's life destroys one's testimony.

7. He lost his *dignity*. The worshipers decided to have Samson "make us sport" (v. 25). Samson had changed from a champion to a clown in their eyes.

8. He lost his *life*. Although Samson sought and got vengeance, it cost him his life.

I think the preacher was right when he said, "Sin would have few takers if its consequences occurred immediately."

DON'T
DESPISE GODLY PARENTS

A wise son maketh a glad father: but a foolish man despiseth his mother. Proverbs 15:20

READ JUDGES 13:1-12

S amson's life shows us that even an individual with many blessings and advantages can make bad choices. Samson had devout parents. His mother recognized that the angelic messenger was from God. How would you feel if your birth had been announced by an angel? Samson shouldn't have had struggles knowing what to do in life, since the divine messenger said what his purpose would be.

Samson's father was a godly man. Upon hearing about the angel's message, Manoah's immediate impulse was to pray. He prayed that the "man of God" would teach him and his wife how to train and relate to the promised son. He wanted divine guidance, saying, "How shall we order the child, and how shall we do unto him?" (Judges 13:12). In other words, how shall we direct and instruct our son in what he should do?

Manoah was a man of faith. Judges 13:17 records that he said to the angel, "*when* thy sayings come to pass," not *if* the sayings came to pass. Both of Samson's parents worshiped the Lord and talked of Him.

Unfortunately, Samson didn't seem to appreciate his training or his parents. When Samson went down to Timnath and saw an attractive heathen woman, he went down both geographically and spiritually. When he desired to marry the Philistine woman, he didn't consult with his parents but ordered them to "get her for me to wife" (Judges 14:2).

There was also a lack of communication between Samson and his parents. After killing a lion, "he told not his father or his mother what he had done" (Judges 14:6).

How sad when children reject the godly teaching and example of their parents.

LESSONS FROM SAMSON

*And what shall I more say? for the time would fail me to tell of
Gedeon, and of Barak, and of Samson, and of Jephthae; of David
also, and Samuel, and of the prophets. Hebrews 11:32*

READ JUDGES 15:3-20

In view of Samson's sins and mistakes, you may be surprised to find
him listed among the heroes of faith in Hebrews 11. (See verse
above.) His inclusion in the list tells us how God takes note of
one's faith. In response to the apostles' aspiration, "Lord, increase our
faith" (Luke 17:5), Jesus mentioned the power of faith, even though it
is small—the size of a mustard seed.

Samson's life also teaches us the futility of seeking revenge. There
is no human passion that promises so much and pays so little. Notice
the pattern of trying to "get even." First, he put a combination of a
riddle and dare to the Philistines. They didn't play fair, so he was
the loser. He killed thirty Philistines to pay for his loss in the challenge. Samson left his wife for a while and when he returned, she
was no longer available. This made Samson angry, so he put three
hundred fiery-tailed foxes in the Philistine fields. They tried to get

even by burning his wife. To get even, he smote the Philistines in a great slaughter.

He thought that would finish the vengeance. He said, "Though ye have done this, yet will I be avenged of you, and after that I will cease" (Judges 15:7). But they came after him "to do to him as he hath done to us" (Judges 15:10). As explained in the daily reading, Samson was tied up. But he broke the ropes as the Philistines approached, found the jawbone of an ass, and slew a thousand men. Then the Philistines got even via Delilah's trickery and made him a prisoner. Ultimately, both Samson and the Philistines died when Samson pulled the house down. Revenge is the sword that wounds the one who wields it.

MORE
LESSONS FROM SAMSON

Keep thyself pure. 1 Timothy 5:22

READ GALATIANS 6:7-10

A young man who was living a sinful life was asked, "Are you getting a kick out of your way of life?"

"A kick?" he replied. "I'm getting a kickback."

The daily reading states the spiritual law of sowing and reaping. Samson sowed sin and reaped "losses." There's no crop failure for sin.

Samson's life teaches us the lesson expressed in Proverbs 6:27. "Can a man take fire in his bosom, and . . . not be burned?"

Samson's life teaches us the need to flee fornication. Samson conquered the Philistines, but he was conquered by lust. His first recorded words in the Bible are, "I have seen a woman." He seems to have become attracted by her appearance not her character. He had a history of immorality—visiting a harlot (Judges 16:1) and then loving Delilah. It may be significant that the first thing the Philistines did to him was put out his eyes—those eyes would never wander again.

Proverbs 6:32, 33 says, "But whoso committeth adultery with a woman lacketh understanding: he that doeth it destroyeth his own soul. A wound and dishonour shall he get; and his reproach shall not be wiped away." Joseph, another hero of faith, was much wiser for he was able to "flee youthful lusts" (2 Timothy 2:22).

Samson's life also demonstrates that a person can lose out spiritually and not realize it. After yielding to sin and then telling Delilah the secret of his strength, "he wist not that the LORD was departed from him" (Judges 16:20). First Corinthians 10:12 warns the believer, "Let him that thinketh he standeth take heed lest he fall."

Finally, don't despise your spiritual heritage. Samson had many advantages, including godly parents, yet he made a mess of his life.

A Jump of Faith
Tim Whatley

By Juliann Good

Imagine a dense jungle in the tropics. Gigantic trees, twisting vines, and lush foliage create a world of vivid green. Toucans, cockatoos, and other birds twitter among the leaves. Wild pigs snuffle the forest floor. Tree kangaroos scamper along branches a hundred feet in the air. Pitcher plants coax insects or lizards into a slippery death by drowning.

261

There are no concrete cities here—no cars, no electric lights, no telephones, no roads, or bridges. In fact, this jungle is so remote that you would need to hike for nearly a month from the nearest road to get there!

Does such a remote jungle exist? Yes! It is in Papua, a province of Indonesia.

Indonesia is a country made up of islands scattered between the Indian Ocean and the Pacific Ocean, right on the equator. It is a land of dense jungles, rugged mountains, and snaking rivers. Most of its millions of people have never heard about Jesus Christ.

In this country of Indonesia, Tim Whatley grew up as a son of a missionary. All his life, Tim had sensed that someday God would ask him to bring the Gospel to a people who had never heard it before. The thought thrilled him. To be the messenger of Jesus to an area plunged in Satan's darkness! To speak His name to ears who had never heard it before!

He had watched his parents preach God's Word to an Indonesian tribe called the Lauje. He had seen God transform the Lauje people, and God pressed into his heart the desire to bring the Good News to another people.

And so in 1998, Tim, his wife Kathy, and their children left their home in Ontario, Canada, and flew to Indonesia. They wanted to find a people who had never heard the Gospel, live among them, and learn their language and culture well enough to communicate God's message. "Lord, which people are you going to send us to?"

About one month after arriving in Indonesia, someone knocked on their door one evening. "Come in," Tim called.

Their visitor was a pilot from a nearby mission agency. "You'll never guess what I saw yesterday," he said, straddling the chair Tim pushed toward him. "I was flying lower than normal because of the weather. The clouds pushed me lower and lower, and I ended up flying through this X-shaped valley." He described his location and then shocked his listeners with his next statement. "I was low enough to easily see the ground, and I saw houses and gardens."

"Wait a minute!" Tim interrupted. "Houses and gardens? Nobody lives in that part of Indonesia."

The pilot leaned forward. "Nobody knows it," he said, pointing at Tim. "But there's a tribe in there! I know it! I saw their houses!"

"Kathy," Tim cried, grabbing her around the waist. "I think God has just brought us our people!"

Indeed He had. Over the months that followed, Tim and his fellow missionaries made plans to reach the "X-ray people," as they dubbed them.

The remote jungle described at the beginning of this story housed a secret—a secret not discovered until 1998. Living in its green depths was a tribe of people called the Moi. No one knew they existed. The government of Indonesia had no record of them. They had zero contact with the outside world, completely isolated in their jungle home.

The Moi lived in thatch-roofed houses made of sticks tied together with vines. Their houses were clustered together in little hamlets scattered throughout the jungle. They grew bananas and sweet potatoes in their gardens. The men hunted cassowary birds, tree kangaroos, and wild pigs for meat. Because they had no cooking pots or knives, they used sharp bamboo splinters to cut and cooked their food directly in the coals or steamed it in bundles of leaves and hot rocks.

They used stone tools and handmade bows and arrows. They started their fires with flint and bamboo. The tribe owned only a few metal axes, which they had acquired from somewhere many years before, but they were worn almost to the handle. Stone axes cannot cut trees down, so in order for gardens to grow, Moi men climbed the trees and chopped off their limbs, leaving only tall spikes.

The Moi people had lovely brown skin and black hair. Women wore short skirts made of bark, men wore a gourd tied about the waist, and children wore no clothes.

The Moi people did not know God. They had never heard of Jesus. They lived in constant fear of evil spirits. Satan had the Moi in his enslaving grip, and Satan is a cruel, cruel taskmaster. Anytime a snake bit or a scorpion stung or an arrow wounded someone, the Moi believed that evil spirits had entered the injured person's body. To draw out the evil spirits, they would slice the victim's body with as many as thirteen large slices. Often the victim died from blood loss.

The Moi believed that evil spirits lived in water. If someone became sick, he would refuse to drink water. Consequently, many sick people died a senseless death of dehydration. Expectant mothers also refused to drink water in case an evil spirit entered the baby. This meant that Moi babies were sickly, and many died. If twins were born, one of the babies was considered to be an evil spirit. The twins' mother was forced to choose her strongest baby and kill it. (The healthiest baby was considered to be the evil spirit eating the weaker baby.)

Moi men often had more than one wife. But husbands and wives did not trust each other. A husband would be fearful of his wife: *What if she curses me? What if she curses my other wife's child?* Likewise, women feared their husbands. Girls got married at the ages of eight to twelve. Their husbands often beat them.

The Moi were murderers. Many men had killed several wives. Sometimes a man would kill his brother in order to take his wife. If a man died, he was not buried until the people figured out why he died. Who had killed him? Who cursed him? Somebody must have!

Obviously, the Moi were not happy. Their lives were ruled by fear and hatred. They desperately needed Jesus to change their hearts and bring them peace and love.

But no one knew they existed! No one knew their language, and they knew no one else's language. They had no chance of hearing God's Word or getting to know Jesus.

But though the world did not know the Moi, God did! And He was about to raise up a faithful missionary team to bring them His message. One bright day the natives would watch, terrified, as a thundering steel bird descended from the skies, bearing within it God's faithful messengers.

It was July 2000. In the living room of their Indonesian house, Tim Whatley's family huddled in a tearful embrace. Tim's eyes were blurred with tears as he cuddled one-year-old Alyssa and three-year-old Tyler. *Will I ever see them again?*

He knelt before his eldest son, five-year-old Brandt. "You take good care of Mommy while I'm gone, okay?" His voice choked as he gathered Brandt in a bear hug.

Tim turned last to his wife Kathy. *Oh, God! This is so hard! What if they kill me? I'll be safe in eternity with You, but what about Kathy and the children? Kathy didn't grow up in Indonesia! She has no family here. Who would look after her?*

Aloud, he spoke bravely into her ear. "Kathy, sweetheart, everything's going to be fine, okay? I'll call you every night. It'll be okay."

Ever since they had discovered the "X-ray people," Tim and Kathy and their fellow missionaries had been making plans to reach them with the Gospel. Three families had committed themselves to live with these people and plant a church—Tim and Kathy, Tim's sister Carolyn and her husband Steve Crockett, and an Indonesian couple, Anderson and Leike Penambunan. After months of intense prayer, they had decided it would be best to fly to them in a helicopter. Four men would make the initial contact. Nobody knew what would happen, but they trusted God.

At first Tim had been very excited. To reach a people who had never heard about God! This was a lifelong dream come true! But the initial excitement gave way to fear. What if the "X-ray people" were cannibals? Many primitive Indonesian tribes were, and it certainly was not in Tim's plans to be eaten!

Now the day had come, and as Tim bade good-bye to his family, nervousness gripped him. What would happen when they opened the helicopter door? Would they be instantly killed and eaten? *Lord, I choose to trust in You,* Tim breathed, waving good-bye. *You are in control, You love the "X-ray people," and even if I'm killed, Your plan is best.*

Tim and his fellow missionaries made a base camp nearer to the jungle where the "X-ray people" lived. As they made final preparations, they needed to decide who would make the first contact. The helicopter would hold four men. One was the pilot, and another pilot, Nate Gordon, needed to operate the radio. That left room for only two more. Tim, Steve, and Anderson decided to draw straws to see which one would stay at base camp and wait for a second flight. The short straw fell to Anderson. Tim and his brother-in-law Steve would take the first flight in.

On the final night before their departure, the missionary team spent a long time in earnest prayer. Everyone felt the nervous tension, but deeper than that, Tim felt a settled calmness. He knew deep in his soul that God was in control. Though panic swelled in his throat when he thought of murderous arrows, he also had peace, the "peace that passes all understanding."

The next morning the four men strapped themselves into the helicopter and lifted off. *Lord, strengthen my weak heart,* Tim prayed. *Use me for Your own glory.*

"Hey, Tim," Nate's voice came through the headset. "Who can run faster—you or your brother-in-law? Because if it's him, you'll be the first in the cooking pot, you know."

Laughter filled the helicopter.

Actually, thought Tim, *I have it all figured out. We land the helicopter. I open the door. I peek out. If they shoot, I slam the door shut and we take off again. I won't even have to get out of this machine if it doesn't look safe.*

The helicopter flew higher and higher into the mountains. Clouds swirled lazily above miles of jungle. And then, suddenly, there they were. Tim gazed down at the telltale "tree spikes"—the de-limbed trees that marked the gardens of the "X-ray people."

"A house! Two houses! Right over there by that big garden," Steve spoke.

As the helicopter dropped lower, Tim could see more gardens and more stick houses. "People!" he exclaimed, spotting some tiny figures.

The pilot's voice crackled through their headsets. "I don't know, guys," he said. "These trees are awfully close together. How are we going to land this bird between them? Let's try this big garden right here." He maneuvered the helicopter above a garden clustered with tree spikes.

"Look at that, everyone!" Nate pointed. "Those are women and children running out of their houses. Looks like they're making a mad dash to hide in the jungle."

"What are the men doing?" Tim asked. Then a chill of horror seized him as he realized. They were lining up in the clearing beneath the helicopter, each carrying a bow and a handful of vicious-looking arrows.

The helicopter hovered right above the treetops now, and the pilot's voice cracked with tension as he spoke. "You all have to help me," he said. "This is going to be a tight squeeze between these trees. You each watch your corner and help me wiggle down. I need twelve inches on each side before my rotor hits a tree."

"Too close on my side!" Nate called out, and the pilot moved over slightly.

"Too close here," Steve announced a second later.

Tim's eyes wandered to the warriors below him. They stood in a semicircle now, bows in position, dark skin gleaming in the sunshine. A fierce sigh shuddered through him. *Lord, is there any other way? I know Jesus became flesh and lived among us, but do we have to live among these people? This doesn't look good. What about Kathy and the children?*

Little by little, slowly and carefully, the pilot eased the helicopter down between the trees. The sound of its whirring rotor and noisy engine echoed in Tim's ears. His palms felt sticky, and he swiped a hand over his sweaty brow.

Then it happened. The skid of the helicopter became wedged in a V-shaped branch twelve feet from the ground.

"We're stuck," the pilot announced grimly. "Pray, everybody!" He gave the helicopter a burst of power.

Vvvv-rrrrrr-oooooooommmm!

Nothing happened.

Vvvv-rrrrrr-oooooooommmm! Vvvvv-rrrrrrr-oooooooommmm!

Still nothing.

"Uh-oh!" said the pilot.

A cold feeling of dread stuck in Tim's throat. He clenched his fists. He bit his lip.

The pilot tried one more time. *Vvvvv-rrrrrrrr-oooooooommmm!*

Pop! The branch snapped and the helicopter broke free.

Yes! Praise the Lord! We're going back home! Tim fought the urge to shout. *This is too tight! It's too dangerous. Those arrows are too big. We tried, Lord. We'll be back another day with another plan. Let's just get out of here.*

But no. God had other plans, and Tim was committed to doing His will. He fought his fear and helped the pilot inch his way lower and lower. He watched the troublemaking V-shaped branch slide past the window.

They were now six feet above the ground. "I'm sorry, guys," the pilot spoke again. "I just cannot go down any farther. You are going to have to jump. I'm really sorry."

Tim shot a horrified glance out the window. The warriors were lined up on his side of the helicopter, about 40 feet away, bows and arrows aimed. *Jump out? You have got to be kidding me.* Tim's heart hammered in his chest. *As soon as I jump out of here, I'm a sitting duck. And a dead duck too, probably.*

But God had everything firmly in control. God loved the "X-ray people" as Tim called them. Even though Tim had no name for these people and could not speak their language, God had sent him with His message of eternal life. Could Tim trust his heavenly Father enough to make that jump of faith?

Steve opened his door and jumped. He and Nate were on the side of the helicopter facing away from the warriors. A second later, Nate jumped too.

Tim took a deep breath. He opened his door and threw out a chain saw (so they could cut down some trees for the pilot). "Don't go up until we tell you it's safe," Tim called to the pilot.

His life was now entirely in God's hands. Could he do it?

Tim jumped.

He stood on the ground a moment later, facing the line of warriors. *Now what, Lord? What do we do now? How will we know what You have planned?*

And then the missionaries witnessed a miracle. They saw the Moi warriors do something they never, ever do. Even today, these Moi men cannot explain why they did what they did. Moi men always, always carry their bows and arrows. Even at church today they stay close to their bows and arrows. It is completely against their nature to lay their weapons down, but that is what they did. They laid down their weapons and walked toward the white strangers.

And the God of the universe, way back at the Tower of Babel, had prepared their language for Tim's trembling heart that day. As they walked toward him, they were saying a word over and over. "Abba, Abba, Abba, Abba, Abba," they said.

Abba! The word soothed Tim's fearful mind. Abba! It was as if God was speaking directly to him, "Relax, Tim. I am your Abba Father, and this is My plan. I am in control; trust Me."

"Abba, Abba, Abba," the men called. They held up the first two fingers of their right hands, and Tim instantly recognized the traditional greeting of many Papuan tribes. He held up the first two fingers of his right hand and "snapped" fingers with each warrior.

Although he couldn't yet know it, "Abba" was the Moi way of saying, "We think we can trust you, and you can trust us."

Tim and his colleagues spent three weeks with the Moi people that first time. The first three or four nights, they slept on the jungle floor under a tarp. After that the Moi invited them to sleep in a men's house.

I can see God at work, Tim marveled as he climbed up into the men's house for the night. *A couple days ago I was afraid these people would kill me. Now they've invited me to sleep inside the house.*

Men's houses were built on stilts two feet off the ground. They had no windows and were sealed tightly to keep the evil spirits out. The men slept with their feet toward the fire pit in the middle of the house. Women slept in their own houses, which were much smaller and built on the ground. With their children, they slept on the dirt floor along with the pigs.

They quickly realized that learning the Moi language would not be easy. Tim knew he needed to learn the nouns first. He picked up a rock and showed it to a young warrior. He listened to what the man said and wrote it down. Then he showed the rock to someone else, hoping he would hear the same sounds. He tried it with *tree, house, pig,* and other words.

"I don't know, Anderson," he said. "I get the feeling these people are purposely trying to trick me. They aren't giving me the same answers. I still have no idea what the word for *tree* is."

"Either that or they don't understand what on earth you're doing by walking around pointing to things," Anderson replied.

Then on the third or the fourth day, the missionaries were sitting with some Moi men when a new man walked in. Tim had not seen him before. When Tim pulled a camera out of his backpack, curiosity crossed the newcomer's face. *"Kassee, Me'embou?"* he asked, pointing toward the camera.

"Kassee, Me'embou?" the newcomer asked again.

Something clicked inside Tim's brain. *He's saying, "What is it?"* Tim thought. A few minutes later, he pointed to a tree and tried the phrase on a young boy. *"Kassee, Me'embou?"*

When the boy replied, Tim felt sure he now had the word for tree. He tried the phrase on someone else and got the same reply.

In this way, little by little, Tim and his coworkers learned the Moi language. But it would be four years before they could speak it fluently.

In October 2000 Tim and Kathy and their children came to live with the Moi people. Anderson and his family also came. They built a house for each family and settled down to life with the Moi. Six months later Steve and Carolyn also arrived and set to work building their family's house.

But one day two chieftains appeared at Tim's house. "Go! Go! You must leave!" they demanded. "Get out! Go away! The spirits are very angry with you."

Tim's knowledge of the Moi language was still very limited, and he struggled to understand the chieftains. "Why?" he asked.

"You are building this house on a spirit trail, and the spirits are very angry," they insisted. "The spirits have said if you want to live here, you must provide a pig sacrifice. If you don't, women and children will begin dying."

Then the chieftains left, leaving Tim and his coworkers with time to think and pray. If they did not sacrifice a pig, every death would be blamed on them. On the other hand, sacrificing a pig would exhibit the same fear of evil spirits that the Moi had. What should they do?

Soon the chieftains returned. "You cannot cut lumber until you sacrifice a pig," they announced. "You are cutting in a sacred forest."

Tim grappled for the right words. "We serve the Jo Spirit," he began. "He sent us here with His message. He is a good spirit, the greatest spirit. He is much stronger than your spirits. We will cut trees, and what happens will be our responsibility."

The Moi chieftains deliberated among themselves and finally replied, "You may cut trees, but it will not go well for you!"

Lord, show these people that You really are much greater than the spirits that rule them, Tim prayed. Then he sent the woodcutters back to work. The woodcutters, Indonesian Papuan men, returned with the chain saw in less than an hour, their faces pale with fright. Something very strange had happened. A chain saw has a crankshaft, which is a cylindrical piece of metal. It is not unusual for it to break in the middle, but this crankshaft had split from end to end—something that is normally impossible.

"We have never seen anything like it. This has never happened before!"

"Well, let's replace it with the crankshaft from another chain saw," Tim replied calmly. "Come back tomorrow and we'll cut some more wood."

The next day the woodcutters went back to work, but they dashed out of the jungle a short while later, trembling with fear. The body of the chain saw had cracked all around in an impossible way. Tim encouraged them to keep working, determined to show the people that his God was stronger than theirs. But he soon realized that they were fighting an intense spiritual war. The carburetor of a chain saw inexplicably broke in half. Their generator died. The most astonishing occurrence happened with a hand planer. While building the two other houses, Tim had used this particular metal hand planer to shape, flatten, and smooth wood. It had always been reliable. But when he used it to work with the lumber from the sacred forest, it mysteriously melted into a clump, which should be a scientific impossibility.

Lord, what shall we do? After praying about it, Tim and his coworkers sensed God wanted them to stop cutting wood in the sacred forest, step back, and watch the Lord do battle. So they stopped cutting wood and waited.

For several weeks they waited. Then one day a group of over forty men gathered in Tim's front yard. The chieftain Tokomati, main witch doctor of the tribe, spoke on behalf of the people. "We are going to kill and sacrifice a pig, and you must be part of this sacrifice," he said. "You must eat the food with us."

Forty pairs of black eyes glittered at Tim. If there ever was a time to boldly proclaim the one true God, this was it. He swallowed hard and addressed the crowd. "I cannot be part of this sacrifice. I told you we have been sent with a message from the *Jo* Spirit. He will not be happy if I show respect to the little spirits. They are weaker than He. I completely trust in Him. But you do not know the *Jo* Spirit, so you will have to sacrifice until you know the *Jo* Spirit."

Utter silence followed. Tokomati put his head down, deep in thought. Tim and his friends prayed silently that God would change the people's minds and reveal Himself to them.

Finally, Tokomati lifted his head and spoke. "If you do not have to sacrifice to the little spirits—our spirits—in this case, then we don't have to either."

The next day people came from throughout the tribe, whooping and shouting, singing, and dancing. They had a loud pig party in Tim's front yard, a joyful celebration of freedom. For the first time in their lives, the Moi people had felt the spiritual oppression lift. They shook their heads, saying, "I don't understand this God. I must hear about this God."

After the party they gave permission to the missionaries to cut wood in the sacred forest. And Tim and his team cut all the wood they needed without a single problem. God had proven Himself supreme over the gods of the Moi.

And the people hungered to know more about the one true Spirit Tim had proclaimed. In 2005 the missionaries had learned the language well enough to begin Bible teaching. They had built a written language for the Moi and begun to translate the Bible. They conducted a Bible class for six months, in which they taught the whole message of the Bible, beginning at Creation.

When they got to the stories of Jesus, the Moi people fell in love with Him. They began to see their own sinfulness. "Get on the radio and tell Jesus to come to our tribe," they begged. "We have killed. We have stolen. We need Him to come and help us."

"Not yet," the missionaries replied. "Just keep listening to the stories."

"Well then, can you bring us some sheep?" the people requested. "We need sheep to sacrifice until Jesus comes to help us."

"Not yet," the missionaries replied. "Just wait until you hear the whole story."

Imagine the joy they felt to see ten Moi people make life-changing commitments to Jesus Christ after that first series of Bible class! The next year they conducted another six-month Bible class. That time one hundred people became believers!

Today there is a strong, growing church in the Moi tribe. Well over one-third of them are believers, and Moi pastors preach the Gospel to their own people.

And Tim and Kathy? They no longer live with the Moi people. Much to their disappointment, Kathy became very, very sick after four years, and they needed to move back home to Ontario. They had planted the Gospel seeds, but God asked them to leave before those seeds sprouted and grew.

The Moi people are not the only ones who have never heard the Gospel. Even in today's world of radio, smartphones, and Internet, it is possible for a person to live his entire life and die without ever hearing the name of Jesus Christ. In fact, this is true for an estimated thirty percent of the people on our planet. Approximately two billion people have never heard the Gospel message. They need someone to tell them.

That is Tim Whatley's passion today. He works for an agency that sends missionaries to tribes who have never heard the Gospel. Perhaps someday God will call you to become a missionary to a people who have never heard about Jesus.

Questions for Review

1. In which country did this story take place?

2. How were the Moi people discovered?

3. How far did Tim need to jump down from the helicopter?

4. What word were the natives saying when they met Tim after he had just jumped from the helicopter?

5. What kind of sacrifice did the native leaders ask Tim to be part of?

Questions for Discussion

1. Why didn't Tim offer a pig sacrifice?

2. What would you have liked or disliked about living with the Moi before the Gospel reached them?

3. If you had been with Tim on the first visit to the Moi people, would you have jumped from the helicopter?

4. Does your family know of any people groups who have not heard the Gospel, or of any missions who try to reach such groups?

5. Why do you think the unusual things with the chain saw, generator, and hand planer were happening?

The author of this story, Juliann Good, and her husband Laverne know Tim personally. Tim kindly reviewed her story to ensure that it is accurate. ~ Howard

SAMUEL

ASKED OF GOD

*Be careful for nothing; but in every thing by prayer
and supplication with thanksgiving let your requests
be made known unto God. Philippians 4:6*

READ 1 SAMUEL 1:9-20

Near the beginning of the twenty-first century, a website was set up to send prayers to God. The site claimed to send prayers via a radio transmitter to star cluster M13, believed by some scientists to be the oldest star group in the universe. Based on Big Bang theories (not Genesis 1), if everything was in one place at the time of the Big Bang, God must have been there too. The website, no longer operational, purported to send fifty thousand prayers a week. The cost was five dollars per prayer or six prayers for twenty-five dollars.

Hannah knew about free access to God and the power of prayer. Concerning her, we might paraphrase James 5:16: "The effectual fervent prayer of a godly *woman* availeth much." Her prayer was so fervent that her spiritual advisor, Eli, thought she was drunk. Her prayer for a son was answered, and she called him *Samuel*, meaning "asked of God."

I wouldn't recommend a website like the one mentioned above. I do recommend Jeremiah 33:3, which states, "Call unto me, and I will answer thee, and show thee great and mighty things, which thou knowest not."

The Bible repeatedly invites us to ask of God. What a privilege! Jesus said, "Ask, and it shall be given you; seek, and ye shall find; knock, and it shall be opened unto you" (Matthew 7:7). Obedience is important in prayer. "And whatsoever we ask, we receive of him, because we keep his commandments, and do those things that are pleasing in his sight" (1 John 3:22).

Perhaps Samuel learned from his mother the privilege of asking God. When Israel was faced with insurmountable odds against the Philistines, after worshiping God via a burnt offering, "Samuel cried unto the LORD for Israel; and the LORD heard him. And as Samuel was offering up the burnt offering, the Philistines drew near to battle against Israel: but the LORD thundered with a great thunder on that day upon the Philistines, and discomfited them; and they were smitten before Israel" (1 Samuel 7:9, 10).

Benjamin Beddome wrote:

> When God inclines the heart to pray,
> He hath an ear to hear;
> To Him there's music in a groan,
> And beauty in a tear.

BUILDING
PROPER SELF-ESTEEM

- -

*Moreover his mother made him a little coat, and brought
it to him from year to year, when she came up with her
husband to offer the yearly sacrifice. 1 Samuel 2:19*

READ 1 SAMUEL 1:21-28

Some parents don't help their children to view themselves with a
proper sense of worth because they don't value the children. In
Tennessee, a couple was arrested for swapping their baby for a
new television. In New Jersey, fourteen-month-old Jimmy was offered
in exchange for a Corvette.

A basic way for parents to teach their children to have a proper view of
self is to have the right appreciation of their worth. Singing songs together
like "Jesus Loves Me" and "Can You Count the Stars of Evening?" and
telling Bible stories like "Jesus and the Children" and "The Boy Who
Shared" can help a child to realize that God cares for and values him.

What are some other practical ways parents may help a growing
child to "think soberly," not more highly or more lowly than he ought
(Romans 12:3)? Let's take a few lessons from Samuel's childhood in
today's reading.

1. Welcome the baby (v. 27). How Hannah desired and treasured Samuel! The idea of being *wanted* ought to be communicated to a child whether he is a toddler or a teen. Even without being told in plain words, a child can sense that he is viewed as a bother or a hindrance to parental plans.

2. Pray for your child. Hannah testified, "for this child I prayed" (v. 27). At times pray audibly, letting your child hear your prayers for him. This reinforces the concept in the child's mind that he is significant to his parents and the Father.

3. View your child as a gift from God. Hannah realized God gave her Samuel (and three more sons and two daughters following). "Lo, children are an heritage of the LORD" (Psalm 127:3). As your child senses that he is a gift from God almighty, he will recognize that he has importance and value.

4. Dedicate your child to God (v. 28). Worthless things are not dedicated, a child will realize.

5. Communicate to the child that he is special. Hannah brought Samuel a special coat. Hand-me-downs have their place, but so do new clothes, especially for the middle child. Our words to, our words about, and our actions toward our children will tell them whether we rate them above, below, or equal to an SUV, laptop, or living room furniture.

ELI'S WISDOM
TOWARD SAMUEL

But when Jesus saw it, he was much displeased, and said unto them, Suffer the little children to come unto me, and forbid them not: for of such is the kingdom of God. Mark 10:14

READ 1 SAMUEL 2:18-21; 3:1-10

Eli had discernment in relating to young Samuel. His attitude and advice show parents ways to help children have a proper view of self.

- Let the child minister before the Lord (1 Samuel 2:18). Significant work (and any for the Lord is significant) helps to give a child a realistic view of himself. Children can pray, sing, and witness of God's love. Let them have an active part in family worship.

- Encourage the child to respond to the Lord. When Samuel heard a voice at bedtime (1 Samuel 3:4-10), Eli didn't answer for him but guided him in an appropriate response. A response to the Lord of reverence, love, and obedience is appropriate at any age.

- Respect privacy. Eli had "his place" (1 Samuel 3:2), and Samuel had a different place. Although children need supervision, they also need "space" as they mature.

- Assign work. Samuel opened the doors of the house of the Lord (1 Samuel 3:15). My wife frequently talked about "Mommy's big helper" to and about our children. For an efficient housekeeper, the temptation is to say, "Oh, you can't do that," knowing that you can do the task faster and better. It is healthy for a child to believe that one has important tasks and can do them.

- Give guidance but don't dominate a growing child.

Some persons grow up feeling they are unimportant to God and others, that they are incapable of doing anything worthwhile, and that everybody can do everything better than they can. They view themselves as "no good." They struggle with feelings of worthlessness and grapple with insecurity.

Some children may create discipline problems in order to be noticed: spilling milk deliberately, upsetting games, or making odd noises in the classroom. Such young people lay rubber on the road, laugh unnecessarily loud (and dress that way too), or may withdraw into a shell. Such adults may exaggerate, attempt to dominate, feel worthless, or have possible suicidal tendencies.

May we help our children to have healthy, Scriptural thoughts about self. Let us "think soberly" about ourselves and build a proper concept of self into our children's consciousness. Christ, who said, "Ye are of more value than many sparrows" (Luke 12:7), bought us with a great price, His precious blood.

SAMUEL'S INTERCESSION

· ·

Moses and Aaron among his priests, and Samuel among them that call upon his name; they called upon the LORD, and he answered them. Psalm 99:6

READ 1 SAMUEL 7:1-13

As Samuel grew, he became a prophet, priest, and civic ruler in Israel. "And Samuel grew, and the LORD was with him, and did let none of his words fall to the ground. And all Israel from Dan even to Beersheba knew that Samuel was established to be a prophet of the LORD" (1 Samuel 3:19, 20).

One of Samuel's contributions to Israel was his intercessory prayer. The daily reading records Samuel's intention to pray for Israel (v. 5), and his crying unto the Lord (v. 9), as well as the results (vv. 10, 11). He also led Israel in remembering God's help.

What a privilege it is for us to be able to say to each other, "I will pray for you."

An American minister became the minister of a London church. On his first Sunday, there were several converts. He preached with power that he had never before experienced. About a year later, he was called to the bedside of an obscure member of his church, a man who was physically challenged, who told him the following story:

"I should not tell you, pastor," he said, "but I know that my time is come, and I do not want my work to cease when I go. I passed through a period of rebellion and spiritual darkness because of my poverty and lameness. It seemed that there was little that I could do for my Master. But God revealed to me that He had given me the privilege of intercession. The Saturday night before you preached your first sermon, I spent all night in prayer for you, and I have done that every Saturday night since. Someone will take up the work that I am about to lay down, surely."

Now the pastor knew what had surely been the secret of his power.

SAMUEL'S FAITHFULNESS

*Be thou faithful unto death, and I will give thee
a crown of life. Revelation 2:10*

READ 1 SAMUEL 7:15-17; 12:1-7

I wonder what Mrs. Samuel thought of her husband's annual circuit mentioned in the daily reading. Perhaps Samuel's frequent absences from the home contributed to his sons' lack of faithfulness. But Samuel himself was a faithful leader.

So outstanding was Samuel's integrity that he could fearlessly challenge his people to find any injustice or partiality in his administration.

Some years ago, a university student worked at a job during the summer vacation to help pay for his education. He worked with an ungodly group of surveyors. The student was a devout Christian. In fact, he was the *only* Christian in that gang of surveyors. When the evening meal was over, the men would gamble and drink and, oftentimes, the atmosphere of the large room where they stayed would be filled with profanity.

On his first night with the gang, before the Christian student retired, he read his Bible and then knelt to pray. Pillows and shoes began to fly about the kneeling form. The praying student was ridiculed and mocked. The foreman of the gang allowed the mockery to go unabated for a moment, but then decency asserted itself in his heart. Leaping to his feet, he said, "The next man who throws a pillow or a shoe or says anything in ridicule of that boy, will be disciplined by me. That boy is genuine. He is more of a man than any of us!" The Christian finished praying. Then he got onto his cot.

That night God seemed to say to him, "You did not deny Me, and I will honor and use you in My service!"

Are you faithful? It may be less difficult to die the martyr's death than to live the courageous Christian life.

SAMUEL'S COURAGE

Behold, God is my salvation; I will trust, and not be
afraid: for the LORD JEHOVAH is my strength and my
song; he also is become my salvation. Isaiah 12:2

READ 1 SAMUEL 13:5-14

When Nikita Khrushchev was dictator in the Soviet Union, he denounced many of the policies and atrocities of his predecessor, Joseph Stalin. Once, as he censured Stalin in a public meeting, Khrushchev was interrupted by a shout from a heckler in the audience.

"You were one of Stalin's colleagues. Why didn't you stop him?"

"Who said that?" yelled Khrushchev. Silence followed as no one in the room moved a muscle. Then Khrushchev replied quietly, "Now you know why."

Samuel courageously confronted the king of Israel, Saul, who stood head and shoulders above him. The daily reading tells how Saul, under pressure of time, offered a sacrifice that was outside his realm of responsibility to offer. Samuel told Saul, "Thou hast done foolishly" (v. 13).

In 1 Samuel 15 we read of another occasion when Samuel needed to confront and correct a very defensive King Saul. He rebuked Saul for his pride, his disobedience, his stubbornness, and his rebellion. He told Saul that God would replace him with a new king. Samuel followed the command that he preached to Israel to fear God, "Only fear the LORD, and serve him in truth with all your heart: for consider how great things he hath done for you" (1 Samuel 12:24).

The Book of Psalms gives us repeated encouragement to conquer fear. Psalm 3:6 says, "I will not be afraid of ten thousands of people, that have set themselves against me round about." Psalm 27:3 says, "Though an host should encamp against me, my heart shall not fear: though war should rise against me, in this will I be confident." Psalm 118:6 says, "The LORD is on my side; I will not fear: what can man do unto me?"

To have courage does not mean a person is oblivious to danger. J. Oswald Sanders wrote, "Courage is that quality of mind which enables men to encounter danger or difficulty with firmness, or without fear or depression of spirits... The highest degree of courage is seen in the person who is most fearful but refuses to capitulate to it."*

Godly courage is not the absence of fear, but the conquest of it through trust in God.

---

* Oswald Sanders, *Spiritual Leadership* (Chicago: Moody Press, 1967), 55

THE IMPORTANCE
OF THE HEART

*Shall not God search this out? for he knoweth
the secrets of the heart. Psalm 44:21*

READ 1 SAMUEL 16:1-7

If you were to look at the heart in your chest, you would see a reddish-brown, pear-shaped organ weighing less than a pound—not a very impressive thing in appearance. It is basically a pump with no bone, cartilage, or glands. But how vital the heart is! It beats about 100,000 times a day, over 30 million times in a year. If the heart stops pumping blood, a person will soon die. The heart sends blood through about 60,000 miles of blood vessels. In a lifetime, it pumps about 500,000 tons of blood.

The Bible refers to the heart as being of crucial importance, possibly because of the importance of the heart to the physical body. "Keep thy heart with all diligence; for out of it are the issues of life" (Proverbs 4:23). The first and great commandment is to "love the Lord thy God with all thine heart" (Matthew 22:37). Jesus also said that good or evil comes from the heart, depending on the heart's condition. "A good man out of the good treasure of the heart bringeth forth good things: and an evil man out of the evil treasure bringeth forth evil things" (Matthew 12:35).

Although observers have some indication of the state of a person's inner self by evaluating his words and actions, only God can truly know his motives, intentions, character, and focus. As the daily reading says, "The LORD said unto Samuel, Look not on his countenance, or on the height of his stature; because I have refused him: for the LORD seeth not as man seeth; for man looketh on the outward appearance, but the LORD looketh on the heart" (1 Samuel 16:7).

What does God see when He looks at your heart? Is it clean? "Create in me a clean heart, O God; and renew a right spirit within me" (Psalm 51:10). Is it deceitful? "The heart is deceitful above all things, and desperately wicked" (Jeremiah 17:9). Is it troubled? "Let not your heart be troubled: ye believe in God, believe also in me" (John 14:1). Is it pure? "Blessed are the pure in heart: for they shall see God" (Matthew 5:8). Is it a broken heart? "The sacrifices of God are a broken spirit: a broken and a contrite heart, O God, thou wilt not despise" (Psalm 51:17).

God will accept a broken heart, but He must have all the pieces.

Missionary With Faith and Fervor
Hudson Taylor

By Howard Bean

Five-year-old Hudson Taylor drank in every word of the story his father was telling. "China has millions of people who don't know Jesus," his father concluded. "Missionaries must go to tell them about Him."

293

Hudson's eyes opened wide. "When I am a man, I will be a missionary and go to China," he declared.

This was exactly what Hudson's parents hoped to hear him say. They had prayed before his birth in 1832 that God would give them a boy who would go to China.

But Hudson was skinny and sickly, unable even to attend school for several years. His parents taught him at their home in England until he was eleven years old.

Hudson's love for reading helped him learn many things. Once, however, it got him into trouble. He did not want to stop reading his book at bedtime. *I'll sneak some candle ends into my pocket so I can read in bed,* he thought. But while he was saying goodnight to his parents, a visitor coaxed Hudson onto his lap and held him a while. Soon Hudson started wiggling restlessly. *The warm fireplace is going to melt my candles!* he worried. *Why doesn't Mother tell me to go to bed?*

Finally, Mother did send him to bed, and Hudson hurried off. When Mother came in several minutes later to tuck him in, she found him still not ready for bed. In the light of the lamp she was carrying, she could see his troubled face and his pocketful of softened balled-up candle ends. Knowing he was caught, he cried with shame and regret.

Hudson and his sister Amelia loved nature. They took long hikes to look for specimens for their insect and flower collections, sometimes accompanied by their father.

At the age of thirteen, Hudson had to begin working with his father in their drugstore. He liked waiting on customers, working with medicines, and reading his father's books on medicine.

In his heart, however, Hudson was unhappy. He didn't enjoy family worship anymore. Listening to his father read God's Word grew boring to him. So did praying. He was not sure there was really a God to pray to. He made worldly friends and learned to scoff and swear.

One afternoon this unsettled boy had some time to himself. Sixteen years old now and still loving books, he looked for something to read. Finally, he picked up a Gospel tract that looked interesting, saying to himself: "There will be a story at the beginning and a sermon at the end. I will read the former and skip the latter."

The tract told about the "finished work of Christ." This got him thinking. He concluded that since Christ's work of providing salvation was finished, all he needed to be saved was to accept Christ. He knelt and prayed, "Jesus, I am a sinner. Forgive me. I accept Christ's salvation."

At the time of his conversion, his mother was seventy-five miles away, but he told his sister Amelia about it and asked her to keep it quiet. When his mother returned home two weeks later, he met her at the door and said he had good news.

"I know," she said, hugging him tightly. "I've been so happy for the past two weeks about the good news you are about to tell me."

"Has Amelia broken her promise?" Hudson asked. "She said she wouldn't tell."

"No, Amelia hasn't talked to me about it. But one afternoon two weeks ago, I felt so burdened for your salvation that I locked myself in my room and decided I would stay there praying until my prayer was answered. I stayed there hour after hour until I felt sure of your salvation."

Now Hudson wanted to help others find Jesus as their Saviour also. He and his sister began handing tracts to people in the neighborhood and telling them about Jesus.

The time came when Hudson heard a call from the Lord, "Go to China." He began at once to prepare. He got up each morning to read and meditate on God's Word. He studied Chinese, Latin, Greek, and Hebrew. He exercised to build up health and strength. He even began sleeping on a hard bed, thinking ahead to times he might have to sleep on the ground in China.

Hudson read that China had many poor, sick people. If he could help their sick bodies, perhaps they would let him help their sick souls also. But to do this, he would need to know more about medicine. He had no idea how or where he could study, but he prayed about it. Soon God led him to a surgeon in the city of Hull who would accept him as his helper. Hudson found Dr. Hardey a good doctor and a pleasant man. Many of his patients thought his good humor helped them more than his medicines did. His work took up so much of his time that he often forgot other things, and he told his new helper: "Hudson, please do remind me when it is time for me to pay you your salary. I'm so busy, you know. I'm quite likely to forget."

Payday came, and Dr. Hardey forgot. Days went by. Should Hudson ask for his money? No, he would ask God. In China he would have only God to ask. He had better start asking here.

Out on the street on his way to his lodging, Hudson suddenly heard a man beside him asking, "Will you come and pray for my wife? She is dying."

The two hurried to a dismal room. Several hungry children stood around their sick mother lying on straw in a corner beside her new baby. After Hudson prayed, the man said, "Sir, you can see what a terrible state we're in. Have mercy, and help us!"

Hudson put his hand in his pocket, took out his last coin (worth about a dollar in our money), and handed it to the man. Then he made his way back to his own simple room, penniless but happy. God had wanted him to give that last coin. God knew where there were more coins.

The next morning Hudson cooked his last porridge and sat down to eat. Before he had finished, the postman came to the door. "Package for you," he called.

What can it be? Hudson wondered. Tearing it open, he found a pair of gloves and a gold coin worth about four dollars.

"The Lord has given me back four times as much money as I gave away!" Truly God had answered his prayer. And later he learned that God had healed the sick woman also.

Trusting God worked! Hudson was sure of this. However, the problem of salary remained. Would the doctor keep on forgetting?

At the end of two weeks, the gift money was spent, the rent was due, and the doctor still had not paid.

Suddenly, on Saturday, Dr. Hardey said, "By the way, Taylor, isn't your salary due?"

"Yes," Hudson answered quietly. "As a matter of fact, it was due two weeks ago."

"I am so sorry! Why didn't you remind me? I just sent all the money I had to the bank."

Then the doctor hurried away to make some calls. Hudson fell on his knees. "God, you know my problem," he prayed. "I have no money to pay my rent or buy food. Help me."

Later Dr. Hardey returned, laughing merrily. "A rich patient just paid his bill," he explained. Then he paid Hudson.

Trusting God had blessed him again!

The Chinese Evangelization Society was preparing to send Hudson to China. One day they sent him word that the time seemed right for him to go. He began packing clothes and books.

On September 19, 1853, at the age of twenty-one, the young missionary stepped aboard a small ship headed for Shanghai, China.

Early in the voyage a terrific storm arose that almost sank the ship. Near the end of the voyage another danger arose: lack of breeze to stir the sails. Worse yet, a strong current in the water dragged the helpless ship toward sand bars and sharp rocks. On the shore, cannibals were lighting fires in preparation for the shipwreck. Captain and sailors strained to turn the ship, but they were no match for the swift current.

"Well, we've done everything that can be done," the captain told Hudson.

Hudson thought, *If only the breeze that usually blows at sunset would blow up now, the ship could be saved. God can make that happen.* He said to the captain, "There's one thing we haven't done."

"What is that?"

Hudson knew that four or five on board were Christians. He suggested, "Let each one of us go to his cabin and pray that God will send a breeze now. He can send it just as easily now as this evening."

The captain, a Christian himself, went to his cabin while Hudson and the other Christians went to theirs.

Soon Hudson got up from his knees, sure that God would send the breeze, and hurried to the deck.

"Let down the corners of the mainsail," he suggested to the officer there.

"What would be the good of that?"

"We have been asking God to send a wind, and it's coming immediately."

"I'd rather see a wind than hear about it," the officer replied roughly. He did glance up, though, and saw the topmost sail flutter faintly.

"Look!" Hudson exclaimed. "The wind is coming!"

"It's only a puff!" the officer said. But he did put down the mainsail. By that time the breeze was filling the sails. The ship slowly turned away from the rocks. Trusting God brought blessings again!

Finally, after five and a half months on the water, the ship anchored near Shanghai in cold, thick fog.

Chilled, bewildered, and lonely, the young missionary stepped off the boat and stood on Chinese soil. Here he was in the country he longed to claim for Christ, but how should he go about settling into it?

For a while he just stood and looked. He gazed at brightly colored signs in the streets but could not read them. He watched coolies swing along with poles across their shoulders and baskets hanging on the ends, but he could not talk with them. He saw pigtailed men lounging in stores and restaurants along the narrow streets, but he could not understand what they were saying. He saw children in the dirty streets, but he had no idea what games they were playing.

Uneasily Hudson set out to find the compound of the London Missionary Society. A long walk brought him there. He rejoiced to find another missionary who could speak English and help him get acquainted with China.

Next came language study. Hour after hour and day after day he sat in a cold room learning to read and write the difficult Chinese language.

It was a great day for Hudson when he could use Chinese well enough to be understood. Now he could visit people and tell them about Jesus.

Hudson decided to begin working in the many towns and villages that lined the Yangtze River. He rented a houseboat and stocked it with food, a cookstove, cookware, bedding, medicine, and doctor's instruments. Also he included tracts, Gospels, and New Testaments to hand out.

Hired servants poled the boat. At towns where he planned to witness, he docked the boat while he walked or let coolies wheel him into town with his bags of books, tracts, and medicines. At some places the people ran from him in fear. At others they gathered around him out of curiosity. Sometimes they listened eagerly as he told them about Jesus. Many who could read accepted tracts and Bible portions readily. And many who were sick or injured gladly accepted his medical help.

At one city Hudson and his missionary companion were badly mistreated. After the two left the boat and started walking toward the city gate, soldiers beat and kicked them and dragged them to the house of the city leader. The leader listened to them tell why they had come and politely accepted a New Testament from them. He even allowed them to preach in the city and hand out tracts.

On the big island of Tsung-Ming the people wanted him to stay. He rented a house, treating the sick and pointing them to the perfect Healer of body and soul. Also he held evening services to teach God's Word. Some became Christians and began bringing others to Christ.

After Hudson had enjoyed six weeks in this way, he was suddenly ordered to leave the island. Native doctors, angry that they were losing patients to his better medicines, complained to government officials and had him ordered off the island.

"Why don't you stay here?" asked two of his missionary friends in the city of Ningpo, where he went for more medical supplies. "You could live in the house we rented near the big pagoda."

Hudson, feeling that God wanted him there, made his home in the attic of that house. This left the downstairs to use as a boys' schoolroom, as a clinic for treating the sick, as a dining room for feeding between forty to seventy hungry Chinese people, and in the evening, as a chapel for teaching the Bible.

Hudson soon learned about a mission school for girls nearby. There he met a most likeable English girl, Maria Dyer, one of the teachers. When he discovered that she trusted God to supply her needs in much the same way he did, he felt God had chosen her to be his wife. She felt that way too, and they were married.

Now instead of one living in the attic, the two worked together for Christ. Maria used the downstairs to teach children. She visited in homes to talk to women about Jesus. Hudson kept on doctoring, feeding, and preaching downstairs.

When the British attacked part of China called Canton, the Chinese became very angry at all Europeans. Some Chinese who had lived in Canton planned to kill all foreigners in Taylor's city of Ningpo. Knowing that a number of foreigners met each Sunday night for worship, the plotters arranged to surround the place and murder them all. Hearing of the plot and that between fifty to sixty Portuguese had already been slain, the missionaries met to ask God to protect them.

At the very time they were praying, the Lord was working. An unknown official came to their rescue and prevented the attack. "This again," Taylor wrote, "we were led to prove that 'Sufficient is His arm alone, And our defense is sure.' "

Over the mantelpiece in Hudson Taylor's home in Ningpo were two scrolls on which were written in Chinese characters: *Ebenezer,* "Hitherto hath the Lord helped us," and *Jehovah Jireh,* "The Lord will provide."

The faith expressed in these mottoes had many severe testings. Quite suddenly, the wife of his missionary associate Dr. Parker died, leaving him with four motherless children. On their account and because his own health was shattered, Dr. Parker felt he must return to Scotland. Now what would the mission do? Dr. Parker was the only doctor in Ningpo. It looked as though the mission dispensary and hospital would have to be closed, for up to that time the expenses had been met by the proceeds of Dr. Parker's practice among the Europeans. This income was now cut off. But Taylor believed that to close the hospital and dispensary on financial grounds would be nothing less than doubting God. He called the hospital assistants together and explained the situation. He said, "If you are prepared to trust God to supply our needs, you are invited to continue your work here. Otherwise you are free to leave. I am confident that His grace is sufficient. Hath not our God said that *whatsoever we ask in the name of the Lord Jesus shall be done?*"

As the weeks passed, supplies decreased. One day the cook said the last bag of rice had been opened. Taylor answered, "Then the Lord's time for helping us must be close at hand." And so it was. Before the rice was completely gone, hundreds of dollars arrived from England. With overflowing hearts the workers went among the patients telling what had occurred and asking, "Have your idols ever delivered you from your troubles or answered prayer after this sort?"

Among those who became followers of Jesus was Mr. Ni. He had been a strong idol worshiper. Now he became a strong Christian and began bringing others to Jesus.

One day Mr. Ni asked Hudson, "How long have you had this good news in your country?"

Ashamed, Hudson answered, "Several hundred years."

"Several hundred years?" Mr. Ni almost shouted. "Is it possible that in your honorable country you have known about Jesus so long and only now have come to tell us? My father looked for the truth for more than twenty years and died without finding it. Oh, why did you people not come sooner?"

This made Hudson want to do everything possible to let China's millions know about Jesus. But he was already an overworked man, and he soon became worn and ill.

Taylor felt that God was telling him to go back to England for a rest. In July of 1860 he boarded a boat for England, taking with him his wife Maria, his baby Grace, and convert Wang.

In England, sickness did not keep this missionary from thinking about the Chinese and praying for them. When he felt able, he started translating the New Testament into Ningpo, a Chinese dialect.

Often while translating, Hudson looked at a large map of China he had placed on the wall. "See," it seemed to say to him, "there are eleven inland provinces without one missionary. Three hundred eighty million Chinese know nothing about the Saviour! They are lost! Every month one million of them die without having heard the way to Heaven."

Hudson began to pray for more missionaries. He prayed for a total of twenty-four.

Before long eight missionaries sailed for China, and soon after, Taylor with his family and Wang and sixteen more missionaries followed. Trusting God was still working! He had sent the twenty-four missionaries!

One time Taylor spoke to a missionary conference near Niagara Falls in Canada. At the same conference another missionary said that he had learned from a certain Christian woman the secret of how to work for Christ twenty-four hours a day all the year round. She had said, "I work twelve hours and when I have a rest, my representative in India, whom I support, begins her day and works the other twelve." He urged those who could not go to the foreign field to support a representative and thus work twenty-four hours a day for Christ. The idea caught fire, not only in this group but in many others. Within a short time enough money was contributed to support dozens of missionaries, and scores of earnest young lives were offered for foreign service.

Hudson knew twenty-four missionaries were still far from enough. He prayed, "Lord, send us seventy new helpers in the next three years." God sent seventy-eight and told him, "Ask Me for one hundred missionaries next year." The following year, 102 went. Hudson told his helpers, "We will ask God for one thousand new missionaries in five years!" He was amazed to welcome 1,153.

Hudson Taylor was often encouraged by thinking of the homecoming that awaited him in the Father's house. As he grew older, he prayed that in God's own time his last climbing footstep would bring him to Heaven. As he read the beautiful promise, "I go to prepare a place for you," his heart responded, "Even so, come, Lord Jesus; come quickly."

Several hours before his death in 1905 in China, Taylor said, "It is a wonderful privilege we have, to be able to bring everything to God in prayer... We should trust Him fully."

Questions for Review

1. In what kind of store did Hudson help his father?

2. What did Dr. Hardey sometimes forget to do?

3. What did Hudson's parents hope he would become?

4. As a teenager in England, why did Hudson sleep on a hard bed?

5. How did God answer the prayer of Hudson and his friends on the ship ride to China?

Questions for Discussion

1. Why do you think Hudson didn't want Amelia to tell their mother about his conversion?

2. How did Hudson learn to trust God?

3. Would you have liked to work for Dr. Hardey?

4. How could you be a missionary for twenty-four hours a day all year long?

5. What are some ways your family can trust God?

Quite a number of books have been written about J. Hudson Taylor. A good short biography that I consulted in writing this story is found in Heroes of Faith on Pioneer Trails *by E. Myers Harrison, published by Moody Press. Some of this story is also adapted from* Hudson Taylor, God's Venture, *by Phyllis Thompson.*

~Howard

DAVID

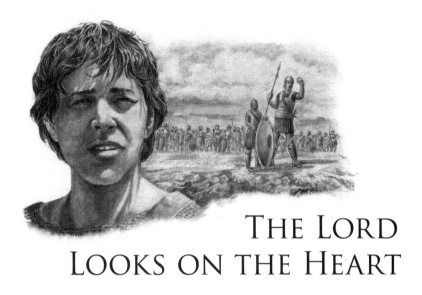

THE LORD
LOOKS ON THE HEART

For the eyes of the LORD run to and fro throughout the
whole earth, to shew himself strong in the behalf of them
whose heart is perfect toward him. 2 Chronicles 16:9

READ 1 SAMUEL 16:8-17

Y ou may hear someone say, "Let's get to the heart of the matter,"
or "I don't have the heart for it." Such expressions indicate the
importance of the heart. What does a paramedic check upon arriving at a medical emergency? The heart has priority.

When Samuel looked for a suitable man to anoint king of Israel, he
looked at physique and appearance. As he sized up Eliab, the oldest of
Jesse's sons, he readily concluded, *This must be the one.* But the Lord told
Samuel that Eliab wasn't suitable for kingship. Outward appearance
wasn't the key. The heart was the crucial criterion. So Abinadab wasn't
the one, nor was Shammah, nor the next four sons. The Lord had selected
the eighth son, the youngest. David's heart was different.

What was special about David's heart that God appreciated? One clue
is found in 1 Samuel 13:14, after God rejected Saul. "The LORD hath
sought him a man after his own heart, and the LORD hath commanded

him to be captain over his people, because thou hast not kept that which the LORD commanded thee." A heart that obeys is essential.

A trustful heart pleases the Lord. "Trust in the LORD with all thine heart" (Proverbs 3:5). David's life also demonstrated trust in the Lord such as when the Lord delivered him from a bear and a lion.

How's your heart? Ask the divine Heart Specialist to check it out.

LESSONS
FROM DAVID'S FAMILY

Children, obey your parents in the Lord: for this is right. Ephesians 6:1

READ 1 SAMUEL 17:12-20

Were there some disadvantages about the home in which you grew up (or are there some negative features about the home in which you are still growing up)? A couple of incidental references to David's childhood home seem to indicate his family was not very wealthy.

Jesse's gift for the king of Israel wasn't very substantial. "And Jesse took an ass laden with bread, and a bottle of wine, and a kid, and sent them by David his son unto Saul" (1 Samuel 16:20). Perhaps Jesse was not a rich man. When big brother Eliab was belittling his youngest brother, he said, "Why camest thou down hither? and with whom has thou left those few sheep in the wilderness?" (1 Samuel 17:28). Coming from a financially poor home need not hinder the development of character; it may, in fact, enhance it.

A second lesson pertains to sibling relationships. Eliab was condescending and mean to David. In his anger he said, "I know the pride, and the naughtiness of thine heart; for thou art come down that thou mightest see the battle" (1 Samuel 17:28). How's that for a lousy attitude toward a brother who had walked miles to deliver some presents from Dad? Eliab accused David of pride, a sinful heart, and of ignoble purpose in coming to Saul's army camp. David merely protested his innocence and moved on. How do you respond to sneers, snubs, and snarls from siblings? Make it your aim to be "kindly affectioned one to another with brotherly love" (Romans 12:10).

A third lesson is obedience to parents. David followed the fifth commandment. "And Jesse said unto David his son, Take now for thy brethren an ephah of this parched corn, and these ten loaves, and run to the camp of thy brethren; and carry these ten cheeses unto the captain of their thousand, and look how thy brethren fare, and take their pledge" (vv. 17, 18). Note David's response: "And David rose up early in the morning" (v. 20). He also acted responsibly by leaving the sheep with a keeper.

Young person, do you come from an ideal home where parents are always fair and exemplary and where siblings are consistently kind and considerate? Probably not. Learn from David's life to have a heart for God in the face of some adverse circumstances.

DAVID
CONFRONTS GOLIATH

*Thou wilt keep him in perfect peace, whose mind is stayed
on thee: because he trusteth in thee. Isaiah 26:3*

READ 1 SAMUEL 17:32-49

I have a good friend who is skillful with a sling. He can accurately
hit a target from fifty yards away, a skill he learned in Mexico.
He taught me how to slip one end of it around a couple of fingers
so that I can easily release it while holding tightly to the other end.
Then the stone is whipped in a big circle as is done "windmill-style"
softball pitching. A smooth stone helps it to go straight to counteract
the scientific principle known as *Bernoulli's effect*. Likely David had
practiced his sling skills hundreds of times. One often can't predict
when a skill may be useful.

What are some other lessons from our daily reading?

Don't try to use someone else's armor. In other words, don't attempt to
be someone else. What works for me may not work for you. Be yourself
as you yield yourself to God and let Him use you.

Face your giants with faith "in the name of the LORD of hosts" (v. 45).
It may be a giant called inferiority complex. It may be the giant of

unemployment. It may be the giant of illness, or a relationship problem, or an exam. Trust in the Lord.

The battle is the Lord's. David was undertaking the impossible-looking task because Goliath had defied God. David wanted all the earth to honor the Lord. He believed God would provide the victory. King Saul thought that Goliath was too big to fight. David thought Goliath was too big to miss.

God can use the weak to do the improbable or the impossible. Paul wrote from God's viewpoint: "My grace is sufficient for thee: for my strength is made perfect in weakness" (2 Corinthians 12:9). For the Christian, to trust is to triumph.

DAVID BEHAVES WISELY

Let no man despise thy youth; but be thou an example
of the believers, in word, in conversation, in charity, in
spirit, in faith, in purity. 1 Timothy 4:12

READ 1 SAMUEL 18:1-16

Reputation is what people think you are. Character is what God knows you are. David's character corresponded to his reputation. He initially was highly regarded by King Saul (v. 2). He was appreciated by all the people, and he was accepted by servants (v. 5). He was deeply loved by Jonathan (v. 1). He was admired and praised by women who met the returning soldiers (v. 7). In fact, "all Israel and Judah loved David" (v. 16).

Sometimes when a person is highly appreciated and honored, it goes to his head. In some cases, pat a man on the back and his head swells. Not so with David. The description "behaved himself wisely" appears four times in chapter 18—in verses 5, 14, 15, and 30.

David acted wisely in public as he moved among Saul's civil servants and among the populace. He had developed his character in solitude—working with sheep, worshiping the Shepherd. He had developed his character in obscurity among Jesse's lonely family in little-known Bethlehem.

David acted wisely when faced by jealousy. It is hard to relate well to a jealous person because jealousy is so unreasonable. It arises because of the talent or popularity of someone who seems to be a rival. Jealousy is dangerous. You may not have a javelin cast at you, but you may have gossip, unkind glances, and evil surmisings cast your way, or be stabbed verbally in the back.

Like David, avoid jealous confrontations as much as possible, humbly accept demotions if necessary, and continue normal life among people (vv. 11, 13). Then the Lord will be with you (v. 14).

Wisdom comes more from living than from studying. True wisdom is the perception of what is truly important.

DAVID FACES DISCOURAGEMENT

*As the hart panteth after the water brooks, so panteth
my soul after thee, O God. Psalm 42:1*

READ 1 SAMUEL 30:1-18

Have you ever faced discouragement? Do you feel down and despondent? Have you got the blues? Do circumstances and negative feelings overwhelm you?

David faced a very discouraging situation. In the events prior to the daily reading, David was on the run from Saul. He barely escaped from a dilemma caused by hiding with the Philistines. When he returned to Ziklag, his base, he and his men found that their families and goods were taken by the Amalekites. David and his men were emotionally drained (v. 4), and David was "greatly distressed" (v. 6). As the depth of this calamity sank in, his people blamed him as the leader and talked of stoning him.

In the face of such difficulties, what did David do? David "encouraged himself in the LORD" (v. 6). How might he have done this? David may have thought of God's attributes—His love, His power, His sovereignty. He may have thought of God's help in the past—against the bear, the

315

lion, the giant, the blood-thirsty king. He may have considered God's promises—to help, to deliver, to strengthen, to provide. He may have counted his blessings from the Lord—His guidance, His forgiveness, His gifts, His answers to prayer.

Then David inquired of the Lord (v. 8). What a privilege we have to pray! Austin Phelps wrote, "Prayer is the preface to the book of Christian living, the text of the new life sermon, the girding on of the armor for battle, the pilgrim's preparation for his journey, and it must be supplemented by action or it amounts to nothing."

God directed David to pursue the enemy. Along the way, he encountered a sick Egyptian slave. David's men helped the Egyptian, and the Egyptian helped them. One of the best ways to overcome discouragement is to find a person in need and help him. Thousands have testified that such actions brought them out of the pit of despondency.

If you face discouraging circumstances, remember to look for the positive, pray, and help others.

ADMIRABLE QUALITIES OF DAVID

The man who was raised up on high, the anointed of the God of Jacob, and the sweet psalmist of Israel. 2 Samuel 23:1

READ 1 SAMUEL 26:1-21

David's life shows a number of commendable character traits:

- *Respect for authority.* Even though King Saul was trying hard to kill David and keep him on the run, David persistently chose to honor the Lord's anointed.

- *Reasonableness.* David asked Saul from the other side of the valley, "Why are you pursuing me? What have I done wrong? Is it the Lord that has stirred you up against me?"

- *Forgiveness.* Not once but twice, David could easily have killed the man who was trying to kill him. Instead of retaliating, David had a forgiving attitude.

- *Versatility.* He could handle a sling, a sword, a staff, and a scepter with skill. He was a shepherd, a musician, a soldier, a poet, and a king.

- *Praise.* David's psalms abound with praise and thanksgiving to the Lord.

- *Courage.* This was evident as he faced a lion, a bear, a giant, and a jealous king.

- *Patience.* After being anointed king by Samuel, he waited on the Lord's time to take the throne.

- *Literary skill.* Of the psalms with titles, seventy-three were written by David (and there are probably others he wrote). He anticipated the coming of the divine Son of David as he wrote the Messianic psalms.

- *Repentance.* When David sinned grievously, as he did with Bathsheba, he genuinely repented. God's mercy is splendidly displayed when one contemplates the depth and breadth of David's sin. As J. Oswald Sanders perceptively wrote: "The comprehensive nature of David's sin appears only on closer examination. It has been pointed out that the breaking of the tenth commandment, coveting his neighbor's wife, led to his breaking the seventh and committing adultery. Soon, in order to break the eighth, stealing what did not belong to him, he broke the sixth and committed murder. He broke the ninth by bearing false witness against his neighbor. He brought dishonor on his parents and thus broke the fifth. Thus he broke all the commandments which refer to loving one's neighbor as one's self. And, of course, in its very nature, his sin dishonored God as well. There is no such thing as a simple sin. Sin is always complicated."*

I admire David's sincere repentance, but, more than that, I appreciate God's mercy and forgiveness.

---

* *Robust in Faith: Men from God's School,* Moody Press, 1965, page 123.

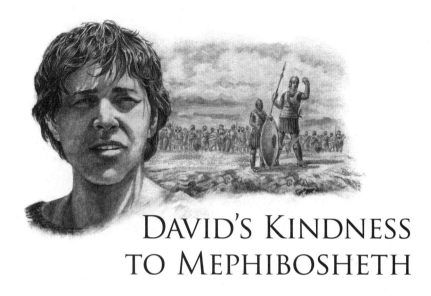

DAVID'S KINDNESS TO MEPHIBOSHETH

Put on therefore, as the elect of God, holy and beloved, bowels of mercies, kindness, humbleness of mind, meekness, longsuffering. Colossians 3:12

READ 2 SAMUEL 9:1-13

Kindness is like snow on a landscape—it beautifies everything it covers. A great man shows his greatness by the kind way he treats the disadvantaged.

David never forgot the kindness of his close friend Jonathan. Jonathan had provided him with clothes, weapons, information in times of danger, emotional support, and undying loyalty. After becoming king, David searched for a way to repay the kindness to Jonathan's family.

It turned out that Jonathan had one living son. Unfortunately, he was lame as a result of falling after his nurse heard of Jonathan's death. Second Samuel 4:4 tells about the misfortune: "And Jonathan, Saul's son, had a son that was lame of his feet. He was five years old when the tidings came of Saul and Jonathan out of Jezreel, and his nurse took him up, and fled: and it came to pass, as she made haste to flee, that he fell, and became lame. And his name was Mephibosheth."

David was pleased to show kindness to Mephibosheth. He restored to him all the land of his lineage and invited Mephibosheth to eat at the king's table indefinitely.

David's attitudes toward Mephibosheth point forward to Christ's attitudes toward people. First, Christ had compassion on humankind, all of whom have been crippled by a Fall (Genesis 3). God calls us into His presence, exalting us on the merits of another (vv. 5, 7). We humble ourselves (v. 6) and bow before our King (v. 8). We view ourselves as servants (v. 8). Furthermore, our King has given us a great inheritance (v. 9).

What an inheritance is ours! Matthew Henry wrote: "Think of going to the Father, to sit down in the *immediate, uninterrupted, and everlasting enjoyment of Him.* Those who love God cannot but be pleased to think of coming to Him, though it be through the valley of the shadow of death. When we go, to be 'absent from the body,' it is to be 'present with the Lord,' like children fetched home from school to their father's house.

"Now come I to Thee whom I have chosen and served, and whom my soul thirsteth after; to Thee the fountain of light and life, the crown and center of bliss and joy; now my longings shall be satisfied, my hopes accomplished, my happiness completed."

Trust in Times of Terror
Sabina Wurmbrand, Robert Haddad, Mentu

by Esther Bean and Howard Bean

Sabina Wurmbrand

Sabina tried to relax on the hard bunk. Every bone and muscle ached.
The day had been long and extremely difficult, but no more than usual.
Every day taxed this malnourished woman to the limit. Her job was to
fill wheelbarrows with earth so male prisoners could push them away.
Their job was harder than hers, but even so, she soon staggered trying
to lift the heavy earth over the side of the wheelbarrow. And for what

purpose? Building a canal, they were told. A good project for wearing out prisoners too. *I am following in the steps of my Israelite forefathers, slaves working on building projects in Egypt,* she thought.

Sabina shifted again. How could one be so tired, yet unable to sleep? "Oh, Lord," she prayed silently. "Bless my loved ones, my Richard, wherever he is. Is he still alive, Lord? And my dear son, my Mihai. He is only eleven years old. Who is taking care of him with his parents in prison? Does he have enough to eat? Where is he sleeping? Will this cause him to become bitter to spiritual things? He's always been so sensitive to You. Oh, Lord, protect him."

"Sabina?" came a voice beside her in the dark. "Why are you here? I hear you mention bits and pieces, but I have questions. I've heard of your husband and his preaching. His name, face, and voice are recognized all over Romania. But I never thought I'd meet you in here."

Sabina turned toward her questioner. *Yes, the new woman,* she thought. *She is obviously not an informer based on her actions. I can speak freely.*

"Well, if you've heard of Richard, my life before my conversion was much like his," she whispered. "I am also Jewish, but we were not practicing Jews. I simply wanted to have a good time in whatever way I could. But when I gave my life to Jesus, everything changed. Instead of pleasing myself, I wanted to please Jesus. Instead of thinking that children would take away from my fun, I had a child, Mihai. We also helped to rescue Jewish children from ghettos during the war. We took in several children to raise for a few years. Instead of thinking only of myself, God opened my eyes to others. Richard and I allowed soldiers from both sides, even Nazi soldiers, to hide in our house and on our property. This was not easy; after all, my entire family had been wiped out by the Nazis. The penalty for hiding a soldier would have been severe. God helped me to see that these were human beings too, and His forgiveness was extended to them as well as to me."

"That's amazing," the fellow prisoner responded. "When you saw Communism taking over, did you think about escaping?"

"Yes, we did consider it, but Richard and I chose to stay in Romania with our church. We believed God had a path of suffering laid out for us, and we asked Him to show us how we could suffer for His name. We knew it was only a matter of time until Richard was arrested. Still, it was very hard for me when I arrived at church one Sunday morning to find he was not there even though he had left 30 minutes earlier than I. We waited, and then I checked with friends, phoned hospitals, and even checked with the police. Even though they said they had no record of him at the police station, I knew he had been arrested. I knew the Lord would take care of him, but it was very difficult to be separated, not knowing where he was or even whether he was still alive."

"How well I understand," the woman said. "And then you were arrested."

"Yes, about two years after Richard. I knew my apartment had been searched by people saying they were from the housing department. I knew they simply wanted to see how many exits there were. But Mihai was at a friend's place, so I knew he'd be safe. I had a friend and a cousin staying with me that night, so I fell asleep. At 5:00 in the morning, they came. Yelling and banging, they barged in and began a search for weapons."

"Weapons?"

"Weapons," Sabina confirmed. "I held up my Bible and told them this was the only weapon I had."

The ladies smiled in the darkness.

"You can guess the rest." Sabina sighed. "Interrogations. Crowded prison cells. Solitary confinement. Food that a person needs to be desperate to eat. Filth everywhere. But Jesus is also here. Do you know Him?"

"I'm not sure I want to. I'm such a wicked woman. You wouldn't talk with me if you knew what I have done."

Sabina smiled. "God delights in taking messes and turning them into miracles. Let me tell you about Him."

"It's the carcer for you!" the guard yelled. "I've been told you did not clap this afternoon in the re-education class."

Sabina's heart sank. She was cold and tired from the week of work and the misty wind coming up from the canal where she had been working. Clothes never really dried. But the carcer was worse yet. A box six feet high, two feet wide, and lined with spikes, this punishment was used frequently. A day's work was bad enough, but to be put into the carcer at night when the body cried out for sleep? Truly, it was torture. One needed to stay awake to avoid injury from hitting the spikes. Then the next day, work again. By this time, one was so tired, the work went more slowly, and then would come the order to go back in the carcer for not getting enough work done.

Yet she had expected some punishment this time. Prison was not simply about punishment; indoctrination—retraining the mind—was a large part as well. The Communists wanted everyone to support their way of thinking—that there is no God, that Communist leaders should be revered, that the communistic belief and way of life was better than any other system in the world.

Every Sunday when the prisoners longed for rest, they needed to attend indoctrination sessions. It was a time to praise the Communist leaders, laugh at religion, and shame those who did not agree with the government. There were speeches given, songs sung, and poems read by prisoners. The humiliation and mocking hurt worse than physical pain.

Sabina had wiggled into the clusters of people standing at the back of the room. Maybe there no one would see that she was not applauding. The words praising Communists and slandering God grated on her ears. Finally, a young woman read a poem dripping with thankfulness to the Soviets for saving Romania from the Nazis.

"Mother Russia, thank you
For what you've done today!
The glorious Red Army
Has shown us all the way... "

Everyone cheered wildly. Informers scanned the crowd, searching for those who didn't show enough enthusiasm or for those who obviously disagreed.

Many times Sabina had been told, "Just fake it. You don't have to agree. What does it really matter? Is resisting worth more punishment?" But she could not clap when she heard God mocked.

The metal carcer was just as difficult as she had remembered. So tiny. So suffocating. So claustrophobic. Only a few holes for air. A slot at the bottom for food.

Sabina knew there would be no rest that night. She began to pray, as she did on other nights when sleep did not come easily. She prayed for the women in the hut she shared, for the prisoners in the camp beyond, and for the millions of prisoners in the Communist world. She prayed for Christians in the West, whom she imagined were praying for their brothers and sisters in chains.

Sabina's feet began to burn with pain. How much longer would she be in here? Hours? How many years could she last in these conditions? Would she stay sane?

Drop. Drop. Drop. Drop. Water was dripping onto the top of the carcer, a lonely sound. Sabina began to count the drops and think of something in the Bible related to each number.

One: There is one God.

Two: There are two tablets of the Law.

Three: God is a Trinity.

Four: Christ will gather His elect from the four corners of the earth.

Five: There are five books of Moses.

Six: The number of the beast in Revelation is 666.

Seven: This is the holy number.

By the time Sabina reached 15 and 16, the numbers meant nothing. The drops continued, so she started over.

Sometimes Sabina lasted till morning; sometimes she passed out for an hour or two, her mind resting at last.

Morning eventually came. Prison life continued. Would she always be beaten? overworked? humiliated? treated as a person of no worth? How long would she last?

Three years. That's how long I've been imprisoned, Sabina mused. *So long to be away from my family. Are they still alive? Will I see them again?* Sabina hacked again at the weeds. Work on the canal had been discontinued due to faulty planning. So now she and five hundred women were tending root crops to prevent erosion.

"Hurry up!" the guard yelled. "Move!"

Sabina didn't dare straighten her back when he was looking. That was sure to be rewarded with the carcer. Her mind traveled over the variety of women she had met in prison. What a place to meet people! There were women from all walks of life—thieves, society ladies, murderers, and Christians all in one cell. There were hard women and others who knew they had hit bottom and were ready to hear about Jesus. Women had confessed all sorts of sins to her, and she had counseled and prayed with them and for them.

Even guards, she thought. *Even with guards I've been able to speak a words of truth and of God. Such as the deputy camp commandant.*

Some time before, Sabina had been brought before a strong, muscular, hard female commandant.

"You must stop!" the commandant yelled. "You have been preaching about God to other prisoners, and you must stop!"

"Nothing can make me stop speaking of God," Sabina replied. "He is my life."

The commandant's face grew red and blotchy. She raised her arm to hit Sabina but stopped abruptly. "Why are you smiling?" she snapped.

"I am smiling because of what I see in your eyes," Sabina replied. "I used to be like you. I was impulsive and angry. Then I learned what it really means to love. I learned about the truth. Since then, I do not hit people."

The commandant's hand dropped.

"If you look into my eyes," Sabina continued, "you will see yourself as God could make you."

The commandant stared and then said quietly, "Get out."

Sabina continued chopping at the baked earth, wondering what God had in store for her next.

Prisoners were being interviewed individually to see if they had learned the lessons the Communists had wanted to teach them in prison. Some women gushed about how much they had learned, saying they had been wrong and now wanted to earn a place in society.

Sabina's turn finally came. Sure enough, there were a few special questions for religious prisoners. The major cleared his throat, "Mrs. Wurmbrand, surely by now you realize that I am more powerful than God. At least, He certainly has not done anything to help you in this office."

The major's assistants smiled at his wit.

"But," he continued, "do you really believe this? Do you understand that God is unnecessary? That you do not need Him? When you get out of here, you will realize the wonderful things that have happened under Communism. Religion is a joke. Do you really understand that?"

Sabina saw the major's hand resting on a file—a file that could contain records about her. She replied, "I see that you are powerful. Probably you have files about me that could decide what will happen to me. But God keeps records too. Neither you nor I would have life without Him. So whether He sets me free or keeps me here, I will accept that as being what is best for me."

The major slammed his hand on the desk. "Ungrateful, Mrs. Wurmbrand! Ungrateful! I see that you have not learned your lessons! I shall make a report showing that! You need more time to change your mind!"

Yet, three days later, Sabina stood in the snow waiting to be released from prison. *The major has power,* she thought. *But I am so glad that I serve a God who has a much higher power than the major!*

Robert Haddad

Robert Haddad worked in a factory in Lebanon in the mid 1970s. One Friday afternoon, a fellow worker placed a picture on his machine that was not fit to be looked at. As a Christian, Robert wanted nothing to do with dirty pictures, so he tore it up. The worker threatened to kill him.

"If you kill me," Robert replied, "I will be transported to the glories of Heaven, but if you die, where will you go?" Then he added, "Jesus loves you and wants to save you, so surrender your heart to Him before death comes, and we will be together in Heaven." Just then the bell rang to signal the end of the workday.

"On Monday, I will kill you with my gun," the man promised.

"I will be here, and the Lord Jesus will be with me," the brave Christian said.

When Robert arrived the following Monday morning, he saw his fellow workers crowded together. They had all known about the threat the previous Friday, and he thought they were talking about what would happen to him. When he came nearer, one shouted, "Do you know what happened to the man who threatened you?"

"No, I don't," Robert replied, "but I thank the Lord that He is with me."

"Well," the other worker said, "the Lord loves you. That man who threatened to kill you on Friday went to his house and dropped dead." Robert then took the chance to tell all the workers about God's love shown in Christ.

It took Robert only about three minutes to walk from his house to the factory. The walk was dangerous in spite of being short, however, because of the civil war going on.

One day Robert's mother said, "I don't think you should go to work today. It's too dangerous."

"The Lord will keep me," Robert assured her. "Let's pray together."

After they prayed, he started off for the factory. He hadn't gone far when he heard guns close by. Suddenly, an armed soldier appeared, asking, "Where are you coming from, and where are you going?"

"I just came from my home, as you can see, and I am going to my work," Robert replied.

"Are you carrying any weapons?"

"Yes, I have a weapon in my bag," Robert answered. The soldier tore the bag open but found only a bottle of drinking water and some food.

"Where's the gun?" he demanded.

Robert smiled and pulled out a New Testament. "This is the weapon."

"Are you mocking me?"

"No, but I believe in Jesus Christ, and His Book is my weapon."

"Don't say that name!" the man ordered. He put his finger on the trigger of his revolver. "I'm going to kill you."

Robert stayed calm. "My weapon is stronger because the Word of God will come out of it and enter your heart. If you believe in it, you will live forever. The Lord gave me the opportunity to tell you about Jesus, the Saviour who loves you."

Again the man shouted, "Don't speak that name!" Robert saw his finger tighten on the trigger and prayed for God to keep him safe.

Suddenly, the soldier smiled nervously. "Are you strong?" he asked.

"In Jesus Christ I am strong," Robert replied.

"Then push my hand down!"

Robert pushed down on his arm but could not move it. Then the soldier suddenly turned and ran away.

"Don't be afraid," Robert called. "Jesus loves you." But the soldier kept running and never looked back.

A few days later Robert heard about a soldier who told his comrades of meeting a man who believed in Christ. "He was a real Christian," the soldier had said. "I wanted to kill him, but my hand was paralyzed and I could not."

Mentu

Mentu's family, like most people in Egypt, were Muslim. His father was a lawyer who advised the government and the president of the country. He taught his children to pray to Allah and to follow the Koran, their holy book. He sent his children to the best schools.

Mentu decided to be a lawyer like his father. He attended a university for several years. When he was about twenty years old, he met some Christians who attended the same university, and they became friends, discussing their beliefs often. Through the influence of these friends, Mentu decided to become a Christian.

In any country, becoming a Christian is very important. But for a Muslim to become a Christian in a Muslim country is very dangerous. Often their families will disown or even kill them, since it is against the law for a Muslim to become a Christian.

Mentu needed to leave his family, so he lived with some other friends. He wanted to learn as much as he could about the Bible and about Christianity. He wrote a book about Christians who lived many, many years ago in Egypt to show that Christianity had been in Egypt before Islam. He knew it was a book that the government would not like.

Sure enough, when the Muslim government found out about the book, they wanted to punish Mentu for writing it. He was arrested and put into prison—a very harsh and cruel prison where guards tried to make people give up thinking the way they wanted to think and do whatever the government told them. Each day, the guards would do something different to the prisoner—things so terrible that they would give children nightmares to hear about. Usually, after seven days, a prisoner was ready to give up and do whatever the guards told them.

The guards did these cruel things to Mentu, trying to get him to give up being a Christian. They also wanted to know the name of the leaders of his group so that they could arrest them too.

Mentu was determined to keep on serving Jesus and give no information about other Christians, but it was difficult. Each night, the guards would tell him what they would do to him the next day. They knew that he would think about it all night long.

One evening they said, "Tomorrow morning we will bring the dogs out to you."

Mentu knew what that meant, and he knew that it was dangerous and frightening. Mentu was a strong, healthy twenty-one-year-old who had been very courageous for God. Still, he was human, and he was scared. All night long he thought about those dogs, and he prayed hard that God would protect him and give him courage in the morning.

In the morning, Mentu sat on the little cot in his cell waiting for the guards. The cell door opened, and a guard entered. With him was a large fierce dog that had been trained to hurt prisoners in certain ways.

Mentu continued to sit on his cot and pray.

The guard gave the dog a command. The dog did not move. The guard gave the command again. The dog arose and walked over to Mentu.

The guard could not understand why the dog did not obey. This had never happened before. The dog always did exactly what the guard told him to do. But not now.

The guard gave one more command. The dog reached up and licked Mentu's face in a friendly way.

The guard knew something was wrong. He ran out of the cell and called a higher officer. When the officer saw what was happening, he immediately took the dog out of the room. Mentu rejoiced, for he knew that God had performed a miracle to save him.

Now the guards, instead of being dangerous, were scared of Mentu. They realized that he served a God who had much more power than they knew what to do with. Their days of torture had not broken Mentu's spirit or his mind.

Although the guards recognized the power of God and needed to change their tactics, they did not release Mentu. They secretly planned to kill him, but he managed to escape the prison and eventually escaped to Israel, the place where he thought he'd be the safest until he could seek asylum in a free country.

Questions for Review

1. What was the name of Sabina's husband?

2. What was the weapon that Sabina had in her apartment?

3. Where did Robert Haddad work?

4. What happened to the factory worker who said he would kill Robert?

5. How did the police try to scare Mentu into denying Christ?

Questions for Discussion

1. In what ways did Sabina suffer? Which was the worst?

2. How is the Bible a Christian weapon?

3. Why do you think the dog was friendly to Mentu?

4. Why is it dangerous for a Muslim to become a Christian?

5. Which of the stories did you like the best—about Sabina or Robert or Mentu?

Sabina was released in 1953 and reunited with her son Mihai. Life was difficult for them, as it is for so many women and children whose family members are in prison. Her husband Richard was released after eight and one-half years of torture and imprisonment. Because he would not stop preaching, he was arrested a second time. He was ransomed from prison in 1964, and the family was able to leave Romania. Richard and Sabina founded Voice of the Martyrs, an organization dedicated to raising awareness of Christians who are being persecuted for Christ.

The information about Robert Haddad is given by James Hefley in the book By Their Blood: Christian Martyrs of the 20th Century *published by Matt Media, Milford, Michigan, 1979.*

Esther Bean wrote the stories about Sabina and Mentu. She heard Mentu speak at a persecution conference in Toronto. The story took place about 1990.

~ Howard

A GREAT
WOMAN

GREAT PERCEPTION

. . . .

*The woman saith unto him, Sir, I perceive
that thou art a prophet. John 4:19*

READ 2 KINGS 4:8-11

A friend who has several children wrote about a mother's perception. "God knew that we mothers need a little extra help. That's why He has given us a special gift. Some would call it a *sixth sense*, the thing that catches that which makes it past the other five. If a mother didn't see it, smell it, feel it, taste it, or hear it, it doesn't mean she doesn't know it. It remains a mystery how a mother can pick up on things without even being able to explain it.

"When our children were young, they really believed I had eyes in the back of my head. *How does Mom always know when we're doing something bad?* they wondered and looked for squinty eyeballs back there. Later they'd depend on those beautiful eyes because *Mom can find everything with her wonderful x-ray vision.*"

The great woman of Shunem was observant and understanding. When the Prophet Elisha came regularly to her town, she noticed he needed food to eat and a place to stay. So she urged Elisha to eat with her and her husband.

She also perceived that Elisha was a holy man of God (v. 9). Christians today are to test the spirits whether they are of God, "because many false prophets are gone into the world" (1 John 4:1).

I am very reluctant to go against my wife's intuition. If she says, "I just don't trust him," or "I think she's putting it on," I've learned she is probably right.

The Shunammite woman also perceived what Elisha needed in his room. She was like the virtuous woman who "stretcheth out her hand to the poor; yea, she reacheth forth her hands to the needy" (Proverbs 31:20). She had the kind of charity that helps people who cannot help in return. Offering good advice is fine, but it's not the same as a helping hand.

GREAT HOSPITALITY

Use hospitality one to another without grudging. 1 Peter 4:9

READ ACTS 16:13-15

A businessman from Chicago called his wife to get her consent to bring home a visitor from Spain as a guest for their evening meal. The family had four children, so the wife had plenty to do without preparing a meal and straightening the house before the Spanish official arrived. However, she agreed, and the meal went well. The foreign official never forgot their kind hospitality.

A number of years later, friends of that family went to Spain as missionaries. Their plans were brought to a standstill by government regulations. When a certain Spanish official realized that the missionaries were friends of the hospitable family from Chicago, he used his influence to clear the obstacles. A church was subsequently begun in that part of Spain, due in part to one meal in Chicago.

Elisha greatly appreciated the hospitality of the couple in Shunem. The Apostle Paul was blessed by the hospitality of Lydia. Christians today should be "given to hospitality" (Romans 12:13). A church leader is to be a "lover of hospitality" (Titus 1:8). My dad wasn't a minister, but my parents invited a lot of visitors at church to my home. If a visitor came to church, more likely than not they received an invitation from my parents. They came not only from Canada and the United States but from around the world.

How should we show hospitality? Invite your guest sincerely and "without grudging" (see verse above). Welcome the guest warmly. Share what you have without embarrassment: it doesn't need to be a five-course meal. Don't avoid hospitality with the excuse, "I'm afraid what I have won't be good enough." Let the food be secondary to fellowship and deepening the relationship. (Take a lesson from Mary and Martha who entertained Jesus.) Make it your aim to minister to others—not to show off your culinary skills. Let your guest leave smoothly. One insightful person said, "Hospitality is the art of making people want to stay without interfering with their departure."

Great Kindness

. . . .

Charity suffereth long, and is kind; charity envieth not; charity vaunteth not itself, is not puffed up. 1 Corinthians 13:4

READ 2 PETER 1:1-7

Kindness always pays, but it pays most when you do not do it for pay. A soldier from Glendale, California, shared some coffee and cakes from home with a hungry old lady in France. His kindness so impressed the lady, whose seven sons were killed by the Nazis, that she willed fifty thousand dollars to the soldier before she died. The bequest was totally unexpected.

The Shunammite woman was very kind to Elisha. She and her husband made a "prophet's room" and kindly added things for his comfort and use—a table, a stool, a candlestick. Elisha recognized and appreciated her thoughtfulness and the extra effort she put forth to make it nice for him.

If your family has the opportunity to host a visiting "prophet," what are some helpful things to provide in his room? A table is very useful for him to have for study and writing his notes. A chair for him to sit on is very helpful. If there is room, a soft chair like a recliner is a nice touch also. Good lighting at the table is an asset. The bed should be of a quality that you wouldn't mind sleeping on it. When my wife and I heard the advice that the hosts should sleep on the guest bed for a night, we did. The next day we ordered a new mattress! If it is cold outside, provide a means of heat in the room.

Kindness is one sign of Christian growth, as indicated in the daily reading.

Henry Wadsworth Longfellow wrote:

Kind hearts are the gardens,
　Kind thoughts are the roots,
Kind words are the flowers,
　Kind deeds are the fruits.
Take care of your garden,
　And keep out the weeds;
Fill it up with sunshine,
　Kind words and kind deeds.

The Shunammite woman certainly took care of her garden well. So should we. Cultivate kindness each day. Men and women are great only when they are kind.

THE REWARDS
OF HOSPITALITY

··

But a lover of hospitality, a lover of good men,
sober, just, holy, temperate. Titus 1:8

READ 2 KINGS 4:12-17

I n the opinion of some who observe church life and congregational
growth, the most influential question that can be asked of a first-
time visitor is, "Would you like to come home with us for dinner?"

You could be hosting someone very special, as Hebrews 13:2 says, "Be
not forgetful to entertain strangers: for thereby some have entertained
angels unawares." What a reward that would be!

A second blessing relates to the experience of sharing God's love with
someone in need. A man saw a young waif gazing through the window
of a bakery in England, hungrily looking at the donuts. He said, "Son,
would you like some of those?"

The boy was startled.

"Oh, yes, I would!"

The American stepped inside and bought a dozen, put them in a bag,
and walked back to where the lad was standing in the foggy cold of the
London morning. He smiled, held out the bag, and said, "Here you are."

As he turned to walk away, the boy tugged on his coat. "Mister, are you God?"

To give to others is godly.

A third blessing is being appreciated. The Shunammite woman, praised in our daily reading, was content. But Elisha was not. He wanted to show appreciation. She and her husband were blessed with a son. There are numerous other ways a hospitable person may be rewarded. Jesus said, "It is more blessed to give than to receive" (Acts 20:35).

God also notices kind hospitality and will reward bountifully in the future. "Then shall the King say unto them on his right hand, Come, ye blessed of my Father, inherit the kingdom prepared for you from the foundation of the world: for I was an hungred, and ye gave me meat: I was thirsty, and ye gave me drink: I was a stranger, and ye took me in" (Matthew 25:34, 35).

John Bunyan, in *Pilgrim's Progress*, wrote:

"He who bestows his goods upon the poor,
   Shall have as much again, and ten times more."

WHEN CHILDREN ARE SICK

*Jesus said unto him, If thou canst believe, all things
are possible to him that believeth. Mark 9:23*

READ 2 KINGS 4:18-24

A young boy was very sick with pneumonia. His parents, who later
became good friends of mine, told me they cared for him the
best they could.

The parents had recently begun attending a spiritually vibrant church
and asked the ministers to visit. The ministry prayed fervently for the
boy's recovery, and eventually the boy did recover. He became one of
my students and has now become an active brother in his congregation.

The daily reading tells of a sick boy and what the parents did about it.
The father sent him to the house to be under his mother's supervision.
She cared for him, but he died. Then she sought help from Elisha.

What should parents in the twenty-first century do when a child
is sick? They should do their best in providing for his physical and
continued needs. I distinctly remember being sick, and my mom taking
my temperature, giving me pain relievers, and especially stroking my
fevered forehead in a comforting way.

I asked a nurse practitioner for the top five things a parent can do for a sick child's care. Here's her response:

1. When an illness begins, the symptoms are often subtle. Don't ignore alarming symptoms such as difficult breathing. Seek medical help for your child.

2. Follow the advice of the medical team that is responsible for the sick child's treatment. Give medications exactly as ordered, and make sure the team knows if you have been giving any other treatment, including "natural" treatments. If you don't agree with the treatment plan, discuss it with the medical personnel.

3. Be there for your sick child. If the child is hospitalized, a parent's presence helps to calm many fears in the strange, scary world of a hospital.

4. Be honest with your child. If your child is going to undergo a painful procedure (even minimal pain such as receiving an injection), don't tell your child that it won't hurt. A much better approach is to honestly tell your child that it will hurt, but it will soon be over.

5. Be proactive before your child is ill or injured: learning CPR or taking a basic first aid course could save your child's life.

THE SHUNAMMITE'S FAITH

Commit thy way unto the LORD; trust also in him;
and he shall bring it to pass. Psalm 37:5

READ 2 KINGS 4:25-37

The story is told of a man, years ago on the frontier, who needed to cross a big river to get some medicines for his wife. It was early winter, and he didn't know how safe the ice was, so he inched along on his hands and knees, hoping the ice would hold his weight.

After a while he heard a rumbling sound that got louder and louder. Looking back, he saw a team of horses pulling a loaded sled over the ice. The man got up and began to jog on his way to get the medicine. He was no longer afraid because he knew the ice was dependable.

God is absolutely trustworthy. He will support the believer. "Trust ye in the LORD for ever: for in the LORD JEHOVAH is everlasting strength" (Isaiah 26:4). With God's everlasting arms beneath us, we can be at peace. "Thou wilt keep him in perfect peace, whose mind is stayed on thee: because he trusteth in thee" (Isaiah 26:3).

The Shunammite's faith is implied by several things mentioned in the daily reading. She laid her dead son on the prophet's bed (v. 21). She came to the man of God, Elisha (v. 25). Her faith was demonstrated by her submission to God's will as shown by her words, "It is well" (v. 26). She was determined to stick with the prophet (v. 31). She had a persistent faith. Faith is the daring of the soul to go farther than it can see.

BE FAIR

*He hath shewed thee, O man, what is good; and what
doth the LORD require of thee, but to do justly, and to love
mercy, and to walk humbly with thy God? Micah 6:8*

READ 2 KINGS 8:1-6

Justice does not always prevail. Research has revealed that less attractive women convicted of a crime receive more severe sentences than do prettier women. The color of a person's skin can also influence the outcome of a trial.

Juries sometimes come to some unfair conclusions. A burglar fell through a skylight while robbing a school. The school was sued and had to pay $260,000 in damages. In another case, a woman claimed she lost her psychic powers after she was injected with dye during a CT scan. She was awarded almost a million dollars in damages. (We might ask: Why didn't she foresee what would happen and just avoid the scan?)

Elisha and the king did as Psalm 82:3 instructs: "Defend the poor and fatherless: do justice to the afflicted and needy."

We can pray that justice prevails for "all that are in authority; that we may lead a quiet and peaceable life in all godliness and honesty"

(1 Timothy 2:2). It is also imperative that we be just and treat others fairly. Proverbs 21:3 says, "To do justice and judgment is more acceptable to the LORD than sacrifice." Employers should be fair to their workers. "Masters, give unto your servants that which is just and equal; knowing that ye also have a Master in heaven" (Colossians 4:1). "That which is altogether just shalt thou follow" (Deuteronomy 16:20). There is no substitute for basic honesty and integrity in one's life.

Man of Narrow Escapes
John Paton

by Howard Bean

"Jesus came to save you from your sins," John Paton said to the villagers on the island of Tanna, among the South Sea Islands. "Jesus can deliver you from the power of evil."

Three witch doctors stood up and interrupted him. "We have the power to kill you by witchcraft," they said, "if we can get a piece of fruit from which you have eaten."

John breathed a prayer as he took a bite out of three plums. He handed one to each of the witch doctors. They began to chant, trying to harm the missionary with their witchcraft. The natives were astounded at his nerve, and even more shocked that he didn't fall over dead. The witch doctors waved their hands and muttered, then rolled up the three plums in leaves, built a sacred fire, and burned them.

"Stir up your gods to help you," John urged. "I'm not dead. I am perfectly well."

After a while, the witch doctors said, "We will call all our sacred men together and kill you before a week has gone by."

Excited, the natives sent messengers each day from different parts of the island, asking if the missionary was ill yet.

The next Sunday, John spoke to the people. "You see that I am perfectly well. Now you must admit that your gods have no power over me. I am protected by the true and living God. He is the only God who can hear and answer prayer. He loves all human beings, despite their great wickedness, and He sent His dear Son Jesus to save from sin all who will believe and follow Him." From that day two of the witch doctors were friendly, but the others were his bitter enemies.

Many other times God responded to John's faith when he faced danger. On one occasion, hundreds of wild natives promised to kill him. A friend warned John and urged him to flee into the bush after dark and hide in the leafy branches of a huge chestnut tree. Up in the tree that night, he heard the men beating the bushes as they searched for him. Later, he wrote, "I heard the frequent discharging of muskets and the yells of the natives. Yet I sat there on one of the branches, safe in the arms of Jesus! Never before, in all my sorrows, did my Lord draw nearer to me and speak more soothingly to my soul. Alone, yet not alone! Had I been a stranger to Jesus and to prayer, my reason would verily have given way, but my comfort and joy sprang from the promise, 'Lo, I am with you always.'"

John Paton had dreamed of taking the Gospel to the Pacific Islands ever since he was a child. John was born in Scotland in 1824, the oldest boy in a family of eleven children. Before he turned twelve years old, he had to stop school and work with his father, who manufactured stockings. Their workday began at six in the morning and lasted until ten at night, with half an hour for breakfast and supper and one hour at noon for dinner. In any meager spare time, John read.

In childhood, he had seen the faith of his father, a strong believer in prayer. One year the potato harvest failed. Other crops were poor too, and many families were in need. While his father was away on a business trip, both food and money gave out entirely. John's mother prayed and assured the children that God would supply their needs in the morning. Sure enough, a basket of food arrived from an unexpected source the next day. Gathering the children around her, the mother said, "My dear children, love our heavenly Father. Tell Him in faith and prayer all your needs, and He will surely supply them, so far as it shall be for your good and His glory."

As a young man, John heard about the need for another missionary to work in the New Hebrides Islands in the South Pacific. "Offer yourself!" God told him.

Not everyone thought he should go. "The cannibals! You will be eaten by cannibals!" an old gentleman declared.

John replied, "Sir, you are getting old now and your own body is soon to be laid in the grave, there to be eaten by worms. If I can live and die serving and honoring the Lord Jesus, it will make no difference to me whether I am eaten by cannibals or by worms; and in the Great Day my resurrected body will arise as fair as yours in the likeness of our risen Redeemer." The old gentleman had nothing more to say.

Soon John and his wife boarded a ship to take the Gospel to the cannibals. After four and a half months at sea, they arrived at the island of Aneityum, where several missionaries, along with a group of Christian believers, welcomed them.

"We have decided to place you on the island called Tanna," they told John.

Tanna, the island of cannibals! Several years earlier two missionaries had started a work here and had to escape for their lives. But John and his wife did not hold back. They had volunteered, and they believed "the place of greatest danger is also the place of greatest need."

Another missionary went along to get them started. He bought some land and helped them put up walls for houses. He bargained with the people for sugarcane leaves to thatch the roofs and for coral to burn to use as lime in plastering the wooden walls. The local people crowded around to watch the work.

One day, men carrying muskets and wearing feathers and paint marched up and down excitedly. John learned that this group of men was preparing to fight another group. Before long he heard the bloodcurdling yells and the thunderous cracking of guns. After the battle he heard that the winners had made a feast of the bodies they had killed.

John shivered. Could such people ever come to love each other? Then he thought of the group of smiling Christians on the island of Aneityum who had once been man-eaters also. Jesus could do for the people of Tanna what He had done for the people of Aneityum.

At first John focused on learning the language and setting it down in writing. Then he began teaching the local people to write, beginning with the chiefs. After they learned, they helped the people learn.

Then came the rainy season with its hordes of mosquitoes. Some mosquitoes carried a deadly disease called malaria. All the missionaries became fevered with malaria. John recovered, but his wife and baby died. He grieved for them, and his faith was tested severely.

As though this were not pain enough for John in his loneliness, the people began blaming him for things that went wrong. A long dry season came. "It is the white man's fault that our yams and bananas cannot grow," the people complained. "His God keeps the rain from coming. Let's send him away! Let's kill him!" they shouted.

John knelt before God and prayed earnestly for rain. Before long the sky grew dark and torrents of rain pelted the ground. To his relief, the people changed their minds about sending him away.

God answered John's prayers for protection many times. Not long after arriving on Tanna, he was almost killed. On New Year's Day, 1861, he had spent the day taking medicine, food, and water to the villagers, hundreds of whom had a nasty type of measles. Those who took the medicine and followed the instructions recovered, but most preferred their own treatments. Dozens of them plunged into the sea, seeking relief from the burning fever, and soon drowned. Others dug holes the length of their body and several feet deep and lay in them, the cool earth feeling pleasant to their fevered bodies. In this useless effort hundreds died, literally in their own graves, and were buried where they lay.

That evening, John and a young missionary knelt in the mission house in fervent prayer, giving their all to Christ and asking for the salvation of the people among whom they lived. They asked for the protecting presence of their Lord, not knowing that even then the house was surrounded by fierce warriors armed with clubs, stones, and muskets, wanting to kill and eat the foreigners whose God, they believed, had brought diseases, hurricanes, and other troubles upon them.

After the worship, the younger missionary stepped out of the door to go to his own house close by. Instantly, he was attacked and fell to the ground screaming, "Look out! They are trying to kill us!" Rushing to the door, John shouted, "Jehovah God sees you and will punish you for trying to murder His servants." Two men swung their clubs at him, but missed, whereupon the entire company fled into the bush.

Sometimes wicked men tried to trick him so they could kill him. John kept several goats for their milk. One day he heard an unusual bleating, as if the goats were being hurt. He hurried to the goat house. Instantly, a band of armed men sprang from the bush, surrounded him, and raised their clubs. "You have escaped from us many times," they said, "but now we are going to kill you!" Lifting his hands and eyes toward Heaven, John committed himself to the Lord. As he prayed, he sensed God's presence. His heart was filled with a tender reassurance, and the cannibals slipped away one after another. "Thus," the missionary reported, "Jesus restrained them once again. His promise is a reality; He is with His servants to support and bless them, even unto the end of the world!"

The natives' hatred then spread to John's native Christian helpers from Aneityum. One day they threw a stone shaped like a scythe at Namuri and almost killed him. John doctored Namuri and begged him to stay at the mission house until he could safely return home. Namuri reminded John that back on his own island of Aneityum, he had once wanted to kill the missionary. Then he added, "If, because of the danger, the missionary had stayed away, I would have remained heathen. But he came and he taught us about Jesus until by the grace of God, I was changed to what I am. Now the same God who changed me can change these poor Tannese to love and serve Him."

John then let Namuri return to his village work. Some time later the man who had thrown the stone clubbed Namuri while he was praying. This time no medical help would save him, and John watched him die, praying for his persecutors. The death of this saint brought both grief and gladness to John. It told him that the salvation of this one soul made all the dangers and suffering among these cannibals worthwhile.

Due to the frequent attacks upon their lives and the murder of Numari, all the teachers from Aneityum except Abraham, returned to their own island. Abraham, formerly a bloodthirsty fighter, determined to stay with the missionary. As hundreds of furious cannibals shouted for their death, the two knelt in prayer. "O Lord," prayed Abraham, "make us strong for Thee and Thy cause, and if they kill us, let us die together in Thy good work."

The warriors formed a circle around the two, urging each other to strike the first blow or fire the first shot. Presently a stone, thrown with great force, grazed Abraham's cheek. He turned his gaze Heavenward and said, "John, I was nearly away to Jesus."

"In that awful hour," John wrote later, "I saw Christ's own words, as if carved in letters of fire upon the clouds of Heaven: 'Whatsoever ye shall ask in My name, that will I do, that the Father may be glorified in the Son.' " As he stood praying, he saw the Lord Jesus hovering close by, watching the scene. An assurance came to him as if a voice from Heaven had spoken, that nothing would happen—not a musket would be fired, not a club strike, not a spear leave the hand in which it was held, not an arrow leave the bow or a stone the fingers—without the permission of Jesus Christ, who rules all nature and restrains even the natives of the South Seas. "If any reader wonders how they were restrained, much more would I, unless I believed that the same Hand that restrained the lions from touching Daniel held back these natives from hurting me."

Later, some chiefs told John, "Your preaching makes us afraid to live like we always have. Unless you quit telling us what we are doing wrong, we will kill you."

One night they tried three times to get into his house to shoot him. Later, he heard that those who tried weakened with fear. John thanked God for making them weak.

When attendance at Sunday services grew to about forty, John began plans to build a church. He bought wood from Aneityum. Since the island of Aneityum was largely Christian then, and the natives wore clothes, they were glad for fifty pairs of trousers in payment for the wood. The trousers had come from the mission in Glasgow, Scotland, where John had served for ten years. In about three months the church building was built.

By this time John knew the Tannese language well enough to prepare a little booklet of Bible verses to hand out. A friend in Scotland had given him a small printing press. Now for the first time he used it, and the result was the very first printing of any part of the Bible in Tannese.

One day an angry group of people surrounded John in his garden, all pointing their guns at him. With a prayer that Jesus would stand between them and him, he continued his work. The circle backed up a short space, then pointed their guns again. None of them shot, however, and after a while they began to leave. Again God had answered prayer.

One morning John was warned that he and his helpers would be eaten that day at a cannibal feast. Quickly, he sent for all his helpers and locked them with himself in the mission house. There they spent the day praying and listening to the tramp of feet outside. At sunset the enemies left. No shots had been fired. No doors or windows had been forced. Again God had protected them.

As time went on, John's enemies grew more and more determined to kill him. Once his dog wakened him during the night to the sight of flames outside. Men were setting fire to the church building and the reed fences between it and the house. John hurried outside with a small tomahawk, cut off the burning fence, and pitched it into the fire. Seeing shadows on the ground, he looked up to find himself surrounded by natives screaming with hatred, brandishing clubs to kill him. Suddenly, they heard the thunderous roar of a strong wind in the distance. Almost immediately it was upon them, blowing the flames away from the house and putting out the fire in a downpour of rain.

"This is God's rain!" they shouted, slinking away.

Another mission worker declared, "If ever in time of need God sent help and protection to His servants in answer to prayer, He has done so tonight."

Next morning a boat from Aneityum arrived. Mission workers there feared for the safety of the workers on Tanna and sent for them.

John said good-bye to Tanna with deep sadness. Were his four years of preaching, praying, witnessing, and suffering to end in failure? He had hoped to see the Tannese turn to Christ and live in peace with each other. Would the day come when he could safely return to finish what he had started?

After a while, the missionaries in Aneityum urged John and his second wife Margaret to start a mission on the island of Aniwa. Again John had to learn a new language. Again he had to build a house. Again he offered medical help to the sick, and many came to him with their ailments.

Since Aniwa was surrounded by coral reefs, the Patons built their house of coral blocks. Many of the local people came to see this strange building. Among the visitors was a chief with his three sons. When one son became ill soon after the visit, the chief blamed John, promising to kill him if the boy died. On hearing this, John hurried to the chief's house and did what he could with his medicines, asking God to help him. When the boy got well, the chief became a grateful friend and listened to the Gospel.

Mr. Paton and his wife rejoiced to welcome a baby boy into their home. At one time when armed natives surrounded the mission house, the little boy slipped away from his parents and ran out among the warriors. When he had hugged and kissed each one, he seated himself on the knee of the ringleader and scolded them all, saying, "Naughty! Naughty!" Their frowns turned to grins, and one by one they slipped away.

The shortage of fresh water on Aniwa became a real problem to John and Margaret. What could they drink, and how could they wash their clothes? Occasional heavy rains furnished good water, but it soon soaked into the loose soil.

Native Aniwans had no water problems. They chewed sugarcane or drank coconut milk when they were thirsty. They went to the ocean to bathe. They did no laundering, for they wore no clothes.

The Patons needed fresh water every day, not just occasionally. For them, cleanliness and health depended on it. John saw no way out but to dig a well. But where? Unless he could strike an underground spring, he would have only a dry hole.

After praying, he felt he should dig near the public path not far from his house. Here others could come for water also.

The head chief of the island wondered what he was doing. John explained that he was digging down for fresh water that he hoped God would send from below.

"Your head is going wrong!" the chief exclaimed. "Rain only comes from above. Wait until the rain comes, and we will save all we possibly can for you."

"I might die before that," John replied. He hired local men to help, paying them with fishhooks.

When they got down to twelve feet, one side of the well caved in. After that, everyone else refused to go down, and John had to dig alone. They stayed at the top and emptied the bucket, which he taught them to draw up by rope and pulley.

At thirty feet he discovered dampness, and one day he said to the chief, "I think God will give us water tomorrow from the hole."

"No," the chief replied, "you will never see rain coming up from the earth on this island. We wonder what is to be the end of this mad work of yours. We expect daily, if you reach water, to see you drop through into the sea, and the sharks will eat you! That will be the end of it; death to you, and danger to us all."

The next day John hurried down the ladder and began digging. Water spurted up. Was it salty or fresh? He tasted it—fresh water! God had answered his prayer.

Excitedly John rushed to his house for a jug and brought up some water to show the chief and all the other curious onlookers.

"Rain! Rain! Yes, it is rain!" the chief exclaimed. "Wonderful is the work of your Jehovah God! No god of Aniwa ever helped us in this way. The world is turned upside down since Jehovah came to Aniwa! But will it always rain up through the earth, or will it come and go like the rain from the clouds?"

John assured them that water would always be in the well, and anyone could get some when he wished.

A wall needed to be built around the inside of the well to prevent any more cave-ins. The people willingly carried coral blocks for John to build the wall. His work was very tiring, and by the time he had curbed twenty feet, he told them he would have to rest a week or more before he could finish. They begged him to rest there and tell them how to finish it. He did, and they curbed the remaining fourteen feet. Then he put a board floor over the top and fitted a rope and bucket for pulling up water.

As John had hoped and prayed, the well became a daily sermon. Others, trying to dig wells of their own, struck coral rock or salt water. They said to him, "You not only used pick and spade, but you prayed to your God. We have learned to dig, but not how to pray, so God will not give us rain from below."

The head chief called his people together on Sunday to John's worship service. With John's permission, he spoke. "Men, women, and children of Aniwa, listen to my words... Whoever expected to see rain coming up through the earth? It has always come from the clouds. Wonderful is the work of this God. No god of Aniwa ever answered prayers as his God has done... From this day, my people, I must worship the God who has opened for us the well. The gods of Aniwa cannot hear. Henceforth I am a follower of his God. Let every man who thinks with me go now and fetch the idols of Aniwa... Let us burn and bury and destroy these things of wood and stone, and let us be taught by him how to serve the God who can hear, who gave us this well, and who will give every other blessing, for He sent His Son Jesus to die for us and to take us to Heaven."

Several brought their idols to the mission house that afternoon and others did so later. There they burned those made of wood and either buried the others or threw them into the ocean.

The little island of Aniwa changed quickly after this. Those who destroyed their idols began praying to God morning and evening and at mealtime. They stopped working on Sunday. They quit stealing. They began bringing orphaned children to the Patons to have them trained for Jesus. Soon all the orphans on the island had been brought, and John built two orphanages, one for girls and one for boys. Many of those children grew up to become evangelists and teachers who took the Gospel to their own people.

John started a school to teach the people to read. Then he printed small booklets of Scripture passages. The people were thrilled when they could look at a booklet and say, "It speaks my words."

Church services had been held from the beginning under a banyan tree or in a hut. Now with most of the people on the island turning to Christ, a church building was needed. John appealed to the people to build one, and they agreed. Men cut trees into lumber. Women and children brought sugarcane leaves for the thatched roof. John oversaw the work, and the building went up quickly.

Later, John was asked to divide his time between working on Aniwa and traveling over the world to tell about the New Hebrides Mission. In old age he lived in Melbourne, Australia, still speaking and writing about the mission. With great joy he saw his son Frank go to Tanna, along with other missionaries who were willing to work there again. Before he died in 1907 at the age of 83, he rejoiced to see a Christian congregation on Tanna, among whom were some who had once tried to kill him.

Questions for Review

1. Why did John take a bite out of three plums?

2. Why did John spend a night up in a tree?

3. How did a strong wind help save John's life?

4. How did John's little boy save the lives of his parents?

5. How did rain come from a hole in the ground?

Questions for Discussion

1. What do you think was the most remarkable answer to John's prayers?

2. How had the faith of John's parents influenced him?

3. How did the well become a "sermon"?

4. Were any of John Paton's adventures familiar to you?

5. What are some answers to prayer that your family has seen?

A good short biography of John Paton is found in Heroes of Faith in Pioneer Trails *by E. Myers Harrison, published by Moody Press, Chicago, Illinois, 1945. For writing this story, I mainly used his autobiography* John G. Paton: Missionary to the New Hebrides *edited by his brother James Paton. ~Howard*

TITLES, VERSES, AND READINGS

NOAH

TITLES	VERSES	READINGS
Noah Found Grace	1 Corinthians 15:10	Genesis 6:1-8
Noah Walked With God	Hebrews 11:5	Genesis 6:9-22
Noah Had Faith and Fear	Hebrews 11:7	Genesis 7:1-10
Noah Obeyed	Ezekiel 14:20	Genesis 7:11-23
Noah Preached and Persevered	2 Peter 2:5	Matthew 24:35-44
Noah's Faith Was Rewarded	Genesis 9:1	Genesis 8:15-22
Noah Was Perfect, Yet Imperfect	1 Corinthians 10:12	Genesis 9:18-29

ABRAHAM

TITLES	VERSES	READINGS
Test of Leaving Family	Hebrews 11:8	Genesis 12:1-9
Test of Truthfulness	Zechariah 8:16	Genesis 12:14-20
Test of Unselfishness	1 Corinthians 10:33	Genesis 13:1-18

TITLES	VERSES	READINGS
Test of Patience	James 5:10	Genesis 15:1-6; 16:1-6
Test of Faith	Hebrews 11:11	Genesis 17:1-8, 15-19
Test of Befriending Strangers	Romans 12:13	Genesis 18:1-15
Test of Obedience	Hebrews 11:17	Genesis 22:1-6

ISAAC

TITLES	VERSES	READINGS
Is Anything Too Hard for God?	Jeremiah 32:17	Genesis 18:9-15
Isaac's Trust and Submission	Romans 12:1	Genesis 22:1-13
A Unique Courtship	Proverbs 3:5	Genesis 24:61-67
He Loved Her	Genesis 24:67	Genesis 24:1-14
Parental Favoritism	Ephesians 6:4	Genesis 27:30-35, 41-46
Live at Peace	Romans 12:18	Genesis 26:12-28
Isaac, a Man of Faith	2 Chronicles 20:20	Matthew 8:5-13

JACOB

TITLES	VERSES	READINGS
Jacob Values the Birthright	Numbers 23:19	Genesis 25:19-34
Jacob Lacks Faith and Integrity	Proverbs 12:22	Genesis 27:15-29
The Staircase to Heaven	John 1:51	Genesis 28:10-22
Facing Fears and the Future	Psalm 34:4	Genesis 32:1-13
Wrestling With God	Acts 12:5	Genesis 32:24-32
Keys to Reconciliation	Matthew 5:9	Genesis 33:1-16
Faith and the Future	Hebrews 11:21	Genesis 47:28-31

JOSEPH

TITLES	VERSES	READINGS
Joseph and Jesus: Relating to Siblings	Mark 6:3	Genesis 37:1-11
Joseph and Jesus: Relating to Parents	Luke 2:51	Genesis 37:12-28
Joseph and Jesus: Purity	Hebrews 7:26	Genesis 39:1-12
Joseph and Jesus: Falsely Accused	Matthew 27:12	Genesis 39:13-20
Joseph and Jesus: Faithful	Hebrews 3:1, 2	Genesis 39:21-23; 40:1-8
Joseph and Jesus: Exalted	Mark 16:19	Genesis 41:37-46
Joseph and Jesus: Forgiveness	Luke 23:24	Genesis 50:15-21

MOSES

TITLES	VERSES	READINGS
Moses the Baby	Hebrews 11:23	Exodus 2:1-10
Moses the Prince	Hebrews 11:24	Exodus 2:11-15
Moses the Shepherd	Exodus 3:14	Exodus 3:1-12
Moses the Leader	Exodus 14:31	Exodus 14:10-18
Moses the Teacher	Luke 12:15	Deuteronomy 6:5-15
Moses the Intercessor	Romans 8:34	Numbers 14:11-21
Moses the Deceased	Mark 9:4	Deuteronomy 34:1-10

RAHAB

TITLES	VERSES	READINGS
Rahab's Faith	Hebrews 11:31	Joshua 2:1-13

TITLES	VERSES	READINGS
The Scarlet Cord	Zechariah 13:1	Joshua 2:14-22
God's Mercy	Lamentations 3:22	John 8:1-11
Rahab, a Type of the Sinner	1 Timothy 1:15	Joshua 6:1-5, 20-23
Faith That Works	Acts 9:36	James 2:14-26
Hall of Shame	Matthew 11:19	Matthew 1:1-6, 18-21
Lessons From Rahab	Jeremiah 29:13	1 Corinthians 6:9-11, 19, 20

GIDEON

TITLES	VERSES	READINGS
A Brave Coward	Deuteronomy 31:6	Judges 6:1-14
Gideon Finds Peace	John 16:33	Judges 6:15-24
Faith in Action	James 2:17	Judges 6:25-35
Faith and the Fleece	Deuteronomy 6:16	Judges 6:36-40
Gideon Conquers His Fears	Psalm 27:1	Judges 7:1-15
Faith Conquers	Hebrews 11:32-34	Judges 7:16-25
The Good and the Bad	1 Timothy 4:16	Judges 8:1-3, 22-35

JEPHTHAH

TITLES	VERSES	READINGS
Getting Past the Past	Philippians 3:13	Judges 11:1-11
Make Peace by Persuasian	James 3:17	Judges 11:12-15
Appreciate God's Providence	Psalm 125:2	Judges 11:16-28
Have Faith	1 John 5:4	Judges 11:29-33

TITLES	VERSES	READINGS
Don't Be Rash	Proverbs 29:20	Acts 19:35-41
A Living Sacrifice	Romans 12:1	Judges 11:34-40
ID'd By One's Speech	Matthew 12:37	Judges 12:1-6

SAMSON

TITLES	VERSES	READINGS
Samson's Strength	Ephesians 6:10	Judges 13:24—14:9
A Strong Weak Man	1 Peter 2:11	Judges 16:1-9
Compromise Can Kill	1 Corinthians 15:33	Judges 16:10-20
What Samson Lost	Proverbs 11:3	Judges 16:21-30
Don't Despise Godly Parents	Proverbs 15:20	Judges 13:1-12
Lessons From Samson	Hebrews 11:32	Judges 15:3-20
More Lessons From Samson	1 Timothy 5:22	Galatians 6:7-10

SAMUEL

TITLES	VERSES	READINGS
Asked of God	Philippians 4:6	1 Samuel 1:9-20
Building Proper Self-Esteem	1 Samuel 2:19	1 Samuel 1:21-28
Eli's Wisdom Toward Samuel	Mark 10:14	1 Samuel 2:18-21; 3:1-10
Samuel's Intercession	Psalm 99:6	1 Samuel 7:1-13
Samuel's Faithfulness	Revelation 2:10	1 Samuel 7:15-17; 12:1-7
Samuel's Courage	Isaiah 12:2	1 Samuel 13:5-14
The Importance of the Heart	Psalm 44:21	1 Samuel 16:1-7

DAVID

TITLES	VERSES	READINGS
The Lord Looks on the Heart	2 Chronicles 16:9	1 Samuel 16:8-17
Lessons from David's Family	Ephesians 6:1	1 Samuel 17:12-20
David Confronts Goliath	Isaiah 26:3	1 Samuel 17:32-49
David Behaves Wisely	1 Timothy 4:12	! Samuel 18:1-16
David Faces Discouragement	Psalm 42:1	1 Samuel 30:1-18
Admirable Qualities of David	2 Samuel 23:1	1 Samuel 26:1-21
David's Kindness to Mephibosheth	Colossians 3:12	2 Samuel 9:1-13

A GREAT WOMEN

TITLES	VERSES	READINGS
Great Perception	John 4:19	2 Kings 4:8-11
Great Hospitality	1 Peter 4:9	Acts 16:13-15
Great Kindness	1 Corinthians 13:4	2 Peter 1:1-7
The Rewards of Hospitality	Titus 1:8	2 Kings 4:12-17
When Children Are Sick	Mark 9:23	2 Kings 4:18-24
The Shunammite's Faith	Psalm 37:5	2 Kings 4:25-37
Be Fair	Micah 6:8	2 Kings 8:1-6

Christian Light Publications is a nonprofit, conservative Mennonite publishing company providing Christ-centered, Biblical literature including books, Gospel tracts, Sunday school materials, summer Bible school materials, and a full curriculum for Christian day schools and homeschools. Though produced primarily in English, some books, tracts, and school materials are also available in Spanish.

For more information about the ministry of CLP or its publications, or for spiritual help, please contact us at:

Christian Light Publications
P. O. Box 1212
Harrisonburg, VA 22803-1212

Telephone—540-434-0768
Fax—540-433-8896
E-mail—info@clp.org
www.clp.org